Sources of
World Societies

Volume 2: Since 1450

Twelfth Edition

THE COMPANION READER FOR
A HISTORY OF WORLD SOCIETIES

TWELFTH EDITION

Merry E. Wiesner-Hanks
Patricia Buckley Ebrey
Roger B. Beck
Jerry Dávila
Clare Haru Crowston
John P. McKay

bedford/st.martin's
Macmillan Learning
Boston | New York

Vice President: Leasa Burton
Senior Program Director: Michael Rosenberg
Senior Executive Program Manager: William J. Lombardo
Director of Content Development: Jane Knetzger
Senior Development Editor: Leah R. Strauss
Assistant Editor: Julia Bell
Director of Media Editorial: Adam Whitehurst
Media Editor: Mollie Chandler
Senior Marketing Manager: Melissa Rodriguez
Senior Director, Content Management Enhancement: Tracey Kuehn
Senior Managing Editor: Michael Granger
Assistant Content Project Manager: Natalie Jones
Senior Workflow Project Manager: Jennifer Wetzel
Production Supervisor: Brianna Lester
Director of Design, Content Management: Diana Blume
Interior Design: Lumina Datamatics, Inc.
Cover Design: William Boardman
Director of Rights and Permissions: Hilary Newman
Text Permissions Manager, Lumina Datamatics, Inc.: Elaine Kosta
Executive Permissions Editor: Robin Fadool
Photo Researcher: Bruce Carson
Director of Digital Production: Keri deManigold
Executive Media Project Manager: Michelle Camisa
Copyeditor: Susan Zorn
Composition: Lumina Datamatics, Inc.
Cover Image: © The Alfredo Ramos Martínez Research Project/Christie's Images/
    Bridgeman Images
Printing and Binding: LSC Communications

Library of Congress Control Number: 2020938581

ISBN: 978-1-319-30358-7

Printed in the United States of America.

1   2   3   4   5   6   25   24   23   22   21   20

Acknowledgments

Acknowledgments and copyrights appear on the same page as the text and art selections they cover; these acknowledgments and copyrights constitute an extension of the copyright page.

For information, write: Bedford/St. Martin's, 75 Arlington Street, Boston, MA 02116

PREFACE

We are pleased to publish this new edition of *Sources of World Societies*. With a parallel chapter structure and documents hand-picked to extend the textbook, this reader is designed to complement *A History of World Societies*, Twelfth Edition. The primary sources in this document collection span prehistory to the present, capturing the voices of individuals within the context of their times and ways of life, while enriching the cross-cultural fabric of history as a whole. Now with new visual sources and an emphasis on historical thinking skills, *Sources* draws from the records of rulers and subjects alike, men and women, philosophers, revolutionaries, economists, laborers, and artists, among others, to present a textured view of the past. *Sources of World Societies* animates the past for students, providing resonant accounts of the people and events that changed the face of world history, from myths of creation to accounts of hardship and conflict, from a local to a global scale.

Sources of World Societies includes both written and visual sources, many chosen by the authors of the companion textbook to align the readings with the chapter topics and textbook themes. We have compiled this document collection with one goal in mind: to make history's most classic and compelling voices accessible to students, from the most well-known thinkers and documentarians of their times to the galvanized or introspective commoner. While students have access to the formative documents of each era, lesser-heard voices reveal life as the great majority of people lived it. In Chapter 32, for example, students can juxtapose the National Party of South Africa's policy and justification of apartheid with Nelson Mandela's speech supporting armed struggle to fight apartheid.

We have aimed to provide just enough background to enable students' own analysis of the sources at hand. Each chapter contains an average of five sources, including a feature called Viewpoints that allows students to compare and contrast two or three sources that voice different perspectives on the same theme or topic. Chapter-opening paragraphs briefly review the major events of the time and place the documents that follow within the framework of the corresponding textbook chapter. A concise headnote for each document provides context about the author and the circumstances surrounding the document's creation, while gloss notes supply clarification to aid comprehension of unfamiliar terms and references. Each document is followed by Reading and Discussion Questions that spur student analysis of the material, while chapter-concluding Comparative Questions encourage students to contemplate the relationships among the sources within and, when called for, between the chapters. All of the questions in

Sources aim to connect events of the past with students' own evolving understandings of power and its abuses, of the ripple effects of human agency, and of the material conditions of life. The excerpts range in length to allow for a variety of class assignments.

New to This Edition

To parallel a new environmental theme of the textbook, we have added new documents to reflect environmental concerns, from a Wandjina cave painting (Chapter 1) to Greta Thunberg's address to the United Nations Climate Action Summit in 2019 (Chapter 33).

We have included a greater emphasis on the voices of women across class and time with selections such as Christine de Pizan's excerpt from *The Treasure of the City of Ladies* (1405), in which an upper-class woman provides moral and practical advice to the wives of artisans (Chapter 14); and a 2004 interview with Wang Xingjuan for the Global Feminisms Project, which sheds light on how economic reforms affected women in China in the 1980s (Chapter 32).

Additional new text sources include Benjamin of Tudela, from *Book of Travels* (Chapter 9); Peter the Great's *Edicts and Decrees* (Chapter 18); José María Morelos's "Sentiments of the Nation" (Chapter 22); Flora Tristan's *The Workers' Union* (Chapter 23); and Mary Seacole's *Wonderful Adventures of Mrs. Seacole in Many Lands* (Chapter 27). In response to reviewers' feedback, we have trimmed the length of some text excerpts to better highlight their key points.

Also in response to reviewers' comments, this edition includes many new images that lend themselves more effectively to analysis and discussion. New visual sources include images of lesser-known individuals in new styles of art (Chapter 5); industrialization and technological advances (Chapter 26); and hardships in the aftermath of war (Chapter 28). The importance of individual experience is highlighted in a letter from a Babylonian copper merchant (Chapter 2); an image depicting court lady and renowned poet Koōgimi (Chapter 12); and the photograph *One Man Demo*, which depicts one man's struggle during the Great Depression (Chapter 30).

Acknowledgments

We extend our gratitude to those instructors who reviewed the previous edition: Dr. Thomas C. Doumaux, Pitt Community College; Steven C. Eames, Saint Anselm College; Jonathan Gentry, Kennesaw State University; Nicole A. Jacoberger, Camden County College; Brian C. Johnson, Kilgore College; Suzanne Linebaugh, Harrisburg Area Community College; Kathryn L. Mapstone, Bunker Hill Community College; J. Stratton, Bakersfield College; and Michael Tafel, DePaul University.

CONTENTS

Sources of
World Societies

Volume 2: Since 1450

16

The Acceleration of Global Contact

1450–1600

Although long-standing trade routes meant that many of the world's civilizations were in contact with one another before 1500, this interaction accelerated drastically in the sixteenth century when Europe became a much larger player in world trade. Europe began establishing trade routes to the newly discovered Americas and sent Christian missionaries to all corners of the globe. The sources in this chapter examine European perceptions of the globe in the early years of exploration, as well as contrasting European and indigenous perspectives on this era of contact and conquest.

16-1 | The World as Europeans Knew It in 1502
World Map (1502)

Created in 1502, this map shows the world as Europeans knew it ten years after the voyages of Christopher Columbus. The African coastline is rendered in extraordinarily accurate detail. Trading destinations in India and Southeast Asia are also clearly indicated. The Americas, however, remain a rough sketch, a largely imagined place, not a known one. Nonetheless, the map offers a glimpse of the future. In 1494, Spain and Portugal signed the Treaty of Tordesillas, which established a line of demarcation running north-south (the heavy line on the left side of the map running through modern-day Brazil). All non-European territories to the west of the line were to be Spanish. All those to the east were to be Portuguese. As you examine the map, think about what it reveals about the European age of expansion. How does it tell the story of the previous century of exploration? What does it suggest about the course of conquests yet to come?

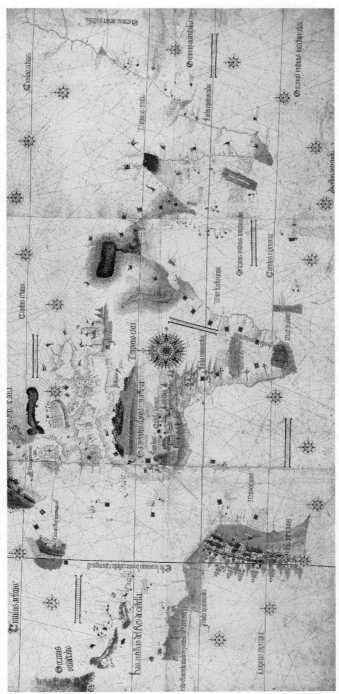

DEA Picture Library/De Agostini/Getty Images

READING AND DISCUSSION QUESTIONS

1. How would you explain the prominence of Africa on the map? How did Europeans develop such an accurate sense of its coastline?

2. What were the larger implications of the Treaty of Tordesillas? What does it tell you about the importance the Spanish and Portuguese attached to the discoveries and achievements of the fifteenth century?

VIEWPOINTS

The Motives of Columbus and His Patrons

The year 1492 was a momentous one in Spanish history. With the fall of the Muslim state of Granada, Ferdinand of Aragon and Isabella of Castile completed the Christian *reconquista* (reconquest) of the Iberian Peninsula. Having driven the "infidels" from their last Iberian stronghold, they turned to the "enemy within," issuing a proclamation expelling all Jews from their lands. It was at this moment, fired with a crusading spirit and eager to gain access to the wealth of Asia, that Ferdinand and Isabella chose to sponsor the exploratory westward voyage of Christopher Columbus. Keep this larger context in mind as you read the documents included in this feature. How does this history help explain the motives and expectations of Columbus and his patrons?

16-2 | Columbus Defends His Accomplishments

CHRISTOPHER COLUMBUS, *Letter from the Third Voyage* (1493)

When King Ferdinand and Queen Isabella decided to fund Columbus's expeditions, they were not engaging in an act of charity. They were making an investment. This is not to say that their motives were strictly material. Both were devout Catholics and were committed to spreading the faith. Nonetheless, Columbus claimed that he knew a faster route to Asia, and to late-fifteenth-century Europeans, Asia meant, first and foremost, a highly profitable trade in luxury goods. Thus when Columbus failed to deliver on his implied promise to deliver fabulous wealth, he knew he would have to explain himself. As you read the letter, think about Columbus's intended audience. How did he seek to refute his critics? Why did he feel he had to?

Cecil Jane, ed. and trans., *Select Documents Illustrating the Four Voyages of Columbus* (London: Hakluyt Society, 1967).

Most serene and most high and most powerful princes, the king and queen, our sovereigns: The Holy Trinity moved Your Highnesses to this enterprise of the Indies, and of His infinite goodness, He made me the messenger thereof, so that, being moved thereunto, I came with the mission to your royal presence, as being the most exalted of Christian princes and so ardently devoted to the Faith and to its increase. The persons who should have occupied themselves with the matter held it to be impossible, for they made of gifts of chance their riches and on them placed their trust.

On this matter I spent six or seven years of deep anxiety, expounding, as well as I could, how great service might in this be rendered to the Lord, by proclaiming abroad His holy name and His faith to so many peoples, which was all a thing of so great excellence and for the fair fame of great princes and for a notable memorial for them. It was needful also to speak of the temporal gain therein, foreshadowed in the writings of so many wise men, worthy of credence, who wrote histories and related how in these parts there are great riches. And it was likewise necessary to bring forward in this matter that which had been said and thought by those who have written of the world and who have described it. Finally, Your Highnesses determined that this enterprise should be undertaken.

Here you displayed that lofty spirit which you have always shown in every great affair, for all those who had been engaged on the matter and who had heard the proposal, one and all laughed it to scorn, save two friars who were ever constant.

I, although I suffered weariness, was very sure that this would not come to nothing, and I am still, for it is true that all will pass away, save the Word of God, and all that He has said will be fulfilled. And He spake so clearly of these lands by the mouth of Isaiah, in many places of his Book, affirming that from Spain His holy name should be proclaimed to them.

And I set forth in the name of the Holy Trinity, and I returned very speedily, with evidence of all, as much as I had said, in my hand. Your highnesses undertook to send me again, and in a little while I say that, . . . by the grace of God, I discovered three hundred and thirty-three leagues of Tierra Firme,[1] the end of the East, and seven hundred islands of importance, over and above that which I discovered on the first voyage, and I circumnavigated the island of Española, which in circumference is greater than all Spain, wherein are people innumerable, all of whom should pay tribute.

Then was born the defaming and disparagement of the undertaking which had been begun there, because I had not immediately sent caravels laden with gold, no thought being taken of the brevity of the time and the other many obstacles which I mentioned. And on this account, for my sins or, as I believe that it will be, for my salvation, I was held in abhorrence and was opposed in whatever I said and asked.

---

[1]**Tierra Firme:** The mainland.

For this cause, I decided to come to Your Highnesses, and to cause you to wonder at everything, and to show you the reason that I had for all. And I told you of the peoples whom I had seen, among whom or from whom many souls may be saved. And I brought to you the service of the people of the island of Española, how they were bound to pay tribute and how they held you as their sovereigns and lords. And I brought to you abundant evidence of gold, and that there are mines and very great nuggets, and likewise of copper. And I brought to you many kinds of spices, of which it would be wearisome to write, and I told you of the great amount of brazil[2] and of other things, innumerable.

READING AND DISCUSSION QUESTIONS

1. What religious implications did Columbus attach to his voyages? Why do you think he chose to highlight the opportunity his discoveries created for the spread of Catholicism?

2. What material advantages did Columbus claim would result from his discoveries? How might his readers have responded to his claims?

16-3 | Spanish Ambitions in the New World
THEODORE DE BRY, *Columbus at Hispaniola* (ca. 1590)

In his letters to King Ferdinand and Queen Isabella, Columbus told his side of the story, describing his voyages in ways that were meant both to please his patrons and to emphasize his personal accomplishments. His was not the last word, however. In the decades following Columbus's death, the motives behind his expeditions and the subsequent Spanish colonization of the Americas became matters of considerable debate. For example, this late-sixteenth-century engraving by the Protestant artist and engraver Theodore de Bry contains all of the motives mentioned by Columbus (see Document 16-2) but presents them in a way that offers an implicit rebuke to the Genoese explorer. As you examine it, think about its intended message. What did the artist see as the primary motives behind Spanish exploration and colonization? How did he want his viewers to feel about the scenes he included in this engraving?

---

[2]**brazil:** Brazilwood, a very expensive wood that was much sought after in Europe.

READING AND DISCUSSION QUESTIONS

1. Which motive did de Bry portray as most important? How did he indicate this?

2. What importance should we attach to the fact that the cross on the left is being erected by a small group of soldiers? What does the scene tell us about de Bry's views on Spanish missionary work in the Americas?

3. What should we make of the Native Americans fleeing the Spanish ships on the right side of the engraving? What are they afraid of? Did de Bry believe their fears were justified?

VIEWPOINTS COMPARATIVE QUESTIONS

1. What common elements are included in both Columbus's letter and de Bry's engraving? How do those elements combine in each document to tell the story of Columbus's voyages?

2. Why might Europeans have seen Columbus's voyages differently at the beginning of the sixteenth century than they did at the end of the century? What intervening events, both in the Americas and in Europe, might have reshaped European perspectives?

16-4 | Spanish Conquest of the Aztecs

BERNARDINO DE SAHAGÚN, From *General History of the Things of New Spain* (ca. 1545–1578)

A member of the Franciscan order, the Spaniard Bernardino de Sahagún (1499–1590) was one of the earliest missionaries to arrive in New Spain (Mexico). Sahagún believed that in order to convert the indigenous population to Christianity he needed to understand their pre-existing ideas and beliefs. He therefore learned the Aztec language of Nahuatl and worked with indigenous scholars to obtain and record information about Aztec culture and religion. Over thirty years, they compiled this knowledge into an encyclopedic text illustrated with over two thousand drawings, known as the *General History of the Things of New Spain*, or the *Florentine Codex*. It is considered one of the best sources for indigenous perspectives on the events of the conquest; however, it is important to remember Sahagún's role in shaping the text. The excerpt below describes the impact of smallpox on the Aztecs and their suffering in the capital, Tenochtitlan, during the Spanish siege of 1521.

Before the Spanish appeared to us, first an epidemic broke out, a sickness of pustules [smallpox]. . . . Large bumps spread on people; some were entirely covered. They spread everywhere, on the face, the head, the chest, etc. The disease brought great desolation; a great many died of it. They could no longer walk about, but lay in their dwellings and sleeping places, no longer able to move or stir. They were unable to change position, to stretch out on their sides or face down, or raise their heads. And when they made a motion, they called out loudly. The pustules that covered people caused great desolation; very many people died of them, and many just starved to death; starvation reigned, and no one took care of others any longer.

On some people, the pustules appeared only far apart, and they did not suffer greatly, nor did many of them die of it. But many people's faces were spoiled by it, their faces and noses were made rough. Some lost an eye or were blinded.

James Lockart, ed. and trans., *We People Here: Nahuatl Accounts of the Conquest of Mexico* (Berkeley: University of California Press, 1993). Copyright © 1993 by James Lockhart. Used with permission.

This disease of pustules lasted a full sixty days; after sixty days it abated and ended. When people were convalescing and reviving, the pustules disease began to move in the direction of Chalco. And many were disabled or paralyzed by it, but they were not disabled forever. . . . The Mexica warriors were greatly weakened by it.

And when things were in this state, the Spaniards came, moving toward us from Tetzcoco. . . .

[Having resupplied his Spanish/Tlaxcalan army and having constructed a dozen cannon-carrying brigantines for use on the lake, Cortés resumed his offensive against the Aztecs late in 1520. In April 1521 he reached Tenochtitlan and placed the city under a blockade.]

When their twelve boats had come from Tetzcoco, at first they were all assembled at Acachinanco, and then the Marqués [Cortés] moved to Acachinanco. He went about searching where the boats could enter, where the canals were straight, whether they were deep or not, so that they would not be grounded somewhere. But the canals were winding and bent back and forth, and they could not get them in. They did get two boats in; they forced them down the road coming straight from Xoloco. . . .

And the two boats came gradually, keeping on one side. On the other side no boats came, because there were houses there. They came ahead, fighting as they came; there were deaths on both sides and on both sides captives were taken. When the Tenochca who lived in Çoquipan saw this, they fled, fled in fear . . . they took nothing at all with them, they just left all their poor property in fear, they just scattered everything in their haste. And our enemies went snatching things up, taking whatever they came upon. Whatever they hit on they carried away, whether cloaks, lengths of cotton cloth, warrior's devices, log drums, or cylindrical drums. . . .

Once they got two of their boats into the canal at Xocotitlan. When they had beached them, then they went looking into the house sites of the people of Xocotitlan. But Tzilacatazin and some other warriors who saw the Spaniards immediately came out to face them; they came running after them, throwing stones at them, and they scattered the Spaniards into the water. . . .

When they got to Tlilhuacan, the warriors crouched far down and hid themselves, hugging the ground, waiting for the war cry, when there would be shouting and cries of encouragement. When the cry went up, "O Mexica, up and at them!" the Tlappanecatl Ecatzin, a warrior of Otomi rank, faced the Spaniards and threw himself at them, saying "O Tlatelolca warriors, up and at them, who are these barbarians? Come running!" Then he went and threw a Spaniard down, knocking him to the ground; the one he threw down was the one who came first, who came leading them. And when he had thrown him down, he dragged the Spaniard off.

And at this point they let loose with all the warriors who had been crouching there; they came out and chased the Spaniards. . . . Then captives were taken. Many Tlaxcalans, and people of Acolhuacan, Chalco, Xochimilco, etc. [i.e., allies of the Spaniards], were captured. A great abundance were captured and killed. . . .

[Despite this victory, the Aztecs could not overcome the problems of shortages of food, water, and warriors. In mid-July 1521 the Spaniards and their allies resumed their assault. Weakened by smallpox, the Aztecs surrendered on August 13, 1521, after a siege of over three months' duration.]

And all the common people suffered greatly. There was famine; many died of hunger. They no longer drank good, pure water, but the water they drank was salty. Many people died of it, and because of it many got dysentery and died. Everything was eaten: lizards, swallows, maize straw, grass that grows on salt flats. And they chewed at . . . wood, glue flowers, plaster, leather, and deerskin, which they roasted, baked, and toasted so that they could eat them, and they ground up medicinal herbs and adobe bricks. There had never been the like of such suffering. The siege was frightening, and great numbers died of hunger. And bit by bit they came pressing us against the wall, herding us together. . . . There was no place to go; people shoved, pressed and trampled one another; many died in the press.

READING AND DISCUSSION QUESTIONS

1. From whose perspective is this text written? How does it characterize the forces fighting in defense of the Aztec Empire and those fighting to defeat it?

2. How does this text document the unintentional consequences of contact between the people of the Valley of Mexico and the Spanish? What role do those consequences play in the conflict?

16-5 | Blending Indigenous and European Styles

ANDRÉS SÁNCHEZ GALLQUE, *The Mulatto Gentlemen of Esmeraldas* (1599)

This painting depicts the almost life-sized image of a fifty-six-year-old man, Don Francisco de Arobe (middle), and two young men, Don Pedro and Don Domingo, believed to be his sons. De Arobe was the leader of a settlement in the province of Esmeraldas on the north coast of modern-day Ecuador. In this tropic coastal region, Africans who had escaped from slavery in the 1550s joined, intermarried with, and ultimately dominated indigenous communities suffering from population loss due to contact with the Spanish. The title commonly given to the painting, *The Mulatto Gentlemen of Esmeraldas*, suggests that the men were "mulattoes," meaning people of mixed European and African ancestry, whereas they were more likely of mixed indigenous and African descent. The men's fine clothing displays a mixture of European and indigenous styles; they wear imported Spanish silk cloaks, lace collars, and cuffs, combined with Amerindian gold nose- and ear-plugs, and seashell necklaces worn since preconquest times. A Spanish official commissioned the painting in 1599 for the king of Spain to commemorate de Arobe's conversion to Christianity and declaration of loyalty to Spain.

Joseph Martin/Album Photo Press, Madrid, Spain/Newscom

READING AND DISCUSSION QUESTIONS

1. What impression of Don Francisco de Arobe and his sons do you get from this painting, and what elements of the painting convey this impression? What do we learn from the clothing and decorations they are wearing?

2. Why would a Spanish official have commissioned this painting for the king of Spain? What message is he sending to the king with this painting?

▪ COMPARATIVE QUESTIONS ▪

1. Compare and contrast the descriptions of Native Americans offered by Columbus and de Sahagún. How would you explain the differences you note?

2. Compare and contrast de Bry's engraving of Columbus at Hispaniola and Gallque's painting of *The Mulatto Gentlemen of Esmeraldas*. In what ways do the paintings show evolving relations between indigenous people and Europeans, from first contact in 1492 to the end of the sixteenth century?

3. What do the documents included in this chapter, taken together, tell you about the motives behind Spanish exploration and colonization in the New World and the impact on indigenous people?

4. What are the limitations of the paintings and documents in this chapter in their depictions of the experiences of indigenous people?

17

The Islamic World Powers

1300–1800

With the decline of the Mongol Empire in the late thirteenth and fourteenth centuries, powerful new states emerged in south and west Eurasia. By the sixteenth century, three areas had developed into major Islamic empires: the Safavid in Persia, the Ottoman in Anatolia, and the Mughal in India. Their collective territories stretched from eastern Europe and West Africa through present-day Bangladesh. Although these three dynasties were rivals that sometimes waged war against each other, the empires they built shared important characteristics and faced similar challenges. As each state flourished, it made significant political, economic, intellectual, and artistic contributions. Islamic culture was enriched by the states' interactions with one another and with the increasingly mobile peoples of Christian Europe. The following documents provide insight into relations among the Ottoman, Safavid, and Mughal Empires, and shed light on the interplay among religion, law, and society in these empires.

17-1 | An Ottoman Sultan Threatens the Shah of Persia

SULTAN SELIM I, *From a Letter to Shah Ismail of Persia* (1514)

Sultan Selim I (r. 1512–1520) presided over a massive territorial expansion of the Ottoman Empire, conquering much of the Middle East, including the holy cities of Mecca and Medina. After defeating the Mamluk Dynasty in Egypt in 1517, Selim assumed the title of caliph—a political and religious successor to Muhammad—thereby declaring Sunni Ottoman leadership of the Muslim world. The excerpt that follows is from Selim's letter to Shah Ismail of Persia, the young founder of the Shi'ite Safavid Empire and a growing threat to Selim's power. The ensuing conflict in 1514 marked an important moment in Sunni–Shi'ite power struggles in the Islamic world.

John J. Saunders, ed. and trans., *The Muslim World on the Eve of Europe's Expansion* (Englewood Cliffs, N.J.: Prentice-Hall, 1966), pp. 41–43.

The Supreme Being who is at once the sovereign arbiter of the destinies of men and the source of all light and knowledge, declares in the holy book [the Qur'an] that the true faith is that of the Muslims, and that whoever professes another religion, far from being hearkened to and saved, will on the contrary be cast out among the rejected on the great day of the Last Judgment; He says further, this God of truth, that His designs and decrees are unalterable, that all human acts are perforce reported to Him, and that he who abandons the good way will be condemned to hell-fire and eternal torments. Place yourself, O Prince, among the true believers, those who walk in the path of salvation, and who turn aside with care from vice and infidelity. . . .

I, sovereign chief of the Ottomans, master of the heroes of the age; . . . I, the exterminator of idolators, destroyer of the enemies of the true faith, the terror of the tyrants and pharaohs of the age; I, before whom proud and unjust kings have humbled themselves, and whose hand breaks the strongest scepters; I, the great Sultan-Khan, son of Sultan Bayezid-Khan, son of Sultan Muhammad-Khan, son of Sultan Murad-Khan, I address myself graciously to you, Emir Ismail, chief of the troops of Persia, comparable in tyranny to Sohak and Afrasiab [legendary Asian kings], and predestined to perish . . . in order to make known to you that the works emanating from the Almighty are not the fragile products of caprice or folly, but make up an infinity of mysteries impenetrable to the human mind. The Lord Himself says in his holy book: "We have not created the heavens and the earth in order to play a game" [Qur'an, 21:16]. Man, who is the noblest of the creatures and the summary of the marvels of God, is in consequence on earth the living image of the Creator. It is He who has set up Caliphs on earth, because, joining faculties of soul with perfection of body, man is the only being who can comprehend the attributes of the divinity and adore its sublime beauties; but he possesses this rare intelligence, he attains this divine knowledge only in our religion and by observing the precepts of the prince of prophets . . . the right arm of the God of Mercy [Muhammad]; it is then only by practicing the true religion that man will prosper in this world and merit eternal life in the other. As to you, Emir Ismail, such a recompense will not be your lot; because you have denied the sanctity of the divine laws; because you have deserted the path of salvation and the sacred commandments; because you have impaired the purity of the dogmas of Islam; because you have dishonored, soiled, and destroyed the altars of the Lord, usurped the scepter of the East by unlawful and tyrannical means; because coming forth from the dust, you have raised yourself by odious devices to a place shining with splendor and magnificence; because you have opened to Muslims the gates of tyranny and oppression; because you have joined iniquity, perjury, and blasphemy to your sectarian impiety; because under the cloak of the hypocrite, you have sowed everywhere trouble and sedition; because you have raised the standard of irreligion and heresy; because yielding to the impulse of your evil passions, and giving yourself up without rein to the most infamous disorders, you have dared to throw off the control of Muslim laws and to permit lust and rape, the massacre of the most virtuous and respectable men, the destruction of pulpits and temples, the profanation of tombs, the ill-treatment of the ulama,[1] the doctors [teachers] and emirs [military commanders and princes] descended from the Prophet, the repudiation of the Quran, the cursing of the legitimate Caliphs.[2] Now as the first duty of a Muslim and above all of a pious prince is to obey the commandment, "O, you faithful who believe, be the executors of the decrees of God!" the ulama and our doctors have pronounced sentence of death against you, perjurer and blasphemer, and have imposed on every Muslim the sacred obligation to arm in defense of religion and destroy heresy and impiety in your person and that of all your partisans.

Animated by the spirit of this fatwa [religious decree], conforming to the Quran, the code of divine laws, and wishing on one side to strengthen Islam, on the other to liberate the lands and peoples who writhe under your yoke, we have resolved to lay aside our imperial robes in order to put on the shield and coat of mail [armor], to raise our ever victorious banner, to assemble our invincible armies, to take up the gauntlet of the avenger, to march with our soldiers, whose sword strikes mortal blows, and whose point will pierce the enemy even to the constellation of Sagittarius. In pursuit of this noble resolution, we have entered upon the campaign, and guided by the hand of the Almighty, we hope soon to strike down your tyrannous arm, blow away the clouds of glory and grandeur which trouble your head and cause your fatal blindness, release from your despotism your trembling subjects, smother you in the end in the very mass of flames which your infernal jinn [supernatural spirit] raises everywhere along your passage, accomplishing in this way on you the maxim which says: "He who sows discord can only reap evils and afflictions." However, anxious to conform to the spirit of the law of the Prophet, we come, before commencing war, to set out before you the words of the Quran, in place of the sword, and to exhort you to embrace the true faith; this is why we address this letter to you. . . .

We urge you to look into yourself, to renounce your errors, and to march towards the good with a firm and courageous step; we ask further that you give up possession of the territory violently seized from our state and to which you have only illegitimate pretensions, that you deliver it back into the hands of our lieutenants and officers; and if you value your safety and repose, this should be done without delay.

But if, to your misfortune, you persist in your past conduct, puffed up with the idea of your power and your foolish bravado, you wish to pursue the course of your iniquities, you will see in a few days your plains covered with our tents and inundated with our battalions. Then prodigies of valor will be done, and we shall see the decrees of the Almighty, Who is the God of Armies, and sovereign judge of the actions of men, accomplished. For the rest, victory to him who follows the path of salvation!

---

[1]**ulama:** Religious teachers and interpreters of the Qur'an and Muslim law.

[2]**the legitimate Caliphs:** Shi'ites broke with mainstream Islam over a dispute about the early caliphate. They believe that Muhammad's cousin and son-in-law Ali (the fourth caliph) should have been the first caliph. Shi'ites thus believe that the first three caliphs are illegitimate.

READING AND DISCUSSION QUESTIONS

1. What is Selim's principal complaint against Ismail? How does he state it?

2. Where in the letter does Selim use the rhetoric of religion against Ismail, and where does he accuse Ismail of political failings? How do the two arguments work together?

3. What do you think Selim's real purpose was in writing this letter: to give Ismail an opportunity to repent, to provoke Ismail into declaring war, or to justify his own decision to attack Ismail?

17-2 | An Ottoman Admiral at the Mughal Court

SEYDI ALI REIS, From *The Mirror of Countries* (1557)

In 1552, Sultan Suleiman I appointed Seydi Ali Reis (1498–1563) to be admiral of the Ottoman Indian Ocean fleet, with orders to return fifteen Ottoman galleys from the Persian Gulf port of Basra to the fleet's headquarters at Suez on the Red Sea. Battles with the Portuguese, followed by bad weather, cost Seydi Ali Reis all but three of his ships. He found refuge on the Gujarat coast of India, where the sultanate was allied with the Ottomans, and then set out to travel overland to Constantinople. This journey, which brought him through India, Afghanistan, and Persia, would take more than two years (1554–1556), including a sojourn in the court of newly installed Mughal emperor Humayun. A learned man, Seydi Ali Reis wrote important books on astronomy, navigation, and geography. Shortly after his return to Constantinople, he wrote an account of his travels entitled *Mirat il Memalik* (The Mirror of Countries), from which the passage below is excerpted.

. . . in the first days of the Month Shawwal (September) we came to Lahore. The political state of the country was as follows: After the death of Selim Shah a son of Shir Khan, the former Sovereign of Hindustan, Iskender Khan, had come to the throne. When the Padishah Humayun heard this he immediately left Kabul and marched his army to India, took Lahore, and fought Iskender Khan near Sahrand. He won the battle and took 400 elephants, besides several cannon and 400 chariots. Iskender Khan escaped to the fortress of Mankut, and Humayun sent Shah Abul-Maali with a detachment of soldiers after him. Humayun himself proceeded to his residence at Delhi and dispatched his officers to different places.[3] The Ozbeg, Iskender Khan, he sent to Agra, and others to Firuzshah Senbel, Bayana, and Karwitch. War raged on all sides, and when I arrived at

---

Charles F. Horne, ed., *The Sacred Books and Early Literature of the East*, vol. 6 (New York: Parke, Austin, & Lipscomb, 1917), pp. 357–360, 363.

[3]**When the Padishah . . . to different places:** Humayun inherited the throne in 1530 from his father Babur, the founder of the Mughal dynasty, but was deposed and exiled in 1540. The events described in this paragraph, by which Humayun regained power, occurred in early 1555, several months before Seyid Ali Reis's arrival in Delhi.

Lahore the Governor, Mirza Shah, would not let me continue my journey until I had seen the Padishah (Humayun).[4] After sending the latter word of my arrival, he received orders to send me forthwith to Delhi. Meanwhile a whole month had been wasted, but finally we were sent off with an escort. The river Sultanpoor was crossed in boats and after a journey of 20 days we arrived, toward the end of Dulkaada, by the route of Firuzshah in the capital of India, called Delhi.

As soon as Humayun heard of our arrival he sent the Khanikhanan [the commander in chief of the army] and other superior officers with 400 elephants and some thousand men to meet us, and, out of respect and regard for our glorious Padishah [the Ottoman sultan], we were accorded a brilliant reception. That same day the Khanikhanan prepared a great banquet in our honor; and as it is the custom in India to give audience in the evening, I was that night introduced with much pomp and ceremony into the Imperial hall. After my presentation I offered the Emperor a small gift, and a chronogram upon the conquest of India, also two gazels,[5] all of which pleased the Padishah greatly. Forthwith I begged for permission to continue my journey, but this was not granted. Instead of that I was offered a Kulur and the governorship over the district of Kharcha. I refused, and again begged to be allowed to go, but for only answer I was told that I must at least remain for one year, to which I replied: "By special command of my glorious Padishah I went by sea to fight the miserable unbelievers [the Portuguese]. Caught in a terrible hurricane, I was wrecked off the coast of India; but it is now my plain duty to return to render an account to my Padishah, and it is to be hoped that Gujarat will soon be delivered out of the hands of the unbelievers." Upon this Humayun suggested the sending of an envoy to Constantinople, to save my going, but this I could not agree to, for it would give the impression that I had purposely arranged it so. I persisted in my entreaties, and he finally consented, adding, however: "We are now close upon the three months of continuous Birshegal, (i.e., the rainy season). The roads are flooded and impassable, remain therefore till the weather improves. Meanwhile calculate solar and lunar eclipses, their degree of latitude, and their exact date in the calendar. Assist our astrologers in studying the course of the sun, and instruct us concerning the points of the equator. When all this is done, and the weather should improve before the three months are over, then thou shalt go hence."

All this was said solemnly and decisively. I had no alternative, but must submit to my fate. I took no rest, however, but labored on night and day. At last I had accomplished the astronomical observations, and about the same time Agra fell into the hands of the Padishah. I immediately wrote a chronogram for the occasion, which found much favor. One day, during an audience, the conversation turned upon Sultan Mahmud of Bukkur, and I suggested that some

---

[4]**Padishah:** Equivalent to Great King; Seyid Ali uses this term for both the Ottoman emperor and the Mughal emperor.

[5]**gazel (*ghazal*):** A form of short lyric poetry popular in the Muslim world, originating in the eighth century.

official contract (Ahdnameh, i.e., "agreement") should be made with him, to which Humayun agreed. The document was drawn up, and the Emperor dipping his fist in saffron pressed it upon the paper, this being the Tughra, or Imperial signature. Thereupon the document was sent to Sultan Mahmud. The Sultan was much pleased, and both he and his Vizier Molla Yari expressed their thanks for my intervention in a private letter, which I showed to his Majesty, who had entrusted me with the transaction. . . .

One day he (Humayun) asked me whether Turkey was larger than India, and I said: "If by Turkey your Majesty means Rum proper, i.e., the province of Siwas,[6] then India is decidedly the larger, but if by Turkey you mean all the lands subject to the ruler of Rum, India is not by a tenth part as large." "I mean the entire Empire," replied Humayun. "Then," I said, "it appears to me, your Majesty, that the seven regions over which Iskender (i.e. Alexander the Great) had dominion, were identical with the present Empire of the Padishah of Turkey. (. . .)" "But has the ruler of Turkey possession in all these regions?" asked Humayun. "Yes, certainly," I replied; "the first is Yemen, the second Mecca, the third Egypt, the fourth Aleppo, the fifth Constantinople, the sixth Kaffa, and the seventh Ofen and Vienna. In each of these regions the Padishah of Turkey appoints his Beglerbeg and Kadi, who rule and govern in this name. (. . .)" The Sovereign (Humayun) turning to his nobles, said: "Surely the only man worthy to bear the title of Padishah is the ruler of Turkey, he alone and no one else in all the world."

On another occasion I called upon Shahin Bey, the keeper of the Imperial Seal, and asked him to use his influence to obtain permission for me to depart. In order not to come empty-handed I brought him two gazels, and begged him urgently to intercede for me. Shahin Bey promised to do his best, and one day he actually brought me the glad news that my petition had been granted, but that I was expected to offer my request formally in verse. The rainy season was now at an end; I wrote to the monarch, enclosing two gazels, which had the desired effect, for I received not only permission to leave, but also presents and letters of safe conduct.

READING AND DISCUSSION QUESTIONS

1. How was Seydi Ali Reis received by Emperor Humayun? Based on his experience at the Mughal court, how would you characterize the relationship between the Ottoman and Mughal Empires in this period?

2. What role did Seydi Ali Reis play in Mughal affairs during his stay at the emperor's court? How do political events around the time of his visit help explain this role?

3. What evidence does this passage provide of Seydi Ali Reis's attitude toward the Mughals? What does he want his hosts to know about the Ottoman Empire?

---

[6]**Siwas:** Refers to the original home of the Ottoman Dynasty; in India and Central Asia, Rum meant the West, and specifically the Ottoman Empire.

VIEWPOINTS

Women's Role in Ottoman Society

As in ancient Greek and Byzantine society, the common view in the early modern Islamic world was that women should remain at home and avoid contact with men apart from close family members. The term *harem* in Arabic refers to a sacred sanctuary, such as the holy cities of Mecca and Medina. It also refers to the private female quarters of any large household, including the imperial palace. During the early modern period, wives of foreign ambassadors sent home stories of the lively sociability of the imperial harem and the lavish receptions they received from their hostesses. The preference for women to remain in the home did not mean, however, that they were deprived of rights and freedoms. Islamic law provided strict protections for women, especially regarding issues of marriage and divorce and ownership of property. As we see below, women, especially in towns and cities, routinely exercised these rights and appeared in person in public courts to press for justice in law courts.

17-3 | Sociability in the Imperial Harem

Feast for the Valide Sultana with the Presence of Madame Girardin, the French Ambassador (ca. 17th century)

This watercolor painting depicts a feast hosted by the *valide sultan*, or queen mother of the Ottoman sultan, in the late 1680s, attended by the wife of the French ambassador. Dancers and acrobats perform accompanied by a troupe of musicians. The harem is guarded by a "black eunuch." Black eunuchs were enslaved men of African descent who were castrated to prevent sexual relations with women and who then served as bodyguards and messengers for the harem. ("White eunuchs," castrated men of European descent, guarded the sultan's private apartments and ran the palace school.) Like eunuchs, male dwarfs (pictured here as acrobats) were allowed in the harem, since they were not considered to be fully adult males.

Bibliotheque Nationale, Paris, France/Bridgeman Images

READING AND DISCUSSION QUESTIONS

1. Based on this painting, what were important elements of hospitality provided by the queen mother to the French ambassador's wife? Why would these be part of diplomatic relations between the Ottoman Empire and the French kingdom?

2. How is the power and authority of the queen mother visually depicted? How would you describe the position of the "black eunuch"?

3. Who do you think the audience would be for this image, and what do you think they would learn from seeing it?

17-4 | Women in Courts of Law in an Ottoman City
From *The Sharia Court of Anatolian Kayseri* (ca. 17th century)

In accordance with Islamic law, women in the Ottoman Empire enjoyed an impressive range of legal and economic rights. Adult women could inherit property (though generally half as much as their male relatives), lend and borrow money, refuse a proposed husband, and, with their husbands' consent, divorce. In order to defend and enforce these rights, they frequently petitioned Islamic law courts. The cases presented here took place in the early 1600s in the central Anatolian city of Kayseri, which had been brought into the Ottoman Empire in 1515 by Selim I (see Document 17-1).

Documents translated in Ronald C. Jennings, "Women in Early 17th Century Ottoman Judicial Records: The sharia Court of Anatolian Kayseri," *Journal of the Economic and Social History of the Orient*, vol. 18, No. 1 (January 1975), pp. 62, 63, 67, 68, 78, 83, 85, 90, 92, 104. Copyright © 1975 by Brill Publisher. Used with permission; permission conveyed through Copyright Clearance Center, Inc.

Çinar daughter of Bagadasar of Talas village sets forth a claim in the presence of Sefer son of Firoz: He struck me, pulled my hair saying, 'I'll make use of you,' and again struck me. I demand that he be punished according to the *sharia* (Islamic law). Sinan son of Kavan and Sunbul son of Yunus confirm that Sefer knocked Çinar to the ground, pulled her hair, and struck her, and they rescued her from him. Heard in the presence of Husam Beg, representative of the Kayseri Major General.

Melek, Sofya, and Sultan daughters of Kara Beg of Talas set forth a claim in the presence of Haci Huseyn son of Mehmed, large landowner (*dergah-i ali buvab*): Haci Huseyn has in his possession two shares of the seven shares of a field, a garden, and two vineyards that we inherited from our late father. Haci Huseyn claims he bought the fields from their brother Mihail five years earlier, but he has no witnesses and so is restrained. The property is ordered to the sisters.

Gul Ana daughter of Ugurlu of the neighborhood of Bektaş sets forth a claim in the presence of Isa son of Mehmed: My husband Kutluşeh son of Iskender sold one of my vineyards without my permission. I want it. Kutluşeh admits having given Gul Ana the vineyard as *mehr* (dowry) and then having sold it unlawfully for 17 guruş. Mehmed asks that Kutluseh and Gul Ana take oaths that she was not consulted in the sale, and they do. Then the vineyard is ordered restored to Gul Ana.

Gulli daughter of Suleyman sets forth a complaint in the presence of Piyale son of Abdullah: I bought a vineyard at Kanli Yurt with 110 *ak altun* of my own money. My son Mustafa sold it without my permission to Piyale. Piyale says that he bought the vineyard for 9 ½ guruş from Mustafa knowing nothing about Gulli's claim. Two witnesses confirm that Gulli bought the vineyard with her own money.

Mehmed son of Yakub sets forth a claim in the presence of his mother Yasemin daughter of Abdullah: My mother has taken possession of a guesthouse in the neighborhood of Debbaglar that I inherited from my late father. Yasemin says Mehmed's father, her husband Yakub, sold her the guesthouse for 3000 akçe, which was paid in full. Two witnesses confirm her.

Haci Bola bint Huseyn, a legal major, from Salurci Dere village in Amasiyya district sets forth a claim saying: On 28 I Cumadi 1034 [the year 1624 in the Julian calendar] my father Huseyn married me to Spahi Mehmed Beg. When I heard this, I refused to accept it. I want that marriage cancelled and I want to marry this Ibrahim Çelebi son of Keyvan. I did not give my consent to be married to Mehmed. A *fetva* (legal opinion on a point of Islamic law, *fatwa* in Arabic) is presented that if she is of age, her father cannot marry her against her wishes. . . . the marriage is annulled, and permission is given for her to marry Ibrahim Çelebi.

Mehmed son of Haci Ali acknowledges in the presence of Fatma daughter of Turmuş: We were not living together. She renounces claim to all dowry and other conjugal liabilities. I divorce her. Confirmed by Fatma.

Rabia daughter of Ali of Gulluk neighborhood acknowledges in the presence of her husband Abdur-Rahman son of Himmet: He gave me half a house in the neighborhood as dowry but since we are not living together I gave it back to him, and I renounce claim to dowry, alimony, and other conjugal liabilities. He pronounced divorce and I accepted some cloth and 2 guruş as divorce payment. Our little daughter Cemile is to stay with me until she is nine.

Emine Hatun son of Abdus-Selame of Kale'-I pala in Amasya has as representative for the matter her father Abdus-Selam, who sets forth a claim: My daughter Emine's husband Ebu Bekr divorced her. He has gone elsewhere, without providing maintenance for Emine's two children. I want 4 acke per day allotted for them.

Hasan son of Kilic sets forth a claim in the presence of Fatma daughter of Veli: I have been married with Fatma for ten years. I went to another province for a few years, and while I was absent she married Murad. I have a fetva regarding this. Fatma claims that Hasan divorced her when he went to the other province, but she has no proof. Hasan takes an oath that he did not divorce her. The fetva says, Is Zeyd's claim against Hind for marrying Amr while he was away in another province valid? The answer: yes. When proof is demanded of Hasan, two witnesses testify that Hasan and Fatma were married ten years ago and were still married when Hasan went away.

Kadi Mevlana Huseyn Efendi (*efendi* is a courtesy title indicating high social rank, equivalent to "sir") son of Haci Ahmed sets forth a claim in the presence of Osman Beşe son of Abdullah: I was engaged to Haci Himmet's daughter Sitti for 7 or 8 years. In 1017 (1607 in the Julian calendar) Sitti was married to me at Haci Himmet's house. Then, while I was away, Osman Beşe unlawfully took her. Osman claims he became married with Sitti after her father died, knowing nothing about Huseyn. Himmet son of Haci Ahmed and Huseyn son of Ali confirm Huseyn Efendi's assertion that Himmet had married his daughter to him.

Hasan grants his wife maintenance, admits he struck her contrary to the sharia, and divorces her.

When Imam Nu'man son of Abdul-Vehhab and Osman son of Mehmed and Himmet son of Ali testified that this Abdul-Celil Aga struck his wife, he took an oath that he would not strike her contrary to the sharia.

Yakub son of Yakub of the neighborhood of Alaca Suluk sets forth a claim in the presence of his wife Safiye daughter of Hamze: For four months my wife Safiye has not lived with me; she has lived in another place. It is my right to have her with me. Let her be asked. Safiye says Adhmed Efendi, judge (*kadi*) in Ermenak, warned Yakub that if he struck me he would be divorced three times. Yakub accepted this, then he struck me contrary to the sharia, so I became divorced from him. Yakub denies this. However, witnesses former judge (*kadi*) Alaeddin Efendi son of Ahmed and Mahmud son of Alaeddin Halife confirm Safiye. They heard Yakub say that Ahmed Efendi had given him this condition.

Selva daughter of Omer makes a claim in the presence of her husband Suleyman Beşe son of Haci Hasan: Although he paid me in full the 31 guruş he got for selling my slave girl, he took the money from me again. I want it. Suleyman denies taking single ackçe.

READING AND DISCUSSION QUESTIONS

1. Based on these legal cases, what issues were most likely to bring women to court in the seventeenth-century Ottoman Empire?

2. What kinds of legal rights did the courts recognize for women? In what areas did women possess fewer rights than men? What roles did men and women play in these cases? Do you think the women in these cases received fair treatment?

3. What evidence of contemporary attitudes toward women do you find in these documents? What concerns did this society seem to have about how men and women behaved?

VIEWPOINTS COMPARATIVE QUESTIONS

1. How would you compare the portrayal of women's lives in the painting versus the court documents? Are the two depictions complementary or contradictory? What could account for the differences in portrayal?

2. How would you assess the relative usefulness of these two sources for understanding women's lives and gender roles in this society? What are their strengths and limitations as historical sources?

17-5 | A Mughal Emperor Describes His Life and Rule

NURUDDIN SALIM JAHANGIR, From the *Memoirs of Jahangir* (ca. 1580–1600)

Akbar's third son, Prince Salim (1569–1628), succeeded his father as the Mughal sovereign in 1605 and took the name Jahangir, or "World Conqueror." During his reign, he continued many of his father's policies, including limited religious tolerance and wars of territorial expansion. Jahangir found himself locked in a familiar pattern of Mughal succession when his son Khurram rebelled in 1622, just as Jahangir had rebelled against his own father. The passages here are taken from Jahangir's autobiography. In the first section, he presents measures to promote justice and social welfare in the realm. In the second, he describes a hunting trip with his favorite wife, Nūr-Jahān Begam.

After my accession, the first order that I gave was for the fastening up of the Chain of Justice, so that if those engaged in the administration of justice should delay or practice hypocrisy in the matter of those seeking justice, the oppressed might come to this chain and shake it so that its noise might attract attention. Its

---

The Tūzuk-i-Jahangīrī or *Memoirs of Jahangir*, ed. Alexander Rogers and Henry Beveridge (London: Royal Asiatic Society, 1909–1914), pp. 2, 105.

fashion was this: I ordered them to make a chain of pure gold, 30 gaz in length and containing 60 bells. Its weight was 4 Indian maunds, equal to 42 'Irāqī maunds. One end of it they made fast to the battlements of the Shāh Burj of the fort at Agra and the other to a stone post fixed on the bank of the river. I also gave twelve orders to be observed as rules of conduct in all my dominions —

1. Forbidding the levy of cesses [taxes] under the names of tamghā and mīr bah·rī [river tolls], and other burdens which the jāgīrdārs[7] of every province and district had imposed for their own profit.
2. On roads where thefts and robberies took place, which roads might be at a little distance from habitations, the jāgīrdārs of the neighborhood should build sarā'īs [public rest houses], mosques, and dig wells, which might stimulate population, and people might settle down in those sarā'īs. If these should be near a khālisa estate,[8] the administrator of that place should execute the work.
3. The bales of merchants should not be opened on the roads without informing them and obtaining their leave.
4. In my dominions if anyone, whether unbeliever or Musalman, should die, his property and effects should be left for his heirs, and no one should interfere with them. If he should have no heir, they should appoint inspectors and separate guardians to guard the property, so that its value might be expended in lawful expenditure, such as the building of mosques and sarā'īs, the repair of broken bridges, and the digging of tanks and wells.
5. They should not make wine or rice-spirit or any kind of intoxicating drug, or sell them; although I myself drink wine, and from the age of 18 years up till now, when I am 38, have persisted in it. When I first took a liking to drinking I sometimes took as much as twenty cups of double-distilled spirit; when by degrees it acquired a great influence over me I endeavored to lessen the quantity, and in the period of seven years I have brought myself from fifteen cups to five or six. My times for drinking were varied; sometimes when three or four sidereal hours of the day remained I would begin to drink, and sometimes at night and partly by day. This went on till I was 30 years old. After that I took to drinking always at night. Now I drink only to digest my food.
6. They should not take possession of any person's house.
7. I forbade the cutting off the nose or ears of any person, and I myself made a vow by the throne of God that I would not blemish anyone by this punishment.
8. I gave an order that the officials of the Crown lands and the jāgīrdārs should not forcibly take the ryots' [farmers'] lands and cultivate them on their own account.
9. A government collector or a jāgīrdār should not without permission intermarry with the people of the pargana [district] in which he might be.

---

[7]**jāgīrdārs:** Regional rulers whose income came primarily from taxes imposed within their districts.

[8]**khālisa estate:** Land controlled by the state.

10. They should found hospitals in the great cities, and appoint physicians for the healing of the sick; whatever the expenditure might be, should be given from the ḳẖāliṣa establishment.

11. In accordance with the regulations of my revered father, I ordered that each year from the 18th of Rabī'u-l-awwal, which is my birthday, for a number of days corresponding to the years of my life, they should not slaughter animals [for food]. Two days in each week were also forbidden, one of them Thursday, the day of my accession, and the other Sunday, the day of my father's birth. He held this day in great esteem on this account, and because it was dedicated to the Sun, and also because it was the day on which the Creation began. Therefore it was one of the days on which there was no killing in his dominions.

12. I gave a general order that the offices and jāgīrs [land plots] of my father's servants should remain as they were. Later, the mansabs [ranks or offices] were increased according to each one's circumstances by not less than 20 percent to 300 or 400 percent. The subsistence money of the ahadīs was increased by 50 percent, and I raised the pay of all domestics by 20 percent. I increased the allowances of all the veiled ladies of my father's harem from 20 percent to 100 percent, according to their condition and relationship. By one stroke of the pen I confirmed the subsistence lands of the holders of aimas [charity lands] within the dominions, who form the army of prayer, according to the deeds in their possession. I gave an order to Mīrān Ṣadr Jahān, who is one of the genuine Sayyids of India [descendants of Muhammad], and who for a long time held the high office of sadr [ecclesiastical officer] under my father, that he should every day produce before me deserving people [worthy of charity]. I released all criminals who had been confined and imprisoned for a long time in the forts and prisons. . . .

On the 25th the contingent of I'timādu-d-daulah passed before me in review on the plain under the jharoka.[9] There were 2,000 cavalry well horsed, most of whom were Moghuls, 500 foot [soldiers] armed with bows and guns, and fourteen elephants. The bakhshis reckoned them up and reported that this force was fully equipped and according to rule. On the 26th a tigress was killed. On Thursday, the 1st Urdībihisht, a diamond that Muqarrab Khān had sent by runners was laid before me; it weighed 23 surkh, and the jewellers valued it at 30,000 rupees. It was a diamond of the first water, and was much approved. I ordered them to make a ring of it. On the 3rd the mansab [military rank] of Yūsuf Khān was, at the request of Bābā Khurram, fixed at 1,000 with 1,500 horses, and in the same way the mansabs of several of the Amirs [nobles] and mansabdars [officeholders] were increased at his suggestion.[10] On the 7th, as the huntsmen had marked down four tigers, when two watches and three gharis [a length

---

[9]**jharoka:** Balcony used for architectural ornamentation and for spying.

[10]**fixed at 1,000 . . . suggestion:** A system of military ranking that also determined compensation. High-ranking commanders were in one of three classes according to the proportion of horsemen in their unit.

of time] had passed I went out to hunt them with my ladies. When the tigers came in sight Nūr-Jahān Begam submitted that if I would order her she herself would kill the tigers with her gun. I said, "Let it be so." She shot two tigers with one shot each and knocked over the two others with four shots. In the twinkling of an eye she deprived of life the bodies of these four tigers. Until now such shooting was never seen, that from the top of an elephant and inside of a howdah [carriage atop an elephant] six shots should be made and not one miss, so that the four beasts found no opportunity to spring or move. As a reward for this good shooting I gave her a pair of bracelets of diamonds worth 100,000 rupees and scattered 1,000 ashrafis [over her].

READING AND DISCUSSION QUESTIONS

1. What is the purpose of Jahangir's Chain of Justice? What impression does it create of the sovereign?

2. Jahangir's twelve orders deal with a variety of issues. How would you categorize them? Which order is most striking to you, and why?

3. What is the effect of Jahangir's frequent references to gold and jewels in both of these excerpts? What image does that create of him and his realm?

4. In the second excerpt, Jahangir describes both military forces and a hunting expedition with his wives. How would you compare the tone of this passage with his comments about justice and social order?

▪ COMPARATIVE QUESTIONS ▪

1. What do the documents included in this chapter reveal about the role of religion in Islamic imperial government? How was religion used to justify policy? How was it used to legitimize authority?

2. Compare and contrast Selim's letter to Ismail with Seydi Ali Reis's account of his sojourn in the Mughal court. What do we learn from these documents about the Ottoman Empire and its relations with other Islamic powers?

3. How does the passage from the *Memoirs of Jahangir*, specifically the tiger hunt, help provide context for the painting of the Ottoman harem and the law cases involving women? Why was the law so important for establishing government authority?

4. Compare and contrast Selim's letter to Ismail and the excerpts from the *Memoirs of Jahangir*. What did each author see as a ruler's primary duty? How did each go about fulfilling that duty?

18

European Power and Expansion

1500–1750

The seventeenth century was a time of deep crisis for Europe. Due in part to a "Little Ice Age" that brought severe weather conditions, commercial and agricultural sectors suffered from prolonged economic stagnation. In addition, many nations found themselves locked in expensive and devastating internal and external wars. In an effort to cope with these difficulties and to gain advantages in the ruthless continental rivalry, European states extended control over their populations through new forms of taxation, the military, and the state bureaucracy. The following documents reveal the different ways in which European governments engaged with the challenges of the seventeenth century. In countries like England and the Dutch Republic, a system of constitutionalism envisioned political power as a careful balance of many forces. In France, Iberia, and eastern Europe, the doctrine of absolutism stressed the divine and undivided power of the monarch. Despite their differences, both systems represented careful attempts to establish centralized states that claimed sovereignty over their territories and peoples, as well as to expand their territory through the creation of land and maritime empires.

18-1 | Secular and Religious Authority in the Protestant Reformation

MARTIN LUTHER, *"On Secular Authority: How Far Does the Obedience Owed to It Extend?"* (1523)

Though the Protestant Reformation is sometimes equated with Martin Luther, from the beginning it was really a plural movement, and people had different ideas about every aspect

Luther and Calvin on Secular Authority (Cambridge Texts in The History of Political Thought), edited and translated by Harro Höpfl; pp. 9–15, 18. Copyright © 1991 by Cambridge University Press. Reproduced with permission of the licensor through PLSclear.

of doctrine and practice. Some ideas were quite radical, including social and political equality, and in a few places, this extremism led to violence. Luther was horrified and quickly wrote several works explaining that religious beliefs did not justify rebellion. This is one of those writings, in which Luther states unequivocally that God has given both spiritual and secular authorities their power. His words did not stop the German peasants from revolting against their overlords, and Luther sided with the nobles, calling for the rebellious peasants to be killed, which many were. From that point on, the Reformation grew increasingly conservative, and Luther worked with authorities to restore order.

[I]f all the world [*Welt*] were true Christians, that is, if everyone truly believed, there would be neither need nor use for princes, kings, lords, the Sword or law. What would there be for them to do. Seeing that [true Christians] have the Holy Spirit in their hearts, which teaches and moves them to love everyone, wrong no one, and suffer wrongs gladly, even unto death. Where all wrongs are endured willingly and what is right is done freely, there is no place for quarrelling, disputes, courts, punishments, laws or the Sword. And therefore laws and the secular Sword cannot possibly find any work to do among Christians, especially since they of themselves do much more than any laws or teachings might demand. . . .

And for the rest God has established another government, outside the Christian estate and the kingdom of God, and has cast them into subjection to the Sword. So that, however much they would like to do evil, they are unable to act in accordance with their inclinations, or, if they do, they cannot do so without fear, or enjoy peace and good fortune. In the same way, a wicked, fierce animal is chained and bound so that it cannot bite or tear, as its nature would prompt it to do, however much it wants to; whereas a tame, gentle animal needs nothing like chains or bonds and is harmless even without them.

If there were [no law and government], then seeing that all the world is evil and that scarcely one human being in a thousand is a true Christian, people would devour each other and no one would be able to support his wife and children, feed himself and serve God. The world [*Welt*] would become a desert. And so God has ordained the two governments, the spiritual [government] which fashions true Christians and just persons through the Holy Spirit under Christ, and the secular [*weltlich*] government which holds the Unchristian and wicked in check and forces them to keep the peace outwardly and be still, like it or not. It is in this way that St. Paul interprets the secular Sword when he says in Romans 13 [3]: "It [the Sword] is not a terror to good works, but to the wicked." And Peter says [1 Pet. 2:14]: "It is given as a punishment on the wicked." . . .

Therefore care must be taken to keep these two governments distinct, and both must be allowed to continue [their work], the one to make [people] just, the other to create outward peace and prevent evildoing. Neither is enough for the world without the other. Without the spiritual government of Christ, no one can be made just in the sight of God by the secular government [alone]. However, Christ's spiritual government does not extend to everyone; on the contrary, Christians are at all times the fewest in number and live in the midst of the

Unchristian. Conversely, where the secular government or law rules on its own, pure hypocrisy must prevail, even if it were God's own commandments [that were being enforced]. For no one becomes truly just without the Holy Spirit in his heart, however good his works. And equally where the spiritual government rules over a country and its people unaided, every sort of wickedness is let loose and every sort of knavery has free play. For the world in general is incapable of accepting it or understanding it [i.e., the spiritual government]. . . .

I have already said that Christians among themselves and for themselves need no law and no Sword, for they have no use for them. But because a true Christian, while he is on the earth, lives for and serves his neighbor and not himself, he does things that are of no benefit to himself, but of which his neighbor stands in need. Such is the nature of the Christian's spirit. Now the Sword is indispensable for the whole world, to preserve peace, punish sin, and restrain the wicked. And therefore Christians readily submit themselves to be governed by the Sword, they pay taxes, honor those in authority, serve and help them, and do what they can to uphold their power, so that they may continue their work, and that honor and fear of authority may be maintained. [All this] even though Christians do not need it for themselves, but they attend to what others need, as Paul teaches in Ephesians 5[21]. . . .

[Y]ou owe the Sword your service and support, by whatever means are available to you, be it with your body, goods, honor or soul. For this is a work of which you yourself have no need, but your neighbor and the whole world most certainly do. And therefore if you see that there is a lack of hangmen, court officials, judges, lords or princes, and you find that you have the necessary skills, then you should offer your services and seek office, so that authority, which is so greatly needed, will never come to be held in contempt, become powerless, or perish. The world cannot get by without it. . . .

The Sword and power, as a special service rendered to God, are more suited to Christians than to anyone else in the world, and so you should value the Sword and power as much as the married state, or cultivating the soil, or any other trade instituted by God. Just as a man can serve God in the married state, in farming or manual labor, for the benefit of his neighbor, and indeed must do so if his neighbor's need demands it, so too he can serve God by the [exercise of] power, and he ought to do it, when his neighbor needs it. For those are God's servants and laborers who punish evil and protect what is good. But this is to be left to free choice where there is no [absolute] need, just as marrying and engaging in farming are also left to people's choice, where there is no [absolute] need.

READING AND DISCUSSION QUESTIONS

1. In Luther's opinion, why has God given secular authorities power? What is the purpose of government?

2. What does Luther see as the proper relationship between spiritual and secular authorities?

3. What duties do Christians have toward secular government, in Luther's view?

The Sources of Government Authority

At the heart of the debate between absolutists and constitutionalists were differences of opinion on the ultimate source of government authority. For absolutists, the answer was clear. All authority was in the hands of divinely appointed monarchs, and their laws and decisions were to be viewed as direct commandments from God. Moreover, the monarch was the head of a divinely ordered society in which each person played an assigned part in carrying out God's plan. In sharp contrast, constitutionalists saw governments and societies as essentially voluntary associations, at least in their initial formation. Their starting point was not God but the inherent rights of the individual. Society and government existed to protect those rights by providing law and order. In forming governments and entering society, individuals agreed to abide by the rule of law, but only so that freedom could be guaranteed. The documents included in this feature offer an opportunity to compare the ideas of the seventeenth century's leading theorist of absolutism, Jacques-Bénigne Bossuet, with those of the century's leading theorist of constitutionalism, John Locke. As you read the excerpts from their work, pay particular attention to the way in which their central assumptions about the nature of authority shape their views on government, law, and society. How did each believe that government and society came into existence? How did their beliefs about the origins of government and society shape their views on their nature and functions?

18-2 | God's Lieutenants on Earth

JACQUES-BÉNIGNE BOSSUET, *On Divine Right* (ca. 1675–1680)

French absolutism developed in the seventeenth century as a response to a number of crises, including the French Wars of Religion (ca. 1562–1598) and a civil war known as the Fronde (1648–1653). A bishop in the French Catholic Church and tutor to the son of Louis XIV, Jacques-Bénigne Bossuet (1627–1704) was an important architect of French absolutism. Drawing on biblical sources, Bossuet argued in his treatises that monarchs' authority came directly from God. This concept of the divine right of kings implied that any challenge to royal authority was tantamount to sacrilege.

We have already seen that all power is of God. The ruler, adds St. Paul, "is the minister of God to thee for good. But if thou do that which is evil, be afraid; for

---

J. H. Robinson, ed., *Readings in European History*, 2 vols. (Boston: Ginn, 1906), 2:273–277.

he beareth not the sword in vain: for he is the minister of God, a revenger to execute wrath upon him that doeth evil" [Rom. 13:1–7]. Rulers then act as the ministers of God and as his lieutenants on earth. It is through them that God exercises his empire. Think ye "to withstand the kingdom of the Lord in the hand of the sons of David" [2 Chron. 13:8]? Consequently, as we have seen, the royal throne is not the throne of a man, but the throne of God himself. . . .

Moreover, that no one may assume that the Israelites were peculiar in having kings over them who were established by God, note what is said in Ecclesiasticus: "God has given to every people its ruler, and Israel is manifestly reserved to him" [Eccles. 17:14–15]. He therefore governs all peoples and gives them their kings, although he governed Israel in a more intimate and obvious manner.

It appears from all this that the person of the king is sacred, and that to attack him in any way is sacrilege. God has the kings anointed by his prophets with the holy unction in like manner as he has bishops and altars anointed. But even without the external application in thus being anointed, they are by their very office the representatives of the divine majesty deputed by Providence for the execution of his purposes. . . . Kings should be guarded as holy things, and whosoever neglects to protect them is worthy of death. . . .

But kings, although their power comes from on high, as has been said, should not regard themselves as masters of that power to use it at their pleasure; . . . they must employ it with fear and self-restraint, as a thing coming from God and of which God will demand an account. "Hear, O kings, and take heed, understand, judges of the earth, lend your ears, ye who hold the peoples under your sway, and delight to see the multitude that surround you. It is God who gives you the power. Your strength comes from the Most High, who will question your works and penetrate the depths of your thoughts, for, being ministers of his kingdom, ye have not given righteous judgments nor have ye walked according to his will. He will straightway appear to you in a terrible manner, for to those who command is the heaviest punishment reserved. The humble and the weak shall receive mercy, but the mighty shall be mightily tormented. For God fears not the power of any one, because he made both great and small and he has care for both" [Ws. 6:2]. . . .

Kings should tremble then as they use the power God has granted them; and let them think how horrible is the sacrilege if they use for evil a power which comes from God. We behold kings seated upon the throne of the Lord, bearing in their hand the sword which God himself has given them. What profanation, what arrogance, for the unjust king to sit on God's throne to render decrees contrary to his laws and to use the sword which God has put in his hand for deeds of violence and to slay his children! . . .

The royal power is absolute. With the aim of making this truth hateful and insufferable, many writers have tried to confound absolute government with arbitrary government. But no two things could be more unlike, as we shall show when we come to speak of justice.

The prince need render account of his acts to no one. "I counsel thee to keep the king's commandment, and that in regard of the oath of God. Be not hasty to go out of his sight: stand not on an evil thing for he doeth whatsoever pleaseth him. Where the word of a king is, there is power: and who may say unto him,

What doest thou? Whoso keepeth the commandment shall feel no evil thing" [Eccles. 8:2–5]. Without this absolute authority the king could neither do good nor repress evil. It is necessary that his power be such that no one can hope to escape him, and, finally, the only protection of individuals against the public authority should be their innocence. This conforms with the teaching of St. Paul: "Wilt thou then not be afraid of the power? do that which is good" [Rom. 13:3].

I do not call majesty that pomp which surrounds kings or that exterior magnificence which dazzles the vulgar. That is but the reflection of majesty and not majesty itself. Majesty is the image of the grandeur of God in the prince.

God is infinite, God is all. The prince, as prince, is not regarded as a private person: he is a public personage, all the state is in him; the will of all the people is included in his. As all perfection and all strength are united in God, so all the power of individuals is united in the person of the prince. What grandeur that a single man should embody so much!

The power of God makes itself felt in a moment from one extremity of the earth to another. Royal power works at the same time throughout all the realm. It holds all the realm in position, as God holds the earth. Should God withdraw his hand, the earth would fall to pieces; should the king's authority cease in the realm, all would be in confusion.

Look at the prince in his cabinet. Thence go out the orders which cause the magistrates and the captains, the citizens and the soldiers, the provinces and the armies on land and on sea, to work in concert. He is the image of God, who, seated on his throne high in the heavens, makes all nature move. . . .

Finally, let us put together the things so great and so august which we have said about royal authority. Behold an immense people united in a single person; behold this holy power, paternal and absolute; behold the secret cause which governs the whole body of the state, contained in a single head: you see the image of God in the king, and you have the idea of royal majesty. God is holiness itself, goodness itself, and power itself. In these things lies the majesty of God. In the image of these things lies the majesty of the prince.

So great is this majesty that it cannot reside in the prince as in its source; it is borrowed from God, who gives it to him for the good of the people, for whom it is good to be checked by a superior force. Something of divinity itself is attached to princes and inspires fear in the people. The king should not forget this. "I have said,"—it is God who speaks,—"I have said, Ye are gods; and all of you are children of the Most High. But ye shall die like men, and fall like one of the princes" [Ps. 82:6–7]. "I have said, Ye are gods"; that is to say, you have in your authority, and you bear on your forehead, a divine imprint. "You are the children of the Most High"; it is he who has established your power for the good of mankind. But, O gods of flesh and blood, gods of clay and dust, "ye shall die like men, and fall like princes." Grandeur separates men for a little time, but a common fall makes them all equal at the end.

O kings, exercise your power then boldly, for it is divine and salutary for human kind, but exercise it with humility. You are endowed with it from without. At bottom it leaves you feeble, it leaves you mortal, it leaves you sinners, and charges you before God with a very heavy account.

READING AND DISCUSSION QUESTIONS

1. According to Bossuet, what is the nature of monarchical authority? What are its sources and purposes?

2. Why must a prince wield his absolute power carefully?

3. In Bossuet's view, are there any limits on what a king can do? Do all royal acts automatically receive divine sanction?

18-3 | Government and the State of Nature

JOHN LOCKE, From *Two Treatises of Government: Of the Ends of Political Society and Government* (1690)

John Locke (1632–1704) was a physician, philosopher, and teacher with ties to the pro-parliamentary faction of the English government. His writings on political theory provided an important foundation for the development of constitutionalism in England. Under suspicion of taking part in a plot to assassinate Charles II, he fled to Holland in 1683. His return to England coincided with the Glorious Revolution of 1688, and he claimed that his *Two Treatises* endorsed the ascension of William III to the English throne. The excerpt here from his second treatise shows Locke's interest in developing a philosophy of government through the careful investigation of human nature.

Sec. 123. If man in the state of nature be so free, as has been said; if he be absolute lord of his own person and possessions, equal to the greatest, and subject to no body, why will he part with his freedom? Why will he give up this empire, and subject himself to the dominion and control of any other power? To which it is obvious to answer, that though in the state of nature he hath such a right, yet the enjoyment of it is very uncertain, and constantly exposed to the invasion of others: for all being kings as much as he, every man his equal, and the greater part no strict observers of equity and justice, the enjoyment of the property he has in this state is very unsafe, very unsecure. This makes him willing to quit a condition, which, however free, is full of fears and continual dangers: and it is not without reason, that he seeks out, and is willing to join in society with others, who are already united, or have a mind to unite, for the mutual preservation of their lives, liberties, and estates, which I call by the general name, property.

Sec. 124. The great and chief end, therefore, of men's uniting into commonwealths, and putting themselves under government, is the preservation of their property. To which in the state of nature there are many things wanting.

First, There wants an established, settled, known law, received and allowed by common consent to be the standard of right and wrong, and the common measure to decide all controversies between them: for though the law of nature be plain and intelligible to all rational creatures; yet men being biassed by their

John Locke, *Two Treatises of Government* (London: A. Millar et al., 1764), pp. 305–310.

interest, as well as ignorant for want of study of it, are not apt to allow of it as a law binding to them in the application of it to their particular cases.

Sec. 125. Secondly, In the state of nature there wants a known and indifferent judge, with authority to determine all differences according to the established law: for every one in that state being both judge and executioner of the law of nature, men being partial to themselves, passion and revenge is very apt to carry them too far, and with too much heat, in their own cases; as well as negligence, and unconcernedness, to make them too remiss in other men's.

Sec. 126. Thirdly, In the state of nature there often wants power to back and support the sentence when right, and to give it due execution. They who by any injustice offended, will seldom fail, where they are able, by force to make good their injustice; such resistance many times makes the punishment dangerous, and frequently destructive, to those who attempt it.

Sec. 127. Thus mankind, notwithstanding all the privileges of the state of nature, being but in an ill condition, while they remain in it, are quickly driven into society. Hence it comes to pass, that we seldom find any number of men live any time together in this state. The inconveniencies that they are therein exposed to, by the irregular and uncertain exercise of the power every man has of punishing the transgressions of others, make them take sanctuary under the established laws of government, and therein seek the preservation of their property. It is this makes them so willingly give up every one his single power of punishing, to be exercised by such alone, as shall be appointed to it amongst them; and by such rules as the community, or those authorized by them to that purpose, shall agree on. And in this we have the original right and rise of both the legislative and executive power, as well as of the governments and societies themselves.

Sec. 128. For in the state of nature, to omit the liberty he has of innocent delights, a man has two powers.

The first is to do whatsoever he thinks fit for the preservation of himself, and others within the permission of the law of nature: by which law, common to them all, he and all the rest of mankind are one community, make up one society, distinct from all other creatures. And were it not for the corruption and viciousness of degenerate men, there would be no need of any other; no necessity that men should separate from this great and natural community, and by positive agreements combine into smaller and divided associations.

The other power a man has in the state of nature, is the power to punish the crimes committed against that law. Both these he gives up, when he joins in a private, if I may so call it, or particular politic society, and incorporates into any commonwealth, separate from the rest of mankind.

Sec. 129. The first power, viz. of doing whatsoever he thought for the preservation of himself, and the rest of mankind, he gives up to be regulated by laws made by the society, so far forth as the preservation of himself, and the rest of that society shall require; which laws of the society in many things confine the liberty he had by the law of nature.

Sec. 130. Secondly, The power of punishing he wholly gives up, and engages his natural force, (which he might before employ in the execution of the law of nature, by his own single authority, as he thought fit) to assist the executive power of the society, as the law thereof shall require: for being now in a new state, wherein he is to enjoy many conveniencies, from the labor, assistance, and society of others in the same community, as well as protection from its whole strength; he is to part also with as much of his natural liberty, in providing for himself, as the good, prosperity, and safety of the society shall require; which is not only necessary, but just, since the other members of the society do the like.

Sec. 131. But though men, when they enter into society, give up the equality, liberty, and executive power they had in the state of nature, into the hands of the society, to be so far disposed of by the legislative, as the good of the society shall require; yet it being only with an intention in every one the better to preserve himself, his liberty and property; (for no rational creature can be supposed to change his condition with an intention to be worse) the power of the society, or legislative constituted by them, can never be supposed to extend farther, than the common good; but is obliged to secure every one's property, by providing against those three defects above mentioned, that made the state of nature so unsafe and uneasy. And so whoever has the legislative or supreme power of any commonwealth, is bound to govern by established standing laws, promulgated and known to the people, and not by extemporary decrees; by indifferent and upright judges, who are to decide controversies by those laws; and to employ the force of the community at home, only in the execution of such laws, or abroad to prevent or redress foreign injuries, and secure the community from inroads and invasion. And all this to be directed to no other end, but the peace, safety, and public good of the people.

READING AND DISCUSSION QUESTIONS

1. According to Locke, what powers do individuals have in the state of nature? What are some of the inevitable difficulties that arise when living in the state of nature?

2. Once individuals agree to form a government, what powers does the government have? What are its primary obligations?

3. In what ways does the treatise challenge the absolutist tendencies of seventeenth-century English monarchs?

VIEWPOINTS COMPARATIVE QUESTIONS

1. According to each author, what is the ultimate source of political authority? How did each author's views on this subject shape his understanding of the nature of government?

2. What aspects of Locke's theory might Bossuet have found most objectionable? Why? What might Locke have been most critical of in Bossuet's argument? Why?

3. What did each author see as the purpose of government? On what, if anything, might they have agreed?

18-4 | A Depiction of Diplomatic Exchange
JASPER BECX, *Don Miguel de Castro, Emissary of Kongo* (ca. 1643)

In the first half of the seventeenth century, the Dutch Republic challenged Portugal's position in west-central Africa. The Dutch, acting through the Dutch West India Company, formed an alliance with the Christian kingdom of Kongo (formerly an ally of Portugal) in the 1620s and seized Portuguese settlements in Angola in 1641. The following year, the ruler of a province of Kongo sent his cousin, Don Miguel de Castro, as an envoy to seek Dutch assistance in an internal conflict with King Garcia II of Kongo. Don Miguel traveled first to the Dutch colony in northeastern Brazil and then to the Dutch Republic, where he met with the stadtholder himself, Frederick Henry, Prince of Orange. During his stay in the Netherlands, directors of the Dutch West India Company commissioned paintings of Don Miguel and his two servants, some in European and some in Kongolese attire. Don Miguel was pleased enough with his portraits that he asked to take one home with him.

This painting shows Don Miguel dressed in the height of European fashion. He wears a brocaded silk shirt under a studded doublet with a starched white linen collar. Two of the items he wears were gifts from his Dutch hosts: a black felt hat and a sword held by a decorated strap draped across his chest. The portraits of his servants show them carrying an ivory tusk and a woven box, gifts from the Kongolese to the Dutch. Altogether, the three portraits emphasize the reciprocal diplomatic exchange between the two sides.

PHAS/Getty Images

Cécile Fromont, *The Art of Conversion: Christian Visual Culture in the Kingdom of the Kongo* (Chapel Hill: University of North Carolina Press, 2014), pp. 165–167.

READING AND DISCUSSION QUESTIONS

1. Why would the directors of the Dutch West India Company commission portraits of the Kongolese emissary, and why would they choose to have him portrayed this way?

2. How would you interpret Don Miguel's posture and facial expression? What message does he seem to be conveying to the viewer?

3. What can be learned from this painting, and from the context in which it was made, about relations between the Kongo and the Dutch Republic during this period?

18-5 | A Tsar Imposes Western Styles on the Russians

PETER THE GREAT, *Edicts and Decrees* (1699–1723)

Peter the Great's reign (1682–1725) marked Russia's emergence as a major player in European continental rivalries. Russia defeated Sweden in the grueling Great Northern War (1700–1721) and acquired a "window on Europe" at the head of the Gulf of Finland, where Peter built a new capital, St. Petersburg. In order to defeat the Swedes, who had routed his ill-trained army at Narva in 1700, Peter had reformed and modernized his military along western European lines. His enthusiasm for Western technology and tactics extended to other realms, including education, dress, and economic programs, as can be seen from the following excerpts. As you read them, ask yourself why the West was of such interest to Peter. What did he hope to accomplish through his program of westernization?

Decree on the Invitation of Foreigners, 1702

Since our accession to the throne all our efforts and intentions have tended to govern this realm in such a way that all of our subjects should, through our care for the general good, become more and more prosperous. For this end we have always tried to maintain internal order, to defend the state against invasion, and in every possible way to improve and to extend trade. With this purpose we have been compelled to make some necessary and salutary changes in the administration, in order that our subjects might more easily gain a knowledge of matters of which they were before ignorant, and become more skillful in their commercial relations.

We have therefore given orders, made dispositions, and founded institutions indispensable for increasing our trade with foreigners, and shall do the same in the future. Nevertheless we fear that matters are not in such a good condition as we desire, and that our subjects cannot in perfect

Marthe Blinoff, *Life and Thought in Old Russia* (University Park: Pennsylvania State University Press, 1961), pp. 49–50; Eugene Schuyler, *Peter the Great*, vol. 2 (New York: Charles Scribner's Sons, 1884), pp. 176–177; L. Jay Oliva, *Peter the Great* (Englewood Cliffs, N.J.: Prentice-Hall, 1970), p. 50; George Vernadsky et al., *A Source Book for Russian History from Early Times to 1917*, vol. 2 (New Haven, Conn.: Yale University Press, 1972), pp. 329, 347, 357.

quietness enjoy the fruits of our labors, and we have therefore considered still other means to protect our frontier from the invasion of the enemy, and to preserve the rights and privileges of our State, and the general peace of all Christians. . . .

To attain these worthy aims, we have endeavored to improve our military forces, which are the protection of our State, so that our troops may consist of well-drilled men, maintained in perfect order and discipline. In order to obtain greater improvement in this respect, and to encourage foreigners, who are able to assist us in this way, as well as artisans profitable to the State, to come in numbers to our country, we have issued this manifesto, and have ordered printed copies of it to be sent throughout Europe. . . . And as in our residence of Moscow, the free exercise of religion of all other sects, although not agreeing with our church, is already allowed, so shall this be hereby confirmed anew in such manner that we, by the power granted to us by the Almighty, shall exercise no compulsion over the consciences of men, and shall gladly allow every Christian to care for his own salvation at his own risk.

An Instruction to Russian Students Abroad Studying Navigation, 1714

1. Learn how to draw plans and charts and how to use the compass and other naval indicators.
2. Learn how to navigate a vessel in battle as well as in a simple maneuver, and learn how to use all appropriate tools and instruments; namely, sails, ropes, and oars, and the like matters, on row boats and other vessels.
3. Discover . . . how to put ships to sea during a naval battle. . . . Obtain from foreign naval officers written statements, bearing their signatures and seals, of how adequately you are prepared for naval duties.
4. If, upon his return, anyone wishes to receive from the Tsar greater favors, he should learn, in addition to the above enumerated instructions, how to construct those vessels [aboard] which he would like to demonstrate his skills.
5. Upon his return to Moscow, every foreign-trained Russian should bring with him at his own expense, for which he will later be reimbursed, at least two experienced masters of naval science. They [the returnees] will be assigned soldiers, one soldier per returnee, to teach them what they have learned abroad. . . .

Decree on Western Dress, 1701

German [i.e., Western][1] dress shall be worn by all the boyars, okol'nichie,[2] members of our councils and of our court . . . gentry of Moscow, secretaries . . .

---

[1]**German:** At the time "German" referred collectively to western European territories, not only German-speaking ones.

[2]**boyars, okol'nichie:** Nobles of the highest and second-highest rank, respectively.

provincial gentry, boiarskie,[3] gosti,[4] government officials, strel'tsy,[5] members of the guilds purveying for our household, citizens of Moscow of all ranks, and residents of provincial cities . . . excepting the clergy (priests, deacons, and church attendants) and peasant tillers of the soil. The upper dress shall be of French or Saxon cut, and the lower dress—[including] waistcoat, trousers, boots, shoes, and hats—shall be of the German type. They shall also ride German saddles. [Likewise] the womenfolk of all ranks, including the priests', deacons', and church attendants' wives, the wives of the dragoons, the soldiers, and the strel'tsy and their children, shall wear German dresses, hats, jackets, and underwear—undervests and petticoats—and shoes. From now on no one [of the abovementioned] is to wear Russian dress or Circassian coats,[6] sheepskin coats, or Russian peasant coats, trousers, boots, and shoes. It is also forbidden to ride Russian saddles, and the craftsmen shall not manufacture them or sell them at the marketplaces.

Decree on Shaving, 1705

A decree to be published in Moscow and in all the provincial cities: Henceforth, in accordance with this, His Majesty's decree, all court attendants . . . provincial service men, government officials of all ranks, military men, all the gosti, members of the wholesale merchants' guild, and members of the guilds purveying for our household must shave their beards and moustaches. But, if it happens that some of them do not wish to shave their beards and moustaches, let a yearly tax be collected from such persons. . . . Special badges shall be issued to them from the Administrator of Land Affairs [of Public Order] . . . which they must wear. . . . As for the peasants, let a toll of two half-copecks[7] per beard be collected at the town gates each time they enter or leave a town; and do not let the peasants pass the town gates, into or out of town, without paying this toll.

Decree on Promotion to Officer's Rank, 1714

Since there are many who promote to officer rank their relatives and friends—young men who do not know the fundamentals of soldiering, not having served in the lower ranks—and since even those who serve [in the ranks] do so for a few weeks or months only, as a formality; therefore . . . let a decree be promulgated that henceforth there shall be no promotion [to officer rank] of men of noble extraction or of any others who have not first served as privates in the Guards. This decree does not apply to soldiers of lowly origin who, after long

---

[3]**boiarskie:** Sons of boyars.

[4]**gosti:** Merchants who often served the tsar in some capacity.

[5]**strel'tsy:** Members of the imperial guard stationed in Moscow.

[6]**Circassian coats:** Traditional outer garments worn by the people of Circassia, a Russian territory between the Caspian and Black Seas. The style was evidently adopted by the nobility.

[7]**half-copecks:** One-twentieth of a ruble, the basic unit of Russian money.

service in the ranks, have received their commissions through honest service or to those who are promoted on the basis of merit, now or in the future; it applies exclusively to those who have remained in the ranks for a short time, only as a formality, as described above.

Statute for the College of Manufactures, 1723

His Imperial Majesty is diligently striving to establish and develop in the Russian Empire such manufacturing plants and factories as are found in other states, for the general welfare and prosperity of his subjects. He [therefore] most graciously charges the College of Manufactures[8] to exert itself in devising the means to introduce, with the least expense, and to spread in the Russian Empire these and other ingenious arts, and especially those for which materials can be found within the empire; [the College of Manufactures] must also consider the privileges that should be granted to those who might wish to found manufacturing plants and factories.

His Imperial Majesty gives permission to everyone, without distinction of rank or condition, to open factories wherever he may find suitable. . . .

Factory owners must be closely supervised, in order that they have at their plants good and experienced [foreign] master craftsmen, who are able to train Russians in such a way that these, in turn, may themselves become masters, so that their produce may bring glory to the Russian manufactures. . . .

By the former decrees of His Majesty commercial people were forbidden to buy villages [i.e., to own serfs], the reason being that they were not engaged in any other activity beneficial for the state save commerce; but since it is now clear to all that many of them have started to found manufacturing establishments and build plants, both in companies and individually, which tend to increase the welfare of the state . . . therefore permission is granted both to the gentry and to men of commerce to acquire villages for these factories without hindrance. . . .

In order to stimulate voluntary immigration of various craftsmen from other countries into the Russian Empire, and to encourage them to establish factories and manufacturing plants freely and at their own expense, the College of Manufactures must send appropriate announcements to the Russian envoys accredited at foreign courts. The envoys should then, in an appropriate way, bring these announcements to the attention of men of various professions, urge them to come to settle in Russia, and help them to move.

READING AND DISCUSSION QUESTIONS

1. Why do you think Peter decreed that the nobles, merchants, and townspeople wear western European style clothing? Why was it important that even women's and children's underwear be in the western European style?

---

[8]**College of Manufactures:** One of several administrative boards created by Peter in 1717, modeled on Swedish practice.

2. What does Peter's decree encouraging foreign soldiers and artisans to emigrate to Russia and his Statute for the College of Manufactures suggest about the state of Russia's military forces and economy as of the early 1700s?

3. Why didn't Russia have a navy prior to 1700?

4. What, according to Peter, was wrong with the system of promotion in the Russian army, and how did he intend to redress it? What does his decree on promotion suggest about the power and benefits granted to the Russian nobility?

■ COMPARATIVE QUESTIONS ■

1. Compare and contrast the views of Luther and Bossuet on the issue of secular authority. What limitations, if any, do they posit on the authority of secular government? Why would religious leaders be willing to accord so much power to a secular ruler?

2. The question of divinity is conspicuously absent in Locke's excerpt. How might Locke have interpreted Bossuet's theologically based arguments about sovereignty? Is there room for religion in Locke's state of nature?

3. How would Bossuet and Locke analyze Peter the Great's actions and policies? On what basis would they approve or disapprove of the decrees included here?

4. Compare Don Miguel's portrait in European dress to Peter the Great's decree ordering his subjects to wear western European clothing. Were they motivated by similar or different concerns? Why was the issue of dress so important to rulers and diplomats, as well as other elites?

5. Based on these readings, what areas of agreement and differences in opinion existed in seventeenth-century Europe regarding the purpose of government and the role it should play in people's everyday lives?

19

New Worldviews and Ways of Life

1540–1790

Beginning in the sixteenth century, western Europe saw its religion-based notions of the natural and social worlds countered by arguments grounded in reason and observation. Leaders of the Scientific Revolution (ca. 1540–1690) drew on earlier European, Greek, and Arab insights to support their theories and to challenge the church-dominated wisdom of the time. Advances in astronomy, physics, mathematics, and other fields were supported and promoted by the huge profits and increasing technological demands of growing European trade. European intellectuals next turned a critical eye toward society and politics. Those active in the period known as the Enlightenment, which stretched from the late seventeenth to the late eighteenth century, insisted on rational approaches to human relations, drawing on scientific arguments and existing critiques of organized religion in their calls for the reform of societies and governments.

VIEWPOINTS

Debating the Experimental Method

In the early seventeenth century, natural philosophers—members of the branch of philosophy focused on studying the natural world—attacked the methods of Aristotelian philosophy that had dominated the universities since the late medieval era. Whereas the Aristotelian approach focused on deducing truth through formal logic, some scholars began to argue for basing the search for truth on empirical observation and experimentation. This was not the first time philosophers had used experimentation; for example, the Arab scholar known as Alhazen conducted experiments in optics in the tenth century. However, it was in the seventeenth century that the experimental method was formally articulated. This method gained powerful support from institutions such as the Royal Society, which was founded in 1660 in England with an explicit mission to focus on experimentation. This development was not welcomed by all, and some philosophers, including Margaret Cavendish (Document 19-2), objected to what they saw as the denigration of the role of reason and deduction in the search for scientific knowledge.

19-1 | Praise for the Experimental Method

ROBERT HOOKE, *Micrographia* (1665)

Robert Hooke (1635–1703) was a natural philosopher whose work spanned the fields of astronomy, physics, and biology. He studied at Oxford University, where he served as an assistant to the prominent scholar Robert Boyle. In 1662, Boyle helped him obtain the position of curator of experiments at the newly founded Royal Society of London for Improving Natural Knowledge (later known simply as the Royal Society). Along with Boyle, Hooke was a strong advocate of the experimental method, insisting that observation and experimentation were essential to acquiring knowledge. His most important work was *Micrographia* (1665), an account of experiments he had performed with a microscope, in which Hooke became the first to use the term *cell* to describe the basic unit of organic life.

It is the great prerogative of mankind above other creatures, that we are not only able to behold the works of nature, or barely to sustain our lives by them, but we have also the power of considering, comparing, altering, assisting, and improving them to various uses. And as this is the peculiar privilege of humane nature in general, so is it capable of being so far advanced by the helps of art, and experience, as to make some men excel others in their observations, and deductions, almost as much as they do beasts. By the addition of such artificial instruments and methods, there may be, in some manner, a reparation made for the mischiefs and imperfections mankind has drawn upon itself, by negligence, intemperance, and a willful and superstitious deserting the prescripts and rules of nature, whereby every man, both from a derived corruption, innate and born with him, and from his breeding and converse with men, is very subject to slip into all sorts of errors. . . .

These being the dangers in the process of human reason, the remedies of them all can only proceed from the real, the mechanical, the experimental philosophy, which has this advantage over the philosophy of discourse and disputation . . . whereas that [the philosophy of disputation] chiefly aims at the subtlety of its deductions and conclusions without much ground to the first groundwork, which ought to be well laid on the sense and memory, so this [the experimental philosophy] intends the right ordering of them all, and the making them serviceable to each other.

The first thing to be undertaken in this weight work, is a watchfulness over the failings and an enlargement of the dominion, of the senses.

To which end it is requisite, first, that there should be a scrupulous choice, and a strict examination, of the reality, constancy, and certainty of the particulars that we admit. This is the first rise whereon truth is to begin, and here the most severe and most impartial diligence must be employed. . . . The footsteps of nature are to be traced, not only in the ordinary course, but when she seems to be put to her shifts, to make many doublings and turnings, and to use some kind of art in endeavoring to avoid our discovery.

The next care to be taken, in respect of the senses, is a supplying of their infirmities with instruments and, as it were, the adding of artificial organs to the natural. This in one of them has been of late years accomplished with prodigious benefit to all sorts of useful knowledge, by the invention of optical glasses. By the means of telescopes, there is nothing so far distant but may be represented to our view; and by the help of microscopes, there is nothing so small as to scape our inquiry. Hence there is a new visible world discovered to the understanding. By this means the heavens are opened, and a vast number of new stars, and new motions, and new productions appear in them, to which all the ancient astronomers were utterly strangers. By this the Earth itself, which lies so near us, under our feet, shows quite a new thing to use, and in every little particle of its matter. We now behold almost as great a variety of creatures, as we were able before to reckon up in the whole universe itself.

It seems not improbable, but that by these helps the subtlety of the composition of bodies, the structure of their parts, the various texture of their matter, the instruments and manner of their inward motions, and all the other possible appearances of things, may come to be more fully discovered. . . . From whence there may arise many admirable advantages, toward the increase of the operative, and the mechanic knowledge, to which this age seems so much inclined, because we may perhaps be enabled to discern all the secret workings of nature, almost in the same manner as we do those that are the productions of art, and are managed by wheels, and engines, and springs, that were devised by human wit. . . .

The truth is, the science of nature has been already too long made only a work of the brain and the fancy. It is now high time that it should return to the plainness and soundness of observations on material and obvious things. . . .

From hence the world may be assisted with a variety of inventions, new matter for sciences may be collected, the old improved and their rust rubbed away. And as it is by the benefit of senses that we receive all our skill in the works of nature, so they also may be wonderfully benefited by it, and may be guided to an easier and more exact performance of their offices. It is not unlikely, but that we may find out wherein our senses are deficient, and as easily find ways of repairing them.

READING AND DISCUSSION QUESTIONS

1. What dangers does Hooke identify in the use of human reason?

2. Why does Hooke believe that experimental philosophy is superior to the "philosophy of disputation" that relies on reason and deduction?

3. What does Hooke mean when he advocates for adding "artificial organs to the natural"? What examples does he provide of such artificial organs, and what advantages does he think they offer?

19-2 | Questioning the Experimental Method

MARGARET CAVENDISH, *Observations upon Experimental Philosophy* (1666)

Margaret Lucas Cavendish, the Duchess of Newcastle (1623–1673), was one of a small group of women at the heart of the Scientific Revolution. Like other girls in her day, she did not receive a formal education but learned at home from tutors and her brother John, who became a founding member of the Royal Society. While in exile in France during the English Civil War, Cavendish participated in a salon hosted by her husband's family that was attended by eminent philosophers such as Thomas Hobbes and René Descartes. In 1666, she published the most famous of her numerous works, *Observations upon Experimental Philosophy*. In this text, she criticized natural philosophers, including Robert Boyle and Robert Hooke, who had acquired fame for their experimental methods. Cavendish was one of the rare natural philosophers with extensive personal experience with microscopes (discussed in the following passage), having acquired a large collection of them with her husband during their exile in the 1640s. Her skepticism regarding artificial instruments was echoed by other philosophers, including John Locke.

Next, I say, that sense, which is more apt to be deluded than reason, cannot be the ground of reason, no more than art can be the ground of nature. . . . [H]ow can a wise man trust his senses, if either the objects be not truly presented according to their natural figure and shape, or if the senses be defective, either through age, or sickness, or other accidents, which do alter the natural motions proper to each sense? And hence I conclude that experimental and mechanical philosophy cannot be above the speculative part, by reason most experiments have their rise from the speculative, so that the artist or mechanic is but a servant to the student. . . .

   Although I am not able to give a solid judgment of the art of micrography and the several dioptrical instruments belonging thereto, by reason I have neither studied nor practiced that art. Yet of this I am confident, that this same art, with all its instruments, is not able to discover the interior natural motions of any part or creature of nature. Nay, the question is whether it can represent yet the exterior shapes and motions so exactly, as naturally they are, for art does more easily alter than inform.

. . . I do not say, that no glass presents the true picture of an object, but only that magnifying, multiplying, and the like optic glasses, may, and do oftentimes present falsely the picture, because it is not the real body of the object which the glass presents, but the glass only figures or patterns out the picture presented in and by the glass, and there mistakes may easily be committed in taking copies from copies. Nay, artists do confess themselves, that flies, and the like, will appear of several figures or shapes, according to the several reflections, refractions, mediums and positions of several lights, which, if so, how can they tell or judge which is the truest light, position, or medium that does present the object naturally as it is? And if not, then an edge may very well seem flat, and a point of a needle a globe. But if the edge of a knife, or a point of a needle were naturally and really so as the microscope present them, they would never be so useful as they are; for, a flat or broad plain-edged knife would not cut, nor a blunt globe pierce so suddenly another body, neither would nor could they pierce without tearing and rending, if their bodies were so uneven. . . .

Wherefore those that invented microscopes, and such like dioptrical glasses, at first, did, in my opinion, the world more injury than benefit; for this art has intoxicated so many men's brains, and wholly employed their thoughts and bodily actions about phenomena, or the exterior figures of objects, as all better arts and studies are laid aside. . . .

But could experimental philosophers find out more beneficial arts than our fore-fathers had done, either for the better increase of vegetables and brute animals to nourish our bodies, or better and commodious contrivances in the art of architecture to build us houses, or for the advancing of trade and traffic to provide necessaries for us to live, or for the decrease of nice distinctions and sophistical disputes in churches, schools, and courts of judicature, to make men live in unity, peace, and neighborly friendship, it would not only be worth their labor, but as much praise as could be given to them. But, as boys that play with watery bubbles, or fling dust into each other's eyes, or make a hobby-horse of snow, are worthy of reproof rather than praise, for wasting their time with useful sports, so those that addict themselves to unprofitable arts spend more time than they reap benefit thereby. Nay, could they benefit men either in husbandry, architecture, or the like necessary and profitable employments. Yet before the vulgar sort would learn to understand them, the world would want bread to eat, and houses to dwell in, as also clothes to keep them from the inconveniences of inconstant weather.

But truly though spinsters were most experienced in their art, yet they will never be able to spin silk, thread, or wool, etc. from loose atoms; neither will weavers weave a web of light from the sun's rays; nor an architect build a house of the bubbles of water and air (unless they be poetical spinsters, weavers and architects). And if a painter should draw a louse as big as a crab, and of that shape as the microscope presents, can anybody truly imagine that a beggar would believe it to be true? But if he did, what advantage would it be to the beggar? For it does neither instruct him how to avoid breeding them, or how to catch them, or to hinder them from biting. . . .

In short, magnifying-glasses are like a high heel to a short leg, which if it be made too high, it is apt to make the wearer fall, and at the best, can do not more than represent exterior figures in a bigger and so in a more deformed shape and posture than naturally they are. But as for the interior forms and motions of a creature, as I said before, they can no more represent them than telescopes can the interior essence and nature of the sun, and what matter it consists of. . . .

Wherefore the best optic is a perfect natural eye, and a regular sensitive perception; and the best judge is reason; and the best study is rational contemplation joined with the observations of regular sense, but not deluding arts. For art is not only gross in comparison to nature, but, for the most part, deformed and defective, and at best produces mixed or hermaphroditical figures, that is a third figure between nature and art. Which provides that natural reason is above artificial sense, as I may call it. Wherefore, those arts are the best and surest informers, that alter nature least, and they the greatest deluders that alter nature most[.]

READING AND DISCUSSION QUESTIONS

1. What criticism does Cavendish offer to those who rely on sensory perception to study nature? Why does she think reason and speculation are necessary guides for the senses?

2. What does this text reveal about the technological limitations of the mid-seventeenth-century microscope?

3. What specific objections does Cavendish raise on the use of the microscope to observe nature? Why does she think the microscope may offer limited or misleading impressions?

4. Given that Cavendish was one of very few women who played an active role in scientific debates, is there any evidence in this passage of her consciousness of gender?

VIEWPOINTS COMPARATIVE QUESTIONS

1. Who do you think makes the strongest case for their argument, Hooke or Cavendish? What aspects of their argument are the most persuasive, and what are the weakest points?

2. Based on these readings, what did Hooke and Cavendish believe was the aim of scientific inquiry? What impact should natural philosophers strive to have on the world?

3. Compare the visions of science articulated in these documents with the understanding of science that prevails today. How do you think a modern scientist would respond to the ideas presented by Hooke and Cavendish?

19-3 | Science Outside the West

Takyuddin and Other Astronomers at the Galata Observatory (ca. 1581)

The fact that the Scientific Revolution was centered in western Europe does not mean that societies outside of Europe were not interested in science or that they did not help make the Scientific Revolution possible. After all, it was Muslim scholars who preserved Greco-Roman literature and philosophy during the early Middle Ages, providing the West with a critical intellectual foundation for later accomplishments. Moreover, Middle Eastern, Indian, and Chinese rulers all showed considerable interest in the study of nature, offering their patronage to natural philosophers and astronomers. Finally, these same societies all made crucial contributions to the development of scientific and navigational instruments. All of these elements can be seen in this image of Ottoman astronomers at the Galata Observatory, a center of astronomical inquiry built by the Ottoman sultan Suleiman the Magnificent (r. 1520–1566). As you examine the image, think about what it tells you about Ottoman science in the sixteenth century. What clues do the details in the image offer about the scope and focus of Ottoman scientific inquiry?

Print Collector/Getty Images

READING AND DISCUSSION QUESTIONS

1. What does the image reveal about the tools of Ottoman science? What books, instruments, and maps were available to Ottoman scientists?

2. What does the image suggest about the social organization of Ottoman science? How might a facility like the Galata Observatory facilitate the exchange of information between scientists?

19-4 | Faith Without Dogma

VOLTAIRE, From *Dictionnaire Philosophique: "Theist"* (1764)

A major figure of the Enlightenment, Voltaire, or François-Marie Arouet (1694–1778), was a literary genius with a keen sense of social responsibility. His writings were immensely popular during his lifetime, although his satirical voice often earned him enemies among France's religious and political elite. The *Dictionnaire Philosophique* (Philosophical Dictionary) of 1764 is less an encyclopedic reference than a compilation of Voltaire's critical musings on the nature of religion and intolerance in modern society. Here, his entry for "Theist" outlines the principles of theism (or deism, as it is more commonly known) and indicates his strong approval for the Enlightenment emphasis on secular humanism over sectarian doctrine.

The theist is a man firmly persuaded of the existence of a Supreme Being equally good and powerful, who has formed all extended, vegetating, sentient, and reflecting existences; who perpetuates their species, who punishes crimes without cruelty, and rewards virtuous actions with kindness.

The theist does not know how God punishes, how he rewards, how he pardons; for he is not presumptuous enough to flatter himself that he understands how God acts; but he knows that God does act and that he is just. The difficulties opposed to a Providence do not stagger him in his faith, because they are only great difficulties, not proofs: he submits himself to that Providence, although he only perceives some of its effects and some appearances; and judging of the things he does not see from those he does see, he thinks that this Providence pervades all places and all ages.

United in this principle with the rest of the universe, he does not join any of the sects, who all contradict themselves; his religion is the most ancient and the most extended: for the simple adoration of a God has preceded all the systems in the world. He speaks a language which all nations understand, while they are unable to understand each other's. He has brethren from Pekin to Cayenne,[1] and he reckons all the wise his brothers. He believes that religion consists neither in the opinions of incomprehensible metaphysics, nor in vain decorations, but in adoration and justice. To do good—that is his worship: to submit oneself to

M. de Voltaire, *A Philosophical Dictionary* (London: John and Henry L. Hunt, 1824), 6:258–259.

[1]**Pekin to Cayenne:** The cities of Peking (Beijing) and Cayenne, French Guiana.

God — that is his doctrine. The Mahometan [Muslim] cries out to him — "Take care of yourself, if you do not make the pilgrimage to Mecca." — "Woe be to thee," says a Franciscan, "if thou dost not make a journey to our Lady of Loretto."[2] He laughs at Loretto and Mecca; but he succors the indigent and defends the oppressed.

READING AND DISCUSSION QUESTIONS

1. What does Voltaire's treatment of the "theist" reveal about his general attitude toward religion?

2. Is Voltaire concerned more with the theist's beliefs about the divine or with his actions in the world? Explain.

3. Based on this excerpt, what might Voltaire say about atheism? Explain.

19-5 | Kant Challenges His Society to Embrace Reason

IMMANUEL KANT, *What Is Enlightenment?* (1784)

The Prussian professor Immanuel Kant (1724–1804) was perhaps the most influential philosopher of the Enlightenment. In *Critique of Pure Reason* (1781), his best-known work, Kant sought to define what we can know and how we know it, thereby reconciling the previous schools of rationalist and empiricist thought and inspiring philosophical trends to this day. The following excerpt is taken from his "Answer to the Question: What Is Enlightenment?" published in 1784 in a monthly periodical. The short work, more accessible than his 800-page *Critique*, marked his renewed status as a public thinker and spoke to his beliefs about intellectual freedom.

Enlightenment is man's emergence from his self-imposed nonage. Nonage is the inability to use one's understanding without another's guidance. This nonage is self-imposed if its cause lies not in lack of understanding but in indecision and lack of courage to use one's own mind without another's guidance. *Dare to know! (Sapere aude.)* "Have the courage to use your own understanding," is therefore the motto of the enlightenment.

Laziness and cowardice are the reasons why such a large part of mankind gladly remain minors all their lives, long after nature has freed them from external guidance. They are the reasons why it is so easy for others to set themselves up as guardians. It is so comfortable to be a minor. If I have a book that thinks for me, a pastor who acts as my conscience, a physician who prescribes my diet, and so on — then I have no need to exert myself. I have no need to think,

---

Immanuel Kant, "What Is Enlightenment?" trans. Peter Gay, in *Introduction to Contemporary Civilization in the West* (New York: Columbia University Press, 1954), pp. 1071–1076. Copyright © 1954 Columbia University Press. Reprinted with permission of the publisher.

[2]**Loretto:** Probably Loreto, a Catholic shrine in Italy and a popular destination for pilgrimages.

if only I can pay; others will take care of that disagreeable business for me. The guardians who have kindly taken supervision upon themselves see to it that the overwhelming majority of mankind—among them the entire fair sex—should consider the step to maturity not only as hard, but as extremely dangerous. First, these guardians make their domestic cattle stupid and carefully prevent the docile creatures from taking a single step without the leading-strings to which they have fastened them. Then they show them the danger that would threaten them if they should try to walk by themselves. Now, this danger is really not very great; after stumbling a few times they would, at last, learn to walk. However, examples of such failures intimidate and generally discourage all further attempts.

Thus it is very difficult for the individual to work himself out of the nonage which has become almost second nature to him. He has even grown to like it and is at first really incapable of using his own understanding, because he has never been permitted to try it. Dogmas and formulas, these mechanical tools designed for reasonable use—or rather abuse—of his natural gifts, are the fetters of an everlasting nonage. The man who casts them off would make an uncertain leap over the narrowest ditch, because he is not used to such free movement. That is why there are only a few men who walk firmly, and who have emerged from nonage by cultivating their own minds.

It is more nearly possible, however, for the public to enlighten itself; indeed, if it is only given freedom, enlightenment is almost inevitable. There will always be a few independent thinkers, even among the self-appointed guardians of the multitude. Once such men have thrown off the yoke of nonage, they will spread about them the spirit of a reasonable appreciation of man's value and of his duty to think for himself. It is especially to be noted that the public which was earlier brought under the yoke by these men afterward forces these very guardians to remain in submission, if it is so incited by some of its guardians who are themselves incapable of any enlightenment. That shows how pernicious it is to implant prejudices: they will eventually revenge themselves upon their authors or their authors' descendants. Therefore, a public can achieve enlightenment only slowly. A revolution may bring about the end of a personal despotism or of avaricious and tyrannical oppression, but never a true reform of modes of thought. New prejudices will serve, in place of the old, as guidelines for the unthinking multitude.

This enlightenment requires nothing but *freedom*—and the most innocent of all that may be called "freedom": freedom to make public use of one's reason in all matters. Now I hear the cry from all sides: "Do not argue!" The officer says: "Do not argue—drill!" The tax collector: "Do not argue—pay!" The pastor: "Do not argue—believe!" Only one ruler in the world says: "Argue as much as you please, and about what you please, but obey!" We find restrictions on freedom everywhere. But which restriction is harmful to enlightenment? Which restriction is innocent, and which advances enlightenment? I reply: the public use of one's reason must be free at all times, and this alone can bring enlightenment to mankind.

On the other hand, the private use of reason may frequently be narrowly restricted without especially hindering the progress of enlightenment. By "public use of one's reason" I mean that use which a man, as *scholar*, makes of it before the reading public. I call "private use" that use which a man makes of his reason in a civic post that has been entrusted to him. In some affairs affecting the interest of the community a certain [governmental] mechanism is necessary in which some members of the community remain passive. This creates an artificial unanimity which will serve the fulfillment of public objectives, or at least keep these objectives from being destroyed. Here arguing is not permitted: one must obey. Insofar as a part of this machine considers himself at the same time a member of a universal community—a world society of citizens—(let us say that he thinks of himself as a scholar rationally addressing his public through his writings) he may indeed argue, and the affairs with which he is associated in part as a passive member will not suffer. Thus, it would be very unfortunate if an officer on duty and under orders from his superiors should want to criticize the appropriateness or utility of his orders. He must obey. But as a scholar he could not rightfully be prevented from taking notice of the mistakes in the military service and from submitting his views to his public for its judgment. The citizen cannot refuse to pay the taxes levied upon him; indeed, impertinent censure of such taxes could be punished as a scandal that might cause general disobedience. Nevertheless, this man does not violate the duties of a citizen if, as a scholar, he publicly expresses his objections to the impropriety or possible injustice of such levies. A pastor too is bound to preach to his congregation in accord with the doctrines of the church which he serves, for he was ordained on that condition. But as a scholar he has full freedom, indeed the obligation, to communicate to his public all his carefully examined and constructive thoughts concerning errors in that doctrine and his proposals concerning improvement of religious dogma and church institutions. This is nothing that could burden his conscience. For what he teaches in pursuance of his office as representative of the church, he represents as something which he is not free to teach as he sees it. He speaks as one who is employed to speak in the name and under the orders of another. He will say: "Our church teaches this or that; these are the proofs which it employs." Thus he will benefit his congregation as much as possible by presenting doctrines to which he may not subscribe with full conviction. He can commit himself to teach them because it is not completely impossible that they may contain hidden truth. In any event, he has found nothing in the doctrines that contradicts the heart of religion. For if he believed that such contradictions existed he would not be able to administer his office with a clear conscience. He would have to resign it. Therefore the use which a scholar makes of his reason before the congregation that employs him is only a private use, for, no matter how sizable, this is only a domestic audience. In view of this he, as preacher, is not free and ought not to be free, since he is carrying out the orders of others. On the other hand, as the scholar who speaks to his own public (the world) through his writings, the minister in the public use of his reason enjoys unlimited freedom to use his own reason and to speak for himself. That the spiritual guardians of the people should themselves be treated as minors is an absurdity which would result in perpetuating absurdities.

But should a society of ministers, say a Church Council, . . . have the right to commit itself by oath to a certain unalterable doctrine, in order to secure perpetual guardianship over all its members and through them over the people? I say that this is quite impossible. Such a contract, concluded to keep all further enlightenment from humanity, is simply null and void even if it should be confirmed by the sovereign power, by parliaments, and by the most solemn treaties. An epoch cannot conclude a pact that will commit succeeding ages, prevent them from increasing their significant insights, purging themselves of errors, and generally progressing in enlightenment. That would be a crime against human nature, whose proper destiny lies precisely in such progress. Therefore, succeeding ages are fully entitled to repudiate such decisions as unauthorized and outrageous. The touchstone of all those decisions that may be made into law for a people lies in this question: Could a people impose such a law upon itself? Now, it might be possible to introduce a certain order for a definite short period of time in expectation of a better order. But while this provisional order continues, each citizen (above all, each pastor acting as a scholar) should be left free to publish his criticisms of the faults of existing institutions. This should continue until public understanding of these matters has gone so far that, by uniting the voices of many (although not necessarily all) scholars, reform proposals could be brought before the sovereign to protect those congregations which had decided according to their best lights upon an altered religious order, without, however, hindering those who want to remain true to the old institutions. But to agree to a perpetual religious constitution which is not to be publicly questioned by anyone would be, as it were, to annihilate a period of time in the progress of man's improvement. This must be absolutely forbidden.

A man may postpone his own enlightenment, but only for a limited period of time. And to give up enlightenment altogether, either for oneself or one's descendants, is to violate and to trample upon the sacred rights of man. What a people may not decide for itself may even less be decided for it by a monarch, for his reputation as a ruler consists precisely in the way in which he unites the will of the whole people within his own. If he only sees to it that all true or supposed [religious] improvement remains in step with the civic order, he can for the rest leave his subjects alone to do what they find necessary for the salvation of their souls. Salvation is none of his business; it *is* his business to prevent one man from forcibly keeping another from determining and promoting his salvation to the best of his ability. Indeed, it would be prejudicial to his majesty if he meddled in these matters and supervised the writings in which his subjects seek to bring their [religious] views into the open, even when he does this from his own highest insight, because then he exposes himself to the reproach: *Caesar non est supra grammaticos.*[3] It is worse when he debases his sovereign power so far as

---

[3]*Caesar non est supra grammaticos*: Latin for "Caesar is not above the grammarians."

to support the spiritual despotism of a few tyrants in his state over the rest of his subjects.

When we ask, Are we now living in an enlightened age? the answer is, No, but we live in an age of enlightenment. As matters now stand it is still far from true that men are already capable of using their own reason in religious matters confidently and correctly without external guidance. Still, we have some obvious indications that the field of working toward the goal [of religious truth] is now being opened. What is more, the hindrances against general enlightenment or the emergence from self-imposed nonage are gradually diminishing. In this respect this is the age of the enlightenment and the century of Frederick.[4]

A prince ought not to deem it beneath his dignity to state that he considers it his duty not to dictate anything to his subjects in religious matters, but to leave them complete freedom. If he repudiates the arrogant word *tolerant*, he is himself enlightened; he deserves to be praised by a grateful world and posterity as the man who was the first to liberate mankind from dependence, at least on the government, and let everybody use his own reason in matters of conscience. Under his reign, honorable pastors, acting as scholars and regardless of the duties of their office, can freely and openly publish their ideas to the world for inspection, although they deviate here and there from accepted doctrine. This is even more true of every other person not restrained by any oath of office. This spirit of freedom is spreading beyond the boundaries [of Prussia], even where it has to struggle against the external hindrances established by a government that fails to grasp its true interest. [Frederick's Prussia] is a shining example that freedom need not cause the least worry concerning public order or the unity of the community. When one does not deliberately attempt to keep men in barbarism, they will gradually work out of that condition by themselves.

I have emphasized the main point of the enlightenment—man's emergence from his self-imposed nonage—primarily in religious matters, because our rulers have no interest in playing the guardian to their subjects in the arts and sciences. Above all, nonage in religion is not only the most harmful but the most dishonorable. But the disposition of a sovereign ruler who favors freedom in the arts and sciences goes even further: he knows that there is no danger in permitting his subjects to make public use of their reason and to publish their ideas concerning a better constitution, as well as candid criticism of existing basic laws. We already have a striking example [of such freedom], and no monarch can match the one whom we venerate.

But only the man who is himself enlightened, who is not afraid of shadows, and who commands at the same time a well-disciplined and numerous army as guarantor of public peace—only he can say what [the sovereign of] a free state cannot dare to say: "Argue as much as you like, and about what you like, but obey!" Thus we observe here as elsewhere in human affairs, in which almost everything is paradoxical, a surprising and unexpected course of events: a large

---

[4]**the century of Frederick:** In the eighteenth century, Prussia was ruled by three Fredericks: Frederick I (r. 1701–1713), Frederick William I (r. 1713–1740), and Frederick II (r. 1740–1786).

degree of civic freedom appears to be of advantage to the intellectual freedom of the people, yet at the same time it establishes insurmountable barriers. A lesser degree of civic freedom, however, creates room to let that free spirit expand to the limits of its capacity. Nature, then, has carefully cultivated the seed within the hard core—namely, the urge for and the vocation of free thought. And this free thought gradually reacts back on the modes of thought of the people, and men become more and more capable of acting in freedom. At last free thought acts even on the fundamentals of government, and the state finds it agreeable to treat man, who is now more than a machine, in accord with his dignity.

READING AND DISCUSSION QUESTIONS

1. Briefly summarize Kant's definition of *enlightenment*. Why is it so difficult for people to achieve enlightenment?

2. According to Kant, who is responsible for enlightening the populace?

3. What is the difference between "public" and "private" freedoms? What examples does Kant give of each?

■ COMPARATIVE QUESTIONS ■

1. Religion and spirituality are important components of several excerpts in this chapter. How does each author present religion, and to what end? What might the relative absence of religion in some of the texts signify?

2. Voltaire and Kant both invoke religion in their discussions of human interaction and engagement with the world around them. In what ways are their ideas similar, and how do they differ? How do their views of religion pertain to their ideas of enlightenment?

3. What did these authors believe was the purpose of human inquiry? Did they believe in knowledge for the sake of knowledge itself, or did they insist that learning must serve utilitarian purposes?

4. It is often claimed that a central element of both the Scientific Revolution and the Enlightenment was optimism, confidence in the future and in the potential for human progress. What evidence of this do you find in these documents? Is there any evidence of pessimism, or doubt, in these texts?

20

Africa and the World
1400–1800

The fifteenth-century voyages of Portuguese mariners eager to identify and exploit new trade opportunities ushered in an era of violence, exploitation, and slavery on the African continent. However, Africa's story during these four centuries was not simply one of involuntary participation in a European-dominated system of colonization and enslavement. For centuries, diverse African states had played an important role in global trade, and foreign and indigenous influences combined to produce powerful and enduring cultures. Neither was slavery new to African culture. However, the traditional African idea of slavery was transformed by the dehumanizing profit motive of European capitalism and plantation economies. Many coastal societies facilitated the massive transatlantic slave trade by capturing people from the African interior and delivering them to European slave ships. Because of disease, non-navigable rivers, and the power of African armies, the European presence had remained along the African coast during these centuries except in southern Africa. At the end of this period, the first Europeans began moving into the West African interior and soon across the continent, making way for colonization. The documents in this chapter depict both continuity and transformation in African society during this period of European incursion.

20-1 | A Dutch View of an African King

OLFERT DAPPER, *King Alvaro I of Kongo Receiving the Dutch Ambassadors* (1668)

The history of the powerful west-central African state of Kongo was profoundly shaped by European expansion and the emergence of the transatlantic slave trade. Portuguese explorers first arrived in Kongo in 1491. They succeeded in making an alliance with the ruling Kongo empire, converting the royal family to Catholicism. The alliance gave the Kongo empire a short-term advantage over its local and regional rivals, but it proved a disaster in the long run. As the slave trade intensified, Kongo became increasingly unstable, descending into endemic warfare and political disorder. Keep this in mind as you examine this image taken from a late-seventeenth-century Dutch book on Africa. What parts of the story of the interaction between Kongo's leaders and Europeans does it highlight? What parts does it leave out?

Private Collection/Bridgeman Images

READING AND DISCUSSION QUESTIONS

1. How would you characterize the interaction between King Alvaro I and the Dutch ambassadors? What response might the artist have been hoping to evoke in viewers?

2. What importance should we attach to the large chandelier that hangs over the king? What other evidence does the image provide of the importation of European goods into Africa?

3. In the upper left corner of the image, we see a church in the distance. Why might the artist have chosen to include this detail?

Debating the Slave Trade

The British dominated the eighteenth-century transatlantic slave trade, and it was in this period that the trade reached its peak. By the end of the century, however, British public opinion was beginning to turn against the slave trade. Inspired by a complex mix of ideological, religious, and economic motives, antislavery organizations emerged to challenge Britain's involvement in the export of human beings from West Africa to the Americas. The efforts of such groups would culminate in the abolition of the slave trade in the British Empire in 1807 and the abolition of slavery itself in 1833. The two documents included in this feature provide an opportunity to gain a better understanding of the different attitudes that Africans held toward these historic antislavery acts. The first, written by the Asante king who profited from the slave trade, questions the motives of the British for ending it. The second, written by a victim of the trade and an antislavery activist, presents the horror, disorientation, and despair of enslavement in vivid detail. As you read these selections, ask yourself how two people could witness similar events and produce such vastly different accounts.

20-2 | West African Dependence on the Slave Trade

OSEI BONSU, *An Asante King Questions British Motives in Ending the Slave Trade* (1820)

Osei Bonsu was king of the Asante (also written *Ashanti* or *Ashantee*) state in West Africa from about 1801 to 1824. Under his rule, the Asante state expanded and solidified the sophisticated bureaucratic structure inaugurated by his predecessors in the late 1700s. The Asante export economy—based historically on the sale of gold, ivory, and slaves—flourished after initial contact with Europeans. His comments, presented here, were recorded by a British trader named Joseph shortly after the British abolition of the slave trade. They indicate both the profound dependence of many African states on the European slave trade and the complex relationships fostered through that system.

"Now," said the king, after a pause, "I have another palaver [topic of discussion], and you must help me to talk it. A long time ago the great king [the king of England] liked plenty of trade, more than now; then many ships came, and they bought ivory, gold, and slaves; but now he will not let the ships come as before, and the people buy gold and ivory only. This is what I have in my head, so now tell me truly, like a friend, why does the king do so?" "His majesty's question," I replied, "was connected with a great palaver, which my instructions did not authorize me to discuss. I had nothing to say regarding the slave trade." "I know that too," retorted the king; "because, if my master liked that trade, you would have told me so before. I only want to hear what you think as a friend: this is not like the other palavers." I was confessedly at a loss for an argument that might pass as a satisfactory reason, and the sequel proved that my doubts were

David Robinson and Douglas Smith, *Sources of the African Past: Case Studies of Five Nineteenth-Century African Societies* (New York: Africana, 1979), pp. 189–190. Copyright © 1979 by Holmes and Meier Publishers, Inc. Used with permission of Lynne Rienner Publishers, Inc.

not groundless. The king did not deem it plausible, that this obnoxious traffic should have been abolished from motives of humanity alone; neither would he admit that it lessened the number either of domestic or foreign wars.

Taking up one of my observations, he remarked, "The white men who go to council with your master, and pray to the great God for him, do not understand my country, or they would not say the slave trade was bad. But if they think it bad now, why did they think it good before? Is not your law an old law, the same as the Crammo [Muslim] law? Do you not both serve the same God, only you have different fashions and customs? Crammos are strong people in fetische,[1] and they say the law is good, because the great God made the book; so they buy slaves, and teach them good things, which they knew not before. This makes everybody love the Crammos, and they go everywhere up and down, and the people give them food when they want it. Then these men come all the way from the great water [the Niger River], and from Manding, and Dagomba, and Killinga; they stop and trade for slaves, and then go home. If the great king would like to restore this trade, it would be good for the white men and for me too, because Ashantee is a country for war, and the people are strong; so if you talk that palaver for me properly, in the white country, if you go there, I will give you plenty of gold, and I will make you richer than all the white men."

READING AND DISCUSSION QUESTIONS

1. How does this document complicate your understanding of the racial politics of transatlantic slavery and of slavery in the United States?

2. In this document, Osei Bonsu uses Muslims (*Crammos*) as an example of moral behavior toward slaves. How does this illustrate his understanding of international affairs?

3. How does the king's description of how Muslims treat slaves compare with their treatment by European Christians?

4. The narrator notes that Osei Bonsu thought it "implausible" that the slave trade was abolished for purely humanitarian reasons. Do you agree, and why?

20-3 | The Terror of Capture and Enslavement

OLAUDAH EQUIANO, From *The Interesting Narrative of Olaudah Equiano* (1789)

One of the few enslaved Africans able to purchase their freedom, Olaudah Equiano (ca. 1745–1797) drew on his remarkable education and experiences to write an autobiographical account of kidnapping and slavery in Africa and the Americas. It was published with the help of British abolitionists, and he promoted his work in Britain with the equivalent

---

Olaudah Equiano, *The Interesting Narrative of Olaudah Equiano* (London, 1789) in *The Atlantic Slave Trade*, ed. David Northrup (Lexington, Mass.: D. C. Heath, 1994), pp. 78–79.

[1]**fetische:** Fetish, religious practice and observance.

of a modern book tour. Some evidence suggests that Equiano may have been born in South Carolina and therefore would not have experienced life in Africa and the Middle Passage. However, his popular narrative is generally consistent with other accounts of the kidnapping and enslavement of Africans, and its power to inspire the abolitionist movement is unquestioned.

One day, when all our people were gone out to their works as usual, and only I and my dear sister were left to mind the house, two men and a woman got over our walls, and in a moment seized us both, and, without giving us time to cry out, or make resistance, they stopped our mouths, and ran off with us into the nearest wood. Here they tied our hands, and continued to carry us as far as they could, till night came on, when we reached a small house, where the robbers halted for refreshment, and spent the night. We were then unbound, but were unable to take any food; and, being quite overpowered by fatigue and grief, our only relief was some sleep, which allayed our misfortune for a short time. The next morning we left the house, and continued traveling all the day. For a long time we had kept [to] the woods, but at last we came to a road which I believed I knew. I now had some hopes of being delivered; for we had advanced but a little way before I discovered some people at a distance, on which I began to cry out for their assistance; but my cries had no other effect than to make them tie me faster and stop my mouth, and then they put me in a large sack. They also stopped my sister's mouth, and tied her hands; and in this manner we proceeded till we were out of sight of these people. When we went to rest the following night, they offered us some victuals, but we refused it; and the only comfort we had was in being in one another's arms all that night, and bathing each other with our tears. But alas! we were soon deprived of even the small comfort of weeping together.

The next day proved a day of greater sorrow than I had yet experienced; for my sister and I were then separated, while we lay clasped in each other's arms. It was in vain that we besought them not to part us; she was torn from me, and immediately carried away, while I was left in a state of distraction not to be described. I cried and grieved continually; and for several days did not eat anything but what they forced into my mouth. At length, after many days' traveling, during which I had often changed masters, I got into the hands of a chieftain, in a very pleasant country. This man had two wives and some children, and they all used me extremely well, and did all they could to comfort me; particularly the first wife, who was something like my mother. Although I was a great many days' journey from my father's house, yet these people spoke exactly the same language with us. . . .

From the time I left my own nation, I always found somebody that understood me till I came to the sea coast. The languages of different nations did not totally differ, nor were they so copious as those of the Europeans,[2] particularly the English. They were therefore easily learned; and, while I was journeying

---

[2] **nor were they so copious . . . Europeans:** Equiano is saying that African languages had less extensive vocabularies than European languages.

thus through Africa, I acquired two or three different tongues. In this manner I had been traveling for a considerable time, when, one evening, to my great surprise, whom should I see brought to the house where I was but my dear sister! As soon as she saw me, she gave a loud shriek, and ran into my arms—I was quite overpowered; neither of us could speak, but, for a considerable time, clung to each other in mutual embraces, unable to do anything but weep. Our meeting affected all who saw us; and, indeed, I must acknowledge, in honor of those sable destroyers of human rights, that I never met with any ill treatment, or saw any offered to their slaves, except tying them, when necessary, to keep them from running away.

When these people knew we were brother and sister, they indulged us to be together; and the man, to whom I suppose we belonged, lay with us, he in the middle, while she and I held one another by the hands across his breast all night; and thus for a while we forgot our misfortunes, in the joy of being together; but even this small comfort was soon to have an end; for scarcely had the fatal morning appeared when she was again torn from me forever! I was now more miserable, if possible, than before. The small relief which her presence gave me from pain, was gone, and the wretchedness of my situation was redoubled by my anxiety after her fate, and my apprehensions lest her sufferings should be greater than mine, when I could not be with her to alleviate them. . . .

I continued to travel, sometimes by land, sometimes by water, through different countries and various nations, till, at the end of six or seven months after I had been kidnapped, I arrived at the sea coast. . . .

The first object which saluted my eyes when I arrived on the coast, was the sea, and a slave ship, which was then riding at anchor, and waiting for its cargo. These filled me with astonishment, which was soon converted into terror, when I was carried on board. I was immediately handled, tossed up to see if I were sound, by some of the crew, and I was now persuaded that I had gotten into a world of bad spirits, and that they were going to kill me. Their complexions, too, differing so much from ours, their long hair, and the language they spoke (which was very different from any I had ever heard), united to confirm me in this belief. Indeed, such were the horrors of my views and fears at the moment, that, if ten thousand worlds had been my own, I would have freely parted with them all to have exchanged my condition with that of the meanest slave in my own country. When I looked round the ship too, and saw a large furnace of copper boiling, and a multitude of black people of every description chained together, every one of their countenances expressing dejection and sorrow. I no longer doubted of my fate, and, quite overpowered with horror and anguish, I fell motionless on the deck and fainted. When I recovered a little, I found some black people about me, who I believed were some of those who had brought me on board, and had been receiving their pay; they talked to me in order to cheer me, but all in vain. I asked them if we were not to be eaten by these white men with horrible looks, red faces, and long hair. They told me I was not, and one of the crew brought me a small portion of spirituous liquor in a wine glass; but being afraid of him, I would not take it out of his hand. One of the blacks therefore took it from him and gave it to me, and I took a little down my palate, which, instead of reviving me, as they thought it would, threw me into the greatest consternation at the strange feeling it produced, having never tasted any such liquor before. Soon after this, the blacks who brought me on board went off, and left me abandoned to despair. . . .

At last, when the ship we were in, had got in all her cargo, they made ready with many fearful noises, and we were all put under deck, so that we could not see how they managed the vessel. But this disappointment was the least of my sorrow. The stench of the hold while we were on the coast was so intolerably loathsome, that it was dangerous to remain there for any time, and some of us had been permitted to stay on the deck for the fresh air; but now that the whole ship's cargo was confined together, it became absolutely pestilential. The closeness of the place, and the heat of the climate, added to the number in the ship, which was so crowded that each had scarcely room to turn himself, almost suffocated us. This produced copious perspirations, so that the air soon became unfit for respiration, from a variety of loathsome smells, and brought on a sickness among the slaves, of which many died — thus falling victims to the improvident avarice, as I may call it, of their purchasers. This wretched situation was again aggravated by the galling of the chains, now became insupportable, and the filth of the necessary tubs [latrines], into which the children often fell, and were almost suffocated. The shrieks of the women, and the groans of the dying, rendered the whole a scene of horror almost inconceivable. Happily, perhaps, for myself, I was soon reduced so low here that it was thought necessary to keep me almost always on deck, and from my extreme youth I was not put in fetters. In this situation I expected every hour to share the fate of my companions, some of whom were almost daily brought upon deck at the point of death, which I began to hope would soon put an end to my miseries. Often did I think of the many inhabitants of the deep much more happy than myself. I envied them [for] the freedom they enjoyed, and as often wished I could change my condition for theirs. Every circumstance I met with, served only to render my state more painful, and heightened my apprehensions, and my opinion of the cruelty of the whites.

One day they had taken a number of fishes; and when they had killed and satisfied themselves with as many as they thought fit, to our astonishment who were on deck, rather than give any of them to us to eat, as we expected, they tossed the remaining fish into the sea again, although we begged and prayed for some as well we could, but in vain. . . .

One day, when we had a smooth sea and a moderate wind, two of my wearied countrymen who were chained together (I was near them at the time), preferring death to such a life of misery, somehow made through the nettings and jumped into the sea; immediately, another quite dejected fellow, who, on account of his illness, was suffered to be out of irons, also followed their example; and I believe many more would have soon done the same, if they had not been pre-vented by the ship's crew, who were instantly alarmed. . . .

At last we came in sight of the island of Barbadoes, at which the whites on board gave a great shout, and made many signs of joy to us. We did not know what to think of this; but as the vessel grew nearer, we plainly saw the harbor, and other ships of different kinds and sizes, and we soon anchored among them, off Bridgetown. Many merchants and planters now came on board, though it was in the evening. They put us in separate parcels, and examined us atten-tively. They also made us jump, and pointed to the land, signifying we were to go there. We thought by this, we should be eaten by these ugly men, as they appeared to us; and, when soon after we were all put down under deck again, there was much dread and trembling among us, and nothing but bitter cries to be heard all the night from these apprehensions, insomuch, that at last the white people got some old slaves from the land to pacify us. They told us we were not to be eaten, but to work, and were soon to go on land, where we would see many of our country people. This report eased us much. And sure enough, soon after we were landed, there came to us Africans of all languages.

We were immediately conducted to the merchant's yard, where we were all pent up together, like so many sheep in a fold, without regard to sex or age. As every object was new to me, everything I saw filled me with surprise. What struck me first, was, that the houses were built with bricks and stones, and every other respect different from those I had seen in Africa; but I was still more aston-ished on seeing people on horseback.[3] I did not know what this could mean; and, indeed, I thought these people were full of nothing but magical arts. While I was in this astonishment, one of my fellow prisoners spoke to a countryman of his, about the horses, who said they were the same kind they had in their country. I understood them, though they were from a distant part of Africa; and I thought it odd I had not seen any horses there; but afterwards, when I came to converse with different Africans, I found they had many horses amongst them, and much larger than those I then saw.

We were not many days in the merchant's custody, before we were sold in the usual manner, which is this: On a signal given (as the beat of a drum), the buyers rush at once into the yard where the slaves are confined, and make a choice of that parcel they like best. The noise and clamor with which this is attended, and the eagerness visible in the countenances of the buyers, serve not a little to increase the apprehension of terrified Africans, who may well be sup-posed to consider them as the ministers of that destruction to which they think themselves devoted. In this manner, without scruple, are relations and friends separated, most of them never to see each other again.

I remember, in the vessel in which I was brought over, in the men's apartment, there were several brothers, who, in the sale, were sold in different lots; and it was

---

[3]**people on horseback:** Equiano would have been unfamiliar with horses in West Africa, where they were susceptible to sleeping sickness, a lethal disease transmitted by the tsetse fly.

very moving on this occasion, to see and hear their cries at parting. O, ye nominal Christians! might not an African ask you—Learned you this from your God, who says unto you, Do unto all men as you would men should do unto you? Is it not enough that we are torn from our country and friends, to toil for your luxury and lust of gain? Must every tender feeling be likewise sacrificed to your avarice? Are the dearest friends and relations, now rendered more dear by their separation from their kindred, still to be parted from each other, and thus prevented from cheering the gloom of slavery, with the small comfort of being together, and mingling their sufferings and sorrows? Why are parents to lose their children, brothers their sisters, or husbands their wives? Surely, this is a new refinement in cruelty, which, while it has no advantage to atone for it, thus aggravates distress, and adds fresh horrors even to the wretchedness of slavery.

READING AND DISCUSSION QUESTIONS

1. How does Equiano contrast his experiences as a slave in Africa with his experiences aboard the slave ship?

2. To whom does Equiano appeal at the end of his narrative, and on what grounds?

3. At times, Equiano describes people as "white" or "black." At others, he distinguishes between people of his own nation and other "blacks," and elsewhere he refers to "Africans." What is the significance of these different categorizations?

VIEWPOINTS COMPARATIVE QUESTIONS

1. Compare and contrast King Bonsu's and Equiano's attitudes toward the slave trade. What differences do you note? In your opinion, what aspects of their life experiences and positions might explain these differences?

2. Imagine a conversation between these two Africans. How might they argue against each other's viewpoints?

20-4 | Enslaved Africans March to the Sea
Transportation of Slaves in Africa (ca. 1800–1900)

This nineteenth-century painting by an anonymous artist depicts the dynamics of the African slave trade and particularly the conditions and nature of that trade as enslaved Africans were marched to the coast. The painting highlights not only the brutal conditions under which Africans were enslaved and transported to the coast but also the multiple and diverse roles played by Africans in the slave trade. The slavers (the figures holding rifles, a hatchet, or a pistol) are guarding or visibly threatening the enslaved Africans, some of whom are yoked together with a forked wooden device. Victims of violence or deprivation are left alongside the trail, and women and children are clearly visible among the slave ranks.

Photo Josse/Leemage/Getty Images

READING AND DISCUSSION QUESTIONS

1. What differences and similarities are discernible between the traders and the captured slaves? What do their garments, postures, and expressions reveal?

2. What might the artist have intended to communicate with this illustration? To whom?

3. Note that at least two of the figures in the image are holding firearms. What, if anything, does the presence of firearms indicate about the nature of African slavery?

4. The line of enslaved Africans stretches into the far distance and blurs as it recedes. What impression is created by this visual effect, and what does it communicate about the nature of African slavery?

20-5 | Europeans Move Inland

MUNGO PARK, From *Travels in the Interior Districts of Africa* (1799)

By the late 1700s, as the Scientific and Industrial Revolutions advanced, the British began to think beyond the slave trade. They sent out scientists to map the world and merchants to look for sources of raw materials and markets for their mass-produced goods. The great African rivers—the Nile, the Niger, and the Congo—particularly intrigued the scientists. How long were they? Were they connected? Where were their sources? In 1895 a Scottish

Mungo Park, *Travels in the Interior Districts of Africa: Performed in the Years 1795, 1796, and 1797. With an Account of a Subsequent Mission to That Country in 1805* (London: John Murray, 1816), pp. 191–192, 266, 310–311.

naturalist and explorer, Mungo Park, led an expedition to discover the course of the Niger River. He traveled first up the Gambia River, then by land across Senegal, reaching Ségou on the Niger in July 1796. He returned to Scotland in December 1797, and an account of his journey was published in 1799. In this account he theorized that the Niger and Congo merged, and in 1803 he set out again to prove it, but in 1806 he drowned in the Niger River. The excerpts here record his impressions of Ségou and of his surprise at African views of Europeans.

Sego, the capital of Bambarra, at which I had now arrived, consists . . . of four distinct towns; two on the northern bank of the Niger . . . and two on the southern bank. . . . They are all surrounded with high mud walls; the houses are built of clay, of a square form, with flat roofs; some of them have two stories, and many of them are white-washed. Besides these buildings, Moorish mosques are seen in every quarter; and the streets, though narrow, are broad enough for every useful purpose, in a country where wheel carriages are entirely unknown. From the best inquiries I could make, I have reason to believe that Sego contains altogether about thirty thousand inhabitants. The King of Bambara . . . employs a great many slaves in conveying people over the river, and the money they receive . . . furnishes considerable revenue to the king. . . . The canoes . . . are . . . very long and disproportionably narrow, and have neither decks nor masts; they are, however, very roomy; for I observed in one of them four horses, and several people crossing over the river. I could not immediately obtain a passage; and sat down upon the bank of the river; . . . The view of this extensive city; the numerous canoes upon the river; the crowded population and the cultivated state of the surrounding country, formed altogether a prospect of civilization and magnificence, which I little expected to find in the bosom of Africa.

[The Africans] imagine that the world is an extended plain, the termination of which no eye has discovered; it being, they say, overhung with clouds and darkness. They describe the sea as a large river of salt water, on the farther shore of which is situated a country called *Tobaubo doo*; "the land of the white people." At a distance from Tobaubo doo, they describe another country, which they allege is inhabited by cannibals of gigantic size, called *Koomi*. That country they call *Jong sang doo*, "the land where the slaves are sold." But of all countries in the world their own appears to them as the best, and their own people as the happiest; and they pity the fate of other nations who have been placed by Providence in less fertile and less fortunate districts.

[Some slaves were] all very inquisitive; but they viewed me at first with looks of horror, and repeatedly asked if my countrymen were cannibals. They were very desirous to know what became of the slaves after they had crossed the salt water. I told them, that they were employed in cultivating the land; but they would not believe me; and one of them putting his hand upon the ground, said with great simplicity, "have you really such ground as this to set your feet upon?" A deeply rooted idea that the whites purchase Negroes for the purpose of devouring them, or of selling them to others, that they may be devoured hereafter, naturally makes the slaves contemplate a journey towards the coast with great terror.

READING AND DISCUSSION QUESTIONS

1. In what ways might the city of Ségou conflict with European views of Africa at the time?

2. What were the universal thoughts about their homeland that Africans held?

3. How were African views of Europeans similar to European views of Africans at the time?

▪ COMPARATIVE QUESTIONS ▪

1. How might Equiano have reacted to the painting of enslaved Africans marching to the sea? What about Osei Bonsu?

2. How are the two images in this chapter reflective of the readings? Which reading(s) would you attach to each, and why?

3. Although Europeans had had contact with Africans along the coast for over two centuries, in what ways did Mungo Park's expedition to the West African interior signal a new era in European-African relations?

21

Continuity and Change in East Asia

1400–1800

From 1400 to 1800, East Asian countries experienced important changes at all levels of society. Despite the growing presence of Europeans in East Asia, both China and Japan remained relatively free from the influence of European commercial expansion. Chinese thinkers in the Ming and early Qing periods were primarily concerned with internal development and regional conflicts involving other Asian states. In Japan, the work of the three great unifiers—Oda Nobunaga, Toyotomi Hideyoshi, and Tokugawa Ieyasu—ended the chaotic Warring States Period and led to the relative peace of the Tokugawa regime (1603–1867). In both countries, transitions from older to newer political orders were mirrored by changes in society and culture. In China, the fall of the Ming Dynasty and the founding of the Qing Dynasty (1644–1911) by Jurchen invaders from Manchuria (known as the Manchus) occasioned new unrest and social critique. In Japan, the stability of the Tokugawa family's rule fostered domestic economic and cultural advances, and—despite careful control of international contact—afforded Dutch merchants limited but important access to Japanese society. The documents here illustrate not only the political shifts in East Asia but also how the Chinese and Japanese discussed gender and its role in their lives.

21-1 | The Growing British Presence in East Asia

The Viceroy of Canton Giving an Audience to Commodore Anson (1748)

In the mid-eighteenth century, important changes were under way in the East Asian maritime world. The Portuguese had lost considerable ground to the Dutch, and more important in the long run, the British presence in the region was growing. British ambitions were centered on India, but the British were also determined to expand their trade with China. In the 1830s, this determination would lead to war and a humiliating defeat for the Chinese. In the 1740s and 1750s, however, the Chinese saw the British as just another group of foreigners who hoped to grow rich buying and selling Chinese goods. In this illustration from *Anson's Voyage Round the World*, we see the British naval commander and adventurer George Anson in the presence of the viceroy of Canton. As you examine the image, think about the relationship between the British visitors and their Chinese host, and who might have produced this image.

Private Collection/Bridgeman Images

READING AND DISCUSSION QUESTIONS

1. How are Anson and his party dressed? What impression might they have hoped their attire would make on the viceroy?

2. What did the artist want to convey to a British audience? How might a Chinese artist have depicted this ceremony differently?

21-2 | A German Doctor Describes Eighteenth-Century Japan
ENGELBERT KAEMPFER, From *History of Japan* (1727)

Engelbert Kaempfer (1651–1716) was a German physician who traveled extensively in Russia and Asia in the late 1600s. His writings on Japan were published posthumously in 1727 to great public interest, and his exhaustive descriptions of Japanese society, language, environment, culture, and history were so accurate—in many cases—that he earned the suspicion of a later Japanese scholar, who warned in the early 1800s that Kaempfer's careful observations were proof that foreigners should be expelled to prevent espionage. The excerpts here outline his notes on commoners, his understanding of Confucianism, and his description of the Dutch in Japan and their commercial position there.

Judō, the Teaching or the Ways of the Moralists and Philosophers

Judō [Confucianism] literally means the way or method of wise men. *Judōsha*, or *judōshū* in the plural, are their philosophers. They do not actually practice a religion but seek perfection and the greatest good in the contentment of the mind resulting from a virtuous and unblemished life and conduct. They believe in only secular punishment and reward, the consequence of virtue and vice. Thus one ought by necessity practice virtue as nature has given birth to us to lead the just life of people, as opposed to dumb animals.

Their founder, the first whose teaching was made public, was the famous Kōshi [Confucius], born in China 2,238 years ago counting from this fifth year of Genroku, or the 1,692nd year after Christ. He used moral teachings to instruct his disciples in the greatest good and was the first to describe the *Shōgaku*, or book of living ethically, inflicting great damage on the opposing sect of Rōshi [Daoism], flourishing at the time. After him this sect was continued by the much-praised teacher Mōshi [Mencius], who established his philosophical Shisho, or Four Books, in this country. Up to this day they have their adherents in all countries where the characters of their writing system are understood.

Their moral philosophy consists of five articles, which they call *jin, gi, rei, chi, shin. Jin* teaches ethical living (consequently *jinsha*, virtuous person); *gi*, law and concern for justice; *rei*, politeness and civil behavior; *chi*, practical philosophy, politics, political judgment; *shin* concerns man's conscience and sincerity of heart.

They do not believe in the transmigration of souls but in a universal soul, or a force common to the entire world, which absorbs the souls of the dead, like the ocean takes back all water, and in the generation of matter permits them to depart again without differentiation. They associate this world soul, or universal nature, with the godhead and endow it with the attributes of the prime being. They use the word *ten*, heaven, or nature, in the actions and fortunes of life, thanking heaven or nature for their food. I have spoken to others who conceded an intellect or perfect incorporeal being as the governing agent, but not as the originator of nature. As the highest creation of nature it is produced by *in* and *yō*, that is, from the action of heaven and receptivity of the earth, the principles of generation and corruption. In this fashion they also accept other forces as spiritual and believe that the world is eternal and that men and animals were produced from the *in yō* of heaven and the five elements.

Engelbert Kaempfer, *Kaempfer's Japan: Tokugawa Culture Observed*, ed. and trans. Beatrice M. Bodart-Bailey (Honolulu: University of Hawaii Press, 1999), pp. 132–133, 145, 187–188. Reprinted by permission of the publisher.

They have neither temple nor gods, but follow the traditions of their forefathers in observing the memory of and commemorating their dead friends. They venerate their dead friends' *byōsho*, or memorial tablet, according to the customs of their forefathers and in the fashion of other believers by placing meat in front of it, lighting candles, and bowing to the ground (as if they were alive). They celebrate their memory monthly and annually and prepare themselves three days in advance by abstaining from sexual intercourse and all sinful matter, cleaning their body, and putting on new clothes. All this they do as a human gesture, prompted by their grateful and virtuous heart. The body of the dead is kept for three days above ground and placed into a European-style coffin, flat on the back, but the head is raised a little. Presumably to prevent decomposition they sometimes also cover the body with spices and scented herbs. Then they accompany it to the place of burial, where they bury the body in the soil without prior cremation.

Suicide is not only permitted in this sect but is considered an extraordinary act of bravery when committed to preempt the enemy or a shameful death.

These atheistic philosophers will only perform heathen celebrations or special duties for the gods out of common politeness. Instead they strive for virtue, a clean conscience, and honorable behavior in accordance with the teaching of [Roman philosopher] Seneca or our Ten Commandments. Thus they are also capable of looking favorably at the Christian teaching and as a result have come under great suspicion. According to the new laws, which came into effect with the banishment of the Christians, they must, against their will, keep in their houses the image of a god or mount, or paste up, the characters of the name of a god with a pot of flowers and an incense burner placed in front of it. Generally they chose Kannon or Amida, whom, according to the custom of the country, they assign a place behind the hearth. Of their own free will they may have a picture of Kōshi in public places of learning or, in their own homes, the *byōsho* of their parents with the posthumous name of, or characters for, a learned man. In the past this now-suspicious sect comprised the greater part of the population and practically held a monopoly on the sciences and liberal arts. But after the martyrdom of the Christians, their numbers decreased yearly and their books were brought into disrepute, even though those books had been valued by all other believers no less than we [Europeans] do the instructive works of Seneca, Plato, and other heathens.

Some thirty years ago it came to pass that the Lord of Bizen, Inaba, an excellent *judōshi* and patron of the liberal arts, attempted to popularize once again in his fief this sect and its stoic manner of living. He founded an academy, appointed learned men and teachers from all parts of the country, and paid them handsomely. Gaining greater understanding and prompted by example of their superiors, the people no longer wanted to believe in the incomprehensible revelation and fantastic tales or to continue supporting the ignorant rabble of priests, who mostly depended for their living on alms. Consequently these gangs (with which the whole country is packed) nearly died of starvation in this fief. But both the emperor and the shogun were so angered about this matter that they were about to deprive this honest patriot of his inherited fief and would have done so had he not taken the precaution of retiring in favor of his son to prevent his family from falling out of favor. His son, who has governed ever since, demonstrates with his stoic conduct that he is still following his father's path. . . .

The Situation of the City of Nagasaki [. . .]

Houses of the Commoners

The houses of common citizens and residents are of poor structure, small and low. They either have no attic at all or one that is low and practically useless. The roof is covered with pine chips, generally secured only by other chips placed across. Like all other houses in this country, they are constructed of wood and clay walls. Inside, the walls are nicely hung with colored paper, and the floors are neatly spread with thickly padded woven rush mats. Further, they are divided into separate rooms by papered sliding windows. They lack chairs or benches and have only as many household items as are essential for daily cooking. At the back there is merely a narrow space for one's private business, which, however poor, does contain some little plants, carefully grown to provide a focus of interest for the eyes. The houses of people of distinction, the rich, and those handling foreign trade rise to two stories, are spacious, and are partly built in Chinese style with a large building with bare floor at the entrance and a garden at the back. . . .

The Situation of the Dutch

At the beginning of the present seventeenth century, very soon after their ships began to travel to Asia and the establishment of their East India Company, the Dutch, enticed by the fertile trade of the Portuguese, began making annual visits to this, the furthest empire of the world. They arrived at the city and island of Hirado and set up their warehouse and living quarters on a spit of land linked to the city by a bridge. Their admission to Japan was all the quicker and easier, the greater their enmity was toward those whom the ruler felt compelled to drive out of the country. Even though the Portuguese still had a lot of influence with the greatest lords of the country, and did much to prevent the entry of the Dutch, they were finally unable to stop the shogun Ieyasu—or Gongen, after his death—from giving the Dutch access to the country in the year of Christ 1611 with a special *goshuin*, which literally means "lofty cinnabar seal" and is a shogunal permit or pass. It is signed by the councilors of the empire and authorized by the red shogunal seal, from the color of which it also takes its name. With this document they were granted in very clear terms, or characters, free trade and access to all provinces and harbors with favorable recommendations to all subjects of the empire. After the death of the shogun they requested to have their privileges renewed and a new pass issued, against the practice of this nation, which considers upholding the laws of its forefathers a sacred duty. This they received, but while outwardly it appeared to be identical in form and shape, it contained much less advantageous conditions. Meanwhile, from the time they settled in Hirado, the Dutch did what they could to profit from the progressive decline of the Portuguese. They did everything possible to please the court, the source of success or failure, as well as the councilors, the lord of Hirado, and any other great men who might proffer help or hindrance. The Dutch spared no cost nor labor to seek out the world's rarest novelties to pay homage to the Japanese annually and to satisfy the ridiculous passion of the Japanese for various strange animals—which nature did not create the way they imagine them—by bringing in as many as possible from the most distant empires of India, Persia, and Europe. The Dutch showed the utmost subservience in everything, even wrongful impositions, to stay in the good books of this nation and conduct profitable trade. Since they valued their lives, they could show no objection when in 1638 the shogun ordered them to tear down as fast as if they were enemy property their own newly built residence and warehouse on the island of Hirado: valuable stone mansions such as Japan had never seen before. The reason was that the buildings were splendid beyond the custom of the country and had the year of the Christian era on the gable [of their roofs]. Soon afterward, in the same year of 1638, this heathen court had no qualms in inflicting upon them a cursed test to find out whether the orders of the shogun or the love for their fellow Christians had greater power over them. It was a matter of us serving the empire by helping to destroy the native Christians, of whom those remaining, some forty thousand people, in desperation over their martyrdom had moved into an old fortress in the province of Shimabara and made preparations to defend themselves. The head of the Dutch, Koekebecker, himself went to the location with the one remaining vessel (for in the face of the impudent demand the remainder had slipped out of the harbor the previous day) and in fourteen days treated the beleaguered Christians to 426 rough cannon salvos, both from land and sea. Although this assistance resulted neither in surrender nor complete defeat, it broke the strength of the besieged. And because the Japanese had the pleasure to order it, he stripped the vessel of a further six cannons (regardless of the fact that she still had to navigate dangerous seas) that the Japanese insisted had to be lent in addition to the first to carry out their cruel designs.

It is true that this show of total obedience was instrumental in keeping a foothold in the country when the court was considering completely closing it to all Christians. At the same time, however, they gained a bad reputation among the more high-minded at court and throughout the country, for they judged that people who so easily permitted themselves to be used in the destruction of those with whom they basically shared the same belief and the path of Christ—as they had been amply told by the padres from Portugal and Manila—could not be true of heart, honest, and loyal towards a foreign ruler. I was told this by the locals in these very same words. Thus far from earning the trust and deep friendship of this exceedingly suspicious nation by their compliance, the reputation of the Dutch was ruined unjustly, regardless of their merits. Shortly afterward, in 1641, the Dutch, having assisted in the confinement of the Portuguese by word and deed, were to undergo the same experience. For they were told to leave the island of Hirado with all their belongings and to exchange subordination to a lenient territorial lord for directions from a new and zealous administration directly responsible to the shogun, while retiring under strict guard and manifold supervision within the limits of the prison built for the Portuguese. Submission to these proud heathens into such servitude and imprisonment, forgoing all celebrations of feast days and Sundays, all devotion with religious song and prayer, the use of the name of Christ, the symbol of the cross, and all outward proof or signs of being a Christian, and, added to that, good-natured acceptance of their despicable impudence, an affront to any high-minded soul, all that for the love of profit and to gain control of the veins of ore in their mountains.

READING AND DISCUSSION QUESTIONS

1. Kaempfer was criticized for his favorable presentation of a "heathen" culture. How does he address religion in these excerpts?

2. Kaempfer's description of Japan fascinated the European public. What might have particularly intrigued European readers in the early 1700s, and why?

3. What light does Kaempfer's account shed on the Dutch presence in Japan in the seventeenth century?

VIEWPOINTS

Gender in East Asia

Over the course of the early modern period, family and marriage systems in China and Japan converged, with Japan moving closer to the Chinese model of strict subordination of women to men. In both societies, women moved into their husband's house upon marriage. Once there, they were expected to show deference to both their husbands and their in-laws. Deprived of independent wealth by inheritance practices that favored sons over daughters, women had little leverage with which to resist the expectations of their relatives. Women were expected to think of themselves in terms of their roles as daughters, wives, and mothers. The documents included in this feature highlight this subordination, but they also reveal some of its limits. Most women worked in some capacity outside of the home, taking on roles that required more of them than humble acquiescence. Moreover, contemporary observers were aware of the gender inequities in their society and did not always approve of them. As you explore the documents, think about the limits on the subordination of women in Japanese and Chinese society. Why did the reality of gender relations rarely match the ideals?

21-3 | Teaching Values to Japanese Children

KAIBARA EKIKEN AND KAIBARA TŌKEN, *Common Sense Teachings for Japanese Children* and *Greater Learning for Women* (ca. 1700)

Kaibara Ekiken (1630–1714) was a physician, educator, and author from the samurai class during the enforced peace of the Tokugawa period (1603–1867). His works combined Neo-Confucian principles of self-reliance and humaneness with careful and practical attention to life in early modern Japan. His writings were printed and distributed widely, thanks to the vibrant publishing world of urban Tokugawa Japan. The following selections (the second probably coauthored with his wife, Tōken) show his concern with daily life and "common sense" and his interest in maintaining Confucian gender and social roles.

Common Sense Teachings for Japanese Children

In January when children reach the age of six, teach them numbers one through ten, and the names given to designate 100, 1,000, 10,000, and 100,000,000. Let them know the four directions, East, West, North, and South. Assess their native intelligence and differentiate between quick and slow learners. Teach them Japanese pronunciation from the age of six or seven, and let them learn how to write. . . . From this time on, teach them to respect their elders, and let them know the distinctions between the upper and lower classes and between the young and old. Let them learn to use the correct expressions.

When the children reach the age of seven, do not let the boys and girls sit together, nor must you allow them to dine together. . . .

For the eighth year. This is the age when the ancients began studying the book *Little Learning*.[1] Beginning at this time, teach the youngsters etiquette befitting their age, and caution them not to commit an act of impoliteness. Among those which must be taught are: daily deportment, the manners set for appearing before one's senior and withdrawing from his presence, how to speak or respond to one's senior or guest, how to place a serving tray or replace it for one's senior, how to present a wine cup and pour rice wine and to serve side dishes to accompany it, and how to serve tea. Children must also learn how to behave while taking their meals.

Children must be taught by those who are close to them the virtues of filial piety and obedience. To serve the parents well is called filial piety, and to serve one's seniors well is called obedience. The one who lives close to the children and who is able to teach must instruct the children in the early years

David J. Lu, *Japan: A Documentary History* (Armonk, N.Y.: M. E. Sharpe, 1997), pp. 258–261. Trans. copyright © 1997 by David J. Lu. Republished with permission of Taylor & Francis Group LLC - Books; permission conveyed through Copyright Clearance Center, Inc.

[1]*Little Learning*: An instruction book for young children that contained rules of behavior.

of their life that the first obligation of a human being is to revere the parents and serve them well. Then comes the next lesson which includes respect for one's seniors, listening to their commands and not holding them in contempt. One's seniors include elder brothers, elder sisters, uncles, aunts, and cousins who are older and worthy of respect. . . . As the children grow older, teach them to love their younger brothers and to be compassionate to the employees and servants. Teach them also the respect due the teachers and the behavior codes governing friends. The etiquette governing each movement toward important guests—such as standing, sitting, advancing forward, and retiring from their presence—and the language to be employed must be taught. Teach them how to pay respect to others according to the social positions held by them. Gradually the ways of filial piety and obedience, loyalty and trustworthiness, right deportment and decorum, and sense of shame must be inculcated in the children's minds and they must know how to implement them. Caution them not to desire the possessions of others, or to stoop below one's dignity in consuming excessive amounts of food and drink. . . .

Once reaching the age of eight, children must follow and never lead their elders when entering a gate, sitting, or eating and drinking. From this time on they must be taught how to become humble and yield to others. Do not permit the children to behave as they please. It is important to caution them against "doing their own things."

At the age of ten, let the children be placed under the guidance of a teacher, and tell them about the general meaning of the five constant virtues and let them understand the way of the five human relationships.[2] Let them read books by the Sage [Confucius] and the wise men of old and cultivate the desire for learning. . . . When not engaged in reading, teach them the literary and military arts. . . .

Fifteen is the age when the ancients began the study of the *Great Learning*.[3] From this time on, concentrate on the learning of a sense of justice and duty. The students must also learn to cultivate their personalities and investigate the way of governing people. . . .

Those who are born in the high-ranking families have the heavy obligations of becoming leaders of the people, of having people entrusted to their care, and of governing them. Therefore, without fail, a teacher must be selected for them when they are still young. They must be taught how to read and be informed of the ways of old, of cultivating their personalities, and of the way of governing people. If they do not learn the way of governing people, they may injure the many people who are entrusted to their care by the Way of Heaven. That will be a serious disaster. . . .

---

[2]**five constant virtues . . . human relationships:** The *five virtues* are human heartedness, righteousness, propriety, wisdom, and good faith. The *five relationships* are ruler–subject, father–son, husband–wife, older brother–younger brother, and friend–friend.

[3]***Great Learning:*** A chapter in the *Record of Rituals*, one of the four works that came to be known within the Confucian classics as the Four Books.

Greater Learning for Women

Seeing that it is a girl's destiny, on reaching womanhood, to go to a new home, and live in submission to her father-in-law, it is even more incumbent upon her than it is on a boy to receive with all reverence her parents' instructions. Should her parents, through their tenderness, allow her to grow up self-willed, she will infallibly show herself capricious in her husband's house, and thus alienate his affection; while, if her father-in-law be a man of correct principles, the girl will find the yoke of these principles intolerable. She will hate and decry her father-in-law, and the end of those domestic dissensions will be her dismissal from her husband's house and the covering of herself with igno-miny. Her parents, forgetting the faulty education they gave her, may indeed lay all the blame on the father-in-law. But they will be in error; for the whole disaster should rightly be attributed to the faulty education the girl received from her parents.

* * *

More precious in a woman is a virtuous heart than a face of beauty. The vicious woman's heart is ever excited; she glares wildly around her, she vents her anger on others, her words are harsh and her accent vulgar. When she speaks, it is to set herself above others, to upbraid others, to envy others, to be puffed up with individual pride, to jeer at others, to outdo others—all things at variance with the way in which a woman should walk. The only qualities that befit a woman are gentle obedience, chastity, mercy, and quietness.

From her earliest youth a girl should observe the line of demarcation sep-arating women from men. The customs of antiquity did not allow men and women to sit in the same apartment, to keep their wearing apparel in the same place, to bathe in the same place, or to transmit to each other anything directly from hand to hand. A woman . . . must observe a certain distance in her rela-tions even with her husband and with her brothers. In our days the women of lower classes, ignoring all rules of this nature, behave disorderly; they contami-nate their reputations, bring down reproach upon the head of their parents and brothers, and spend their whole lives in an unprofitable manner. Is not this truly lamentable?

* * *

It is the chief duty of a girl living in the parental house to practice filial piety towards her father and mother. But after marriage her duty is to honor her father-in-law and mother-in-law, to honor them beyond her father and mother, to love and reverence them with all ardor, and to tend them with practice of every filial piety. . . . Even if your father-in-law and mother-in-law are inclined to hate and vilify you, do not be angry with them, and murmur not. If you carry piety towards them to its utmost limits, and minister to them in all sincerity, it cannot be but that they will end by becoming friendly to you.

* * *

The great lifelong duty of a woman is obedience. . . . When the husband issues his instructions, the wife must never disobey them. In a doubtful case, she should inquire of her husband and obediently follow his commands. . . .

Should her husband be roused at any time to anger, she must obey him with fear and trembling, and not set herself up against him in anger and forwardness. A woman should look upon her husband as if he were Heaven itself, and never weary of thinking how she may yield to her husband and thus escape celestial castigation.

Her treatment of her servant girls will require circumspection. Those low-born girls have had no proper education; they are stupid, obstinate, and vulgar in their speech. . . . Again, in her dealings with those lowly people, a woman will find many things to disapprove of. But if she be always reproving and scolding, and spend her time in hustle and anger, her household will be in a continual state of disturbance. When there is real wrongdoing, she should occasionally notice it, and point out the path of amendment, while lesser faults should be quietly endured without anger.

READING AND DISCUSSION QUESTIONS

1. What values does Ekiken emphasize for children's education? How are they to be instilled?

2. How is concern for social hierarchy and propriety evident in Ekiken's work on children? In his work on women?

3. What assumptions, if any, does Ekiken make about his likely audience? What gives you that impression?

21-4 | Pleasure and Gender in Tokugawa Edo

TORII KIYONAGA, *Women of the Gay Quarters* (late 18th century)

For Japanese daimyo, Tokugawa-era Edo was a gilded prison. On the one hand, the city boasted an astonishing variety of establishments devoted to providing urban elites with every possible pleasure, luxury, and form of diversion. Providing he had the money to pay for his desires, a daimyo living in Edo could indulge his every whim. On the other hand, the alternate residence system required all daimyo to live in Edo every other year and to leave their families there. Thus, the decision to maintain a residence in Edo, with all the costs that entailed, was not a choice for daimyo but a legal requirement that resulted in the eventual bankruptcy of many once-powerful daimyo families. Think about these issues as you examine this eighteenth-century woodblock print of a wealthy Japanese man surrounded by "women of the gay quarters" of Edo. In what ways might this image comment on the effects of city life on elite Japanese men?

Heritage Images/Getty Images

READING AND DISCUSSION QUESTIONS

1. How would you characterize the lone male figure in the print? What is his relationship to the women who surround him?

2. In your opinion, should we see this image as a reflection of male dominance in Japanese society? Why or why not? What alternative interpretations of the image are possible?

21-5 | Chinese Gender Norms Turned Upside Down

LI RUZHEN (LI JU-CHEN), From *Flowers in the Mirror* (1827)

Li Ruzhen (1763–1830) was a Chinese scholar and novelist in the Qing Dynasty. Objecting to the constraints of the Confucian examination system, he achieved only the lowest official rank of scholarship, but his work in linguistics earned him a reputation as an intellectual. His novel *Flowers in the Mirror* (*Jing Hua Yuan*) is a fantastic and satirical take on Chinese society during the Tang Dynasty (618–907). In this excerpt, the main characters Tang Ao and Merchant Lin have traveled from the Kingdom on Earth to the Country of Women. Their experiences there call attention to gender dynamics during the Qing Dynasty, and especially the practice of foot binding, a popular but controversial procedure in which young girls' feet were tightly bound to keep them small, which was thought to be appealing to men.

When Tang Ao heard that they had arrived at the Country of Women, he thought that the country was populated entirely by women, and was afraid to go ashore. But Old Tuo said, "Not at all! There are men as well as women, only they call men women, and women men. The men wear the skirts and take care of the home, while the women wear hats and trousers and manage affairs outside." . . .

"If the men dress like women, do they use cosmetics and bind their feet?" asked Tang Ao.

"Of course they do!" cried Lin, and took from his pocket a list of the merchandise he was going to sell, which consisted of huge quantities of rouge, face powder, combs and other women's notions. "Lucky I wasn't born in this country," he said. "Catch me mincing around on bound feet!" . . .

Merchant Lin had been told by one of his customers that the "King's uncle" wanted to buy some of his goods. Following instructions, he went to the "Royal Uncle's" Residence in the Palace, and handed his list of merchandise to the gatekeeper. Soon, the gatekeeper came back and said that it was just what the "King" was looking for for his "concubines" and "maids," and asked Lin to be shown into the inner apartments. . . .

Merchant Lin followed the guard inside, and was soon in the presence of the "King." After making a deep bow, he saw that she was a woman of about thirty years old, with a beautiful face, fair skin and cherry-red lips. Around her there stood many palace "maids."

The "King" spoke to Lin in a light voice[,] . . . looking at him with interest as he answered her questions.

"I wonder what she is staring at me like this for," Merchant Lin thought to himself. "Hasn't she ever seen a man from the Kingdom on Earth before?" . . .

In a little time, Merchant Lin was ushered to a room upstairs, where victuals of many kinds awaited him. . . . Several palace "maids" ran upstairs soon, and calling him "Your Highness" kowtowed to him and congratulated him. Before

Li Ju-chen, *Flowers in the Mirror*, trans. and ed. Lin Tai-yi (Berkeley: University of California Press, 1965), pp. 107–113. Reprinted with permission of Peter Owen Publishers.

he knew what was happening, Merchant Lin was being stripped completely bare by the maids and led to a perfumed bath. Against the powerful arms of these maids, he could scarcely struggle. Soon he found himself being anointed, perfumed, powdered and rouged, and dressed in a skirt. His big feet were bound up in strips of cloth and socks, and his hair was combed into an elaborate braid over his head and decorated with pins. . . .

Merchant Lin thought he must be drunk, or dreaming, and began to tremble. He asked the maids what was happening, and was told that he had been chosen by the "King" to be the Imperial Consort, and that a propitious day would be chosen for him to enter the "King's" chambers.

Before he could utter a word, another group of maids, all tall and strong and wearing beards, came in. One was holding a threaded needle. "We are ordered to pierce your ears," he said, as the other four "maids" grabbed Lin by the arms and legs. The white-bearded one seized Lin's right ear, and after rubbing the lobe a little, drove the needle through it.

"Ooh!" Merchant Lin screamed. . . .

Having finished what they came to do, the maids retreated, and a black-bearded fellow came in with a bolt of white silk. Kneeling down before him, the fellow said, "I am ordered to bind Your Highness's feet."

Two other maids seized Lin's feet as the black-bearded one sat down on a low stool, and began to rip the silk into ribbons. Seizing Lin's right foot, he set it upon his knee, and sprinkled white alum powder between the toes and the grooves of the foot. He squeezed the toes tightly together, bent them down so that the whole foot was shaped like an arch, and took a length of white silk and bound it tightly around it twice. One of the others sewed the ribbon together in small stitches. Again the silk went around the foot, and again, it was sewn up.

Merchant Lin felt as though his feet were burning, and wave after wave of pain rose to his heart. When he could stand it no longer, he let out his voice and began to cry. . . .

Before two weeks were over, Lin's feet had begun to assume a permanently arched form, and his toes begun to rot. Daily medical ablutions were given to them, and the pain persisted. . . .

In due course, his feet lost much of their original shape. Blood and flesh were squeezed into a pulp and then little remained of his feet but dry bones and skin, shrunk, indeed, to a dainty size. Responding to daily anointing, his hair became shiny and smooth, and his body, after repeated ablutions of perfumed water, began to look very attractive indeed. His eyebrows were plucked to resemble a new moon. With blood-red lipstick and powder adorning his face, and jade and pearl adorning his coiffure and ears, Merchant Lin assumed, at last, a not unappealing appearance.

READING AND DISCUSSION QUESTIONS

1. What does Li's novel tell us about gender norms in his society? What role were women supposed to play? What about men?

2. How should we see Li's work—as a comedy in which the absurdity of the situation serves to reinforce traditional gender roles, or as a work of social satire and criticism in which the oppression of women is revealed by placing male characters in traditional female roles?

VIEWPOINTS COMPARATIVE QUESTIONS

1. How might Li have responded to Kaibara Ekiken and Kaibara Tōken's advice book? How might they have responded to his work?

2. How do the works included in this feature demonstrate the power of traditional gender norms in Chinese and Japanese society? How do they reveal the limits of that power?

▪ COMPARATIVE QUESTIONS ▪

1. Several of the documents in this chapter address, directly or indirectly, the construction of gender in East Asian societies. Based on these documents, what conclusions can you draw about how men and women related to one another in early modern China and Japan? How did these relations change, and why?

2. Compare and contrast the illustration from *Anson's Voyage Round the World* and Kaempfer's account of the Dutch presence in Japan. What common themes are present in both documents?

3. Both Kaempfer and Li write about the experience of being in a foreign culture. In Li's case, the fictional account is designed as a commentary on his own time and place. How might Kaempfer's writing say as much about his own culture as it does about early modern Japan? In what ways does his writing reflect a European perspective? How might it have been different if written by a Japanese observer?

22

Revolutions in the Atlantic World

1775–1825

Beginning with the American Revolution in 1775, the intellectual projects of the Enlightenment in Europe intersected with the economic logic of overseas colonial empires to generate optimism and upheaval in the Atlantic world. Colonists in British and Spanish America, members of the third estate in France, and slaves in the French colony of Saint-Domingue (Haiti) all used Enlightenment values to justify rebellion. The bloody expression of notions of freedom, equality, and national integrity in the American, French, Haitian, and Latin American Revolutions, along with the Napoleonic wars of conquest in Europe, challenged many aspects of traditional European society at home and in the colonies. However, the endurance of sexual, class-based, and ethnic discrimination and the recurrence of violence and war complicate the era's story of egalitarianism and democracy.

VIEWPOINTS

Defining the Citizen

At the heart of the revolutionary movement that swept France in 1789 was the replacement of the term *subject* with the term *citizen*. Subjects were given their rights by a divinely appointed ruler. Since rights were assigned to subjects at the discretion of the monarch, it followed that not all subjects would necessarily enjoy the same rights and that those rights could be withdrawn at any time. In sharp contrast, the rights of the citizen were the product of natural law and hence universal, immutable, and irrevocable. Government did not exist in order to dispense rights and privileges; it existed to protect them. Likewise, the purpose of the law was not to enforce inequality, but to create conditions in which all citizens could enjoy the full expression of their national rights. However, almost as quickly as this vision was articulated in the Declaration of the Rights of Man and of the Citizen (see Document 22-1), critics noted an important omission in this foundational document of the Revolution. While the authors had taken great care to define the rights of citizens, they had been less precise in identifying which groups were to be included as citizens. Were women to have the same rights as men? Was slavery compatible with the new political order? Think about these questions as you read the selections included in this feature. What traditional social and political structures did the National Assembly challenge? Which were left in place?

22-1 | The National Assembly Presents a New Vision of Government

The Declaration of the Rights of Man and of the Citizen (1789)

On June 17, 1789, during a meeting of the Estates General, the traditional advisory body under the absolutist French monarchy, delegates of the third estate voted to form a new National Assembly of France. They were joined by clergy and noblemen from the first and second estates, one of whom, the Marquis de Lafayette (1757–1834), outlined the Assembly's aims in the Declaration of the Rights of Man. The Assembly approved the document in August, after the Revolution had begun, and trumpeted it throughout Europe and the world. The Declaration is an important codification of Enlightenment ideas that embodies the National Assembly's vision of the relationship between the individual and government.

The representatives of the French people, organized as a National Assembly, believing that the ignorance, neglect, or contempt of the rights of man are the sole cause of public calamities and of the corruption of governments, have determined to set forth in a solemn declaration the natural, inalienable, and sacred rights of man, in order that this declaration, being constantly before all the members of the social body, shall remind them continually of their rights and duties; in order that the acts of the legislative power, as well as those of the executive power, may be compared at any moment with the objects and purposes of all political institutions and may thus be more respected; and, lastly, in order that the grievances of the citizens, based hereafter upon simple and incontestable principles, shall tend to the maintenance of the constitution and redound to the happiness of all.

James Harvey Robinson, ed., *Readings in European History* (Boston: Ginn, 1904), 2:409–411.

Therefore the National Assembly recognizes and proclaims, in the presence and under the auspices of the Supreme Being, the following rights of man and of the citizen:

ARTICLE 1. Men are born and remain free and equal in rights. Social distinctions may be founded only upon the general good.

2. The aim of all political association is the preservation of the natural and imprescriptible rights of man. These rights are liberty, property, security, and resistance to oppression.

3. The principle of all sovereignty resides essentially in the nation. No body nor individual may exercise any authority which does not proceed directly from the nation.

4. Liberty consists in the freedom to do everything which injures no one else; hence the exercise of the natural rights of each man has no limits except those which assure to the other members of the society the enjoyment of the same rights. These limits can only be determined by law.

5. Law can only prohibit such actions as are hurtful to society. Nothing may be prevented which is not forbidden by law, and no one may be forced to do anything not provided for by law.

6. Law is the expression of the general will. Every citizen has a right to participate personally, or through his representative, in its formation. It must be the same for all, whether it protects or punishes. All citizens, being equal in the eyes of the law, are equally eligible to all dignities and to all public positions and occupations, according to their abilities, and without distinction except that of their virtues and talents.

7. No person shall be accused, arrested, or imprisoned except in the cases and according to the forms prescribed by law. Any one soliciting, transmitting, executing, or causing to be executed, any arbitrary order, shall be punished. But any citizen summoned or arrested in virtue of the law shall submit without delay, as resistance constitutes an offense.

8. The law shall provide for such punishments only as are strictly and obviously necessary, and no one shall suffer punishment except it be legally inflicted in virtue of a law passed and promulgated before the commission of the offense.

9. As all persons are held innocent until they shall have been declared guilty, if arrest shall be deemed indispensable, all harshness not essential to the securing of the prisoner's person shall be severely repressed by law.

10. No one shall be disquieted on account of his opinions, including his religious views, provided their manifestation does not disturb the public order established by law.

11. The free communication of ideas and opinions is one of the most precious of the rights of man. Every citizen may, accordingly, speak, write, and print with freedom, but shall be responsible for such abuses of this freedom as shall be defined by law.

12. The security of the rights of man and of the citizen requires public military forces. These forces are, therefore, established for the good of all and not for the personal advantage of those to whom they shall be intrusted.

13. A common contribution is essential for the maintenance of the public forces and for the cost of administration. This should be equitably distributed among all the citizens in proportion to their means.

14. All the citizens have a right to decide, either personally or by their representatives, as to the necessity of the public contribution; to grant this freely; to know to what uses it is put; and to fix the proportion, the mode of assessment and of collection and the duration of the taxes.

15. Society has the right to require of every public agent an account of his administration.

16. A society in which the observance of the law is not assured, nor the separation of powers defined, has no constitution at all.

17. Since property is an inviolable and sacred right, no one shall be deprived thereof except where public necessity, legally determined, shall clearly demand it, and then only on condition that the owner shall have been previously and equitably indemnified.

READING AND DISCUSSION QUESTIONS

1. According to the Declaration, what is the source of individual rights? What traditional ideas about such rights does the Declaration implicitly challenge?

2. Which rights did the authors see as most important? Why? What did they see as the essential elements of a just and prosperous society?

3. What importance should we attach to the fact that the authors failed to include any discussion of race, gender, or social status in the Declaration? Should we assume that men and women of all races and all social backgrounds were intended to be included in the category "citizen"? Why or why not?

22-2 | A Female Author Revises the Declaration of the Rights of Man

OLYMPE DE GOUGES, From *Declaration of the Rights of Woman* (1791)

Olympe de Gouges (1748–1793) was a French playwright who turned to political activism in the late 1780s. In plays and other writings, she advocated for the rights of enslaved people in France's colonies. After her initial enthusiasm with the Revolution, she became

Darline G. Levy, Harriet B. Applewhite, and Mary D. Johnson, eds., *Women in Revolutionary Paris, 1789–1795* (Champaign: University of Illinois Press, 1979), pp. 89–92. Copyright 1979 by the Board of Trustees of the University of Illinois. Used with permission of the University of Illinois Press.

increasingly outspoken on gender equality. She continued to speak out against injustice, opposing the execution of Louis XVI and offering her opinion on factional revolutionary politics. She was arrested for the latter, and—thanks in part to her own refusal to plead ignorance—was executed in November 1793. The pamphlet excerpted here is her best-known work. In it, she skillfully reproduces the form of the Declaration of the Rights of Man and of the Citizen (see Document 22-1) to direct attention to women's rights.

For the National Assembly to decree in its last sessions, or in those of the next legislature:

Preamble

Mothers, daughters, sisters [and] representatives of the nation demand to be constituted into a national assembly. Believing that ignorance, omission, or scorn for the rights of woman are the only causes of public misfortunes and of the corruption of governments, [the women] have resolved to set forth in a solemn declaration the natural, inalienable, and sacred rights of woman in order that this declaration, constantly exposed before all the members of the society, will ceaselessly remind them of their rights and duties; in order that the authoritative acts of women and the authoritative acts of men may be at any moment compared with and respectful of the purpose of all political institutions; and in order that citizens' demands, henceforth based on simple and incontestable principles, will always support the constitution, good morals, and the happiness of all.

Consequently, the sex that is as superior in beauty as it is in courage during the sufferings of maternity recognizes and declares in the presence and under the auspices of the Supreme Being, the following Rights of Woman and of Female Citizens.

Article I

Woman is born free and lives equal to man in her rights. Social distinctions can be based only on the common utility.

Article II

The purpose of any political association is the conservation of the natural and imprescriptible rights of woman and man; these rights are liberty, property, security, and especially resistance to oppression.

Article III

The principle of all sovereignty rests essentially with the nation, which is nothing but the union of woman and man; no body and no individual can exercise any authority which does not come expressly from it [the nation].

Article IV

Liberty and justice consist of restoring all that belongs to others; thus, the only limits on the exercise of the natural rights of woman are perpetual male tyranny; these limits are to be reformed by the laws of nature and reason.

Article V

Laws of nature and reason proscribe all acts harmful to society; everything which is not prohibited by these wise and divine laws cannot be prevented, and no one can be constrained to do what they do not command.

Article VI

The law must be the expression of the general will; all female and male citizens must contribute either personally or through their representatives to its formation; it must be the same for all: male and female citizens, being equal in the eyes of the law, must be equally admitted to all honors, positions, and public employment according to their capacity and without other distinctions besides those of their virtues and talents.

Article VII

No woman is an exception; she is accused, arrested, and detained in cases determined by law. Women, like men, obey this rigorous law.

Article VIII

The law must establish only those penalties that are strictly and obviously necessary, and no one can be punished except by virtue of a law established and promulgated prior to the crime and legally applicable to women.

Article IX

Once any woman is declared guilty, complete rigor is [to be] exercised by the law.

Article X

No one is to be disquieted for his very basic opinions; woman has the right to mount the scaffold; she must equally have the right to mount the rostrum [podium], provided that her demonstrations do not disturb the legally established public order.

Article XI

The free communication of thoughts and opinions is one of the most precious rights of woman, since that liberty assures the recognition of children by their fathers. Any female citizen thus may say freely, I am the mother of a child which belongs to you, without being forced by a barbarous prejudice to hide the truth; [an exception may be made] to respond to the abuse of this liberty in cases determined by the law.

Article XII

The guarantee of the rights of woman and the female citizen implies a major benefit; this guarantee must be instituted for the advantage of all, and not for the particular benefit of those to whom it is entrusted.

Article XIII

For the support of the public force and the expenses of administration, the contributions of woman and man are equal; she shares all the duties and all the painful tasks; therefore, she must have the same share in the distribution of positions, employment, offices, honors, and jobs.

Article XIV

Female and male citizens have the right to verify, either by themselves or through their representatives, the necessity of the public contribution. This can only apply to women if they are granted an equal share, not only of wealth, but also of public administration, and in the determination of the proportion, the base, the collection, and the duration of the tax.

Article XV

The collectivity of women, joined for tax purposes to the aggregate of men, has the right to demand an accounting of his administration from any public agent.

Article XVI

No society has a constitution without the guarantee of rights and the separation of powers; the constitution is null if the majority of individuals comprising the nation have not cooperated in drafting it.

Article XVII

Property belongs to both sexes whether united or separate; for each it is an inviolable and sacred right; no one can be deprived of it, since it is the true patrimony of nature, unless the legally determined public need obviously dictates it, and then only with a just and prior indemnity.

READING AND DISCUSSION QUESTIONS

1. How does de Gouges define "the nation"? What does her definition tell you about her view of the ideal polity?

2. What distinctions, if any, does de Gouges make between the rights of men and the rights of women?

3. Why did de Gouges believe that the full participation of women was necessary in all aspects of the life of the nation?

VIEWPOINTS COMPARATIVE QUESTIONS

1. What ideals are championed both in the Declaration of the Rights of Man and in the Declaration of the Rights of Woman?

2. How might the authors of the Declaration of the Rights of Man have responded to de Gouges's critique? How might they explain their failure to address gender inequality?

22-3 | Robespierre Justifies Terror as a Tool of Revolutionary Change

MAXIMILIEN ROBESPIERRE, *Revolutionary Speech* (February 5, 1794)

Maximilien Robespierre (1758–1794) was one of the most important figures of the French Revolution. His skills as an orator and his control of the influential Committee of Public Safety helped lead to the period known as the Reign of Terror, during which Robespierre and his political allies not only executed political rivals but also encouraged the population through laws and example to practice their own persecution of fellow citizens deemed to be "counterrevolutionary." Thousands were executed by government tribunals without evidence, while many others were killed by mobs. Robespierre himself was executed by members of the National Convention on July 27, 1794. This excerpt from a speech he had delivered to the Convention several months earlier demonstrates Robespierre's extreme commitment to revolutionary values, even to the point of violence.

After having marched for a long time at hazard, and, as it were, carried away by the movement of contrary factions, the representatives of the people have at last formed a government. A sudden change in the nation's fortune announced to Europe the regeneration which had been operated in the national representation; but up to this moment, we must admit that *we have been rather guided in these stormy circumstances by the love of good, and by a sense of the country's wants, than by any exact theory, or precise rules of conduct.*

It is time to distinguish clearly the aim of the revolution, and the term to which we would arrive. It is time for us to render account to ourselves, both of the obstacles which still keep us from that aim, and of the means which we ought to take to attain it.

What is the aim to which we tend?

The peaceful enjoyment of liberty and equality; the reign of that eternal justice, of which the laws have been engraved, not upon marble, but upon the

G. H. Lewes, ed., *The Life of Maximilien Robespierre: With Extracts of His Unpublished Correspondence* (Philadelphia: Carey and Hart, 1849), pp. 270–273.

hearts of all mankind; even in the hearts of the slaves who forget them, or of the tyrants who have denied them! We desire a state of things wherein all base and cruel passions shall be enchained; all generous and beneficent passions awakened by the laws; wherein ambition should be the desire of glory, and glory the desire of serving the country; wherein distinctions should arise but from equality itself; wherein the citizen should submit to the magistrate, the magistrate to the people, and the people to justice; wherein the country assures the welfare of every individual; wherein every individual enjoys with pride the prosperity and the glory of his country; wherein all minds are enlarged by the continual communication of republican sentiments, and by the desire of meriting the esteem of a great people; wherein arts should be the decorations of that liberty which they ennoble, and commerce the source of public wealth, and not the monstrous opulence of some few houses. We desire to substitute morality for egotism, probity for honor, principles for usages, duties for functions, the empire of reason for the tyranny of fashion, the scorn of vice for the scorn of misfortune, pride for insolence, greatness of soul for vanity, the love of glory for the love of money, good citizens for good society, merit for intrigue, genius for cleverness, truth for splendor, the charm of happiness for the *ennui* of voluptuousness, the grandeur of man for the pettiness of the great, a magnanimous people, powerful, happy, for a people amiable, frivolous, and miserable; that is to say, all the virtues and all the miracles of a republic, for all the vices and all the follies of a monarchy.

What is the nature of the government which can realize these prodigies? The democratic or republican government.

Democracy is that state in which the people, guided by laws which are its own work, executes for itself all that it can well do, and, by its delegates, all that it cannot do itself. But to found and consolidate democracy, we must first end the war of liberty against tyranny, and traverse the storm of the revolution. Such is the aim of the revolutionary system which you have organized; you ought, therefore, to regulate your conduct by the circumstances in which the republic finds itself; and the plan of your administration ought to be the result of the spirit of revolutionary government, combined with the general principles of democracy.

The great purity of the French revolution, the sublimity even of its object, is precisely that which makes our force and our weakness. Our force, because it gives us the ascendency of truth over imposture, and the rights of public interest over private interest. Our weakness, because it rallies against us all the vicious; all those who in their heart meditate the robbery of the people; all those who, having robbed them, seek impunity; and all those who have rejected liberty as a personal calamity, and those who have embraced the revolution as a trade, and the republic as a prey. Hence the defection of so many ambitious men, who have abandoned us on our route, because they did not commence the journey to arrive at the same object as we did. We must crush both the interior and exterior enemies of the republic, or perish with her. And in this situation, the first maxim of your policy should be to conduct the people by reason, and the enemies of the people by terror. If the spring of popular government during peace is virtue, the spring of popular government in rebellion is at once both virtue and terror; virtue, without which terror is fatal!

terror, without which virtue is powerless! Terror is nothing else than justice, prompt, secure, and inflexible! It is, therefore, an emanation of virtue; it is less a particular principle, than a consequence of the general principles of democracy, applied to the most urgent wants of the country.

It has been said that terror is the instrument of a despotic government. Does yours then resemble despotism? Yes, as the sword which glitters in the hand of a hero of liberty, resembles that with which the satellites of tyranny are armed! The *government of a revolution is the despotism of liberty against tyranny*. Is force then only made to protect crime? Is it not also made to strike those haughty heads which the lightning has doomed? Nature has imposed upon every being the law of self-preservation. Crime massacres innocence to reign, and innocence struggles with all its force in the hands of crime. Let tyranny but reign one day, and on the morrow there would not remain a single patriot. Until when will the fury of tyranny continue to be called justice, and the justice of the people barbarity and rebellion? How tender they are to oppressors: how inexorable to the oppressed! Nevertheless, it is necessary that one or the other should succumb. Indulgence for the Royalist! exclaimed certain people. Pardon for wretches! No! Pardon for innocence, pardon for the weak, pardon for the unhappy, pardon for humanity!

READING AND DISCUSSION QUESTIONS

1. What are the aims of the French Revolution as Robespierre describes them? Are they achievable goals or unreasonable goals for society? Cite evidence to support your position.

2. How does Robespierre justify his vision of terror? Against whom should terror be directed?

3. Robespierre advocates for democracy. How might he define democracy? How does he imagine terror will help to achieve democracy?

22-4 | A Former Slave Calls on France to Support the Cause of Freedom

FRANÇOIS DOMINIQUE TOUSSAINT L'OUVERTURE, *Letter to the French National Assembly* (1797)

The impact of the French Revolution and the Napoleonic Wars was not limited to Europe. Societies across the Americas were shaken by events in France. In the United States, support or opposition to the Revolution was a key line of division between emerging political parties. In South America, independence movements flared up in colony after colony. And in the sugar

François Dominique Toussaint L'Ouverture, Letter, in C. L. R. James, ed., *The Black Jacobins*, 2d ed. (New York: Vintage Books, 1963), pp. 195–197. Reprinted with permission of Estate of C.L. R. James c/o The Curtis Brown Group.

islands of the Caribbean, oppressed slaves rose in revolt, determined to have their full share in the rights of men. In 1792, after French colonial rulers arrested the leader of a Caribbean slave delegation in Paris, freed slave Toussaint L'Ouverture (1743–1803) emerged as the leader of a massive revolt on the French island of Saint-Domingue (Haiti). In the letter included here, Toussaint L'Ouverture appealed to French leaders to reject calls by the colonial planter class for the re-establishment of slavery in the French colonies and instead to support the cause of liberty.

The impolitic and incendiary discourse of Vaublanc[1] has not affected the blacks nearly so much as their certainty of the projects which the proprietors of San Domingo are planning: insidious declarations should not have any effect in the eyes of wise legislators who have decreed liberty for the nations. But the attempts on that liberty which the colonists propose are all the more to be feared because it is with the veil of patriotism that they cover their detestable plans. We know that they seek to impose some of them on you by illusory and specious promises, in order to see renewed in this colony its former scenes of horror. Already perfidious emissaries have stepped in among us to ferment the destructive leaven prepared by the hands of liberticides [murderers of liberty]. But they will not succeed. I swear it by all that liberty holds most sacred. My attachment to France, my knowledge of the blacks, make it my duty not to leave you ignorant either of the crimes which they meditate or the oath that we renew, to bury ourselves under the ruins of a country revived by liberty rather than suffer the return of slavery.

It is for you, Citizens Directors, to turn from over our heads the storm which the eternal enemies of our liberty are preparing in the shades of silence. It is for you to enlighten the legislature, it is for you to prevent the enemies of the present system from spreading themselves on our unfortunate shores to sully it with new crimes. Do not allow our brothers, our friends, to be sacrificed to men who wish to reign over the ruins of the human species. But no, your wisdom will enable you to avoid the dangerous snares which our common enemies hold out for you. . . .

I send you with this letter a declaration which will acquaint you with the unity that exists between the proprietors of San Domingo who are in France, those in the United States, and those who serve under the English banner. You will see there a resolution, unequivocal and carefully constructed, for the restoration of slavery; you will see there that their determination to succeed has led them to envelop themselves in the mantle of liberty in order to strike it more deadly blows. You will see that they are counting heavily on my complacency in lending myself to their perfidious views by my fear for my children. It is not astonishing that these men who sacrifice their country to their interests are unable to conceive how many sacrifices a true love of country can support in a better father than they, since I unhesitatingly base the happiness of my children on that of my country, which they and they alone wish to destroy.

I shall never hesitate between the safety of San Domingo and my personal happiness; but I have nothing to fear. It is to the solicitude of the French Government that I have confided my children. . . . I would tremble with horror if it

---

[1]**Vaublanc:** The count of Vaublanc was a royalist and proponent of freeing the slaves and giving them citizenship, in opposition to Toussaint L'Ouverture's more moderate views.

was into the hands of the colonists that I had sent them as hostages; but even if it were so, let them know that in punishing them for the fidelity of their father, they would only add one degree more to their barbarism, without any hope of ever making me fail in my duty. . . . Blind as they are! They cannot see how this odious conduct on their part can become the signal of new disasters and irreparable misfortunes, and that far from making them regain what in their eyes liberty for all has made them lose, they expose themselves to a total ruin and the colony to its inevitable destruction. Do they think that men who have been able to enjoy the blessing of liberty will calmly see it snatched away? They supported their chains only so long as they did not know any condition of life more happy than that of slavery. But to-day when they have left it, if they had a thousand lives they would sacrifice them all rather than be forced into slavery again. But no, the same hand which has broken our chains will not enslave us anew. France will not revoke her principles, she will not withdraw from us the greatest of her benefits. She will protect us against all our enemies; she will not permit her sublime morality to be perverted, those principles which do her most honor to be destroyed, her most beautiful achievement to be degraded, and her Decree of 16 Pluviose[2] which so honors humanity to be revoked. But if, to re-establish slavery in San Domingo, this was done, then I declare to you it would be to attempt the impossible: we have known how to face dangers to obtain our liberty, we shall know how to brave death to maintain it.

This, Citizens Directors, is the morale of the people of San Domingo, those are the principles that they transmit to you by me.

My own you know. It is sufficient to renew, my hand in yours, the oath that I have made, to cease to live before gratitude dies in my heart, before I cease to be faithful to France and to my duty, before the god of liberty is profaned and sullied by the liberticides, before they can snatch from my hands that sword, those arms, which France confided to me for the defense of its rights and those of humanity, for the triumph of liberty and equality.

READING AND DISCUSSION QUESTIONS

1. Who is the intended audience of this document? What is Toussaint L'Ouverture trying to convince them to do?

2. What reasons might persuade the French to reimpose slavery in Haiti, and what reasons might they have for defending its abolition?

3. How does Toussaint L'Ouverture use the ideas and rhetoric of the French Revolution to argue for the rights of Haitian slaves?

---

[2]**Decree of 16 Pluviose:** In 1793, French revolutionaries reorganized their calendar to remove the Christian elements; the event marking year one moved from the birth of Jesus to the adoption of the French constitution in 1792. The fifth month, roughly corresponding to April, known for its rains, became Pluviose, which loosely translates as "rainy." The specific decree to which Toussaint L'Ouverture refers abolished slavery in French colonies in April 1794.

22-5 | Declaring Freedom from Colonial Control
JOSÉ MARÍA MORELOS, *"Sentiments of the Nation"* (1813)

The first movement toward independence in Mexico was led by two priests, Miguel Hidalgo and José María Morelos. Hidalgo was a Creole born of Spanish heritage in the Americas, who earned a doctorate in theology as a Jesuit priest. A passionate believer in social and racial equality, Hidalgo began an insurrection in 1810 among poor Creoles and indigenous and mestizo peasants. After Hidalgo was arrested and executed in 1811, another Catholic priest, José María Morelos, emerged as the leader of the insurrection. Morelos, from a modest family of mestizo or Afro-mestizo origins, proved to be a better military leader and more cohesive political thinker than Hidalgo. In 1813, he delivered the document (reproduced here) known as "Sentiments of the Nation" to a congress he had convened to plan a new national government. Morelos was captured, defrocked, and executed by the Spanish in 1815. Nevertheless, unrest continued, and with support from elite Creoles and rebellious armies, the independent Mexican republic was established in 1823.

1. That America is free and independent from Spain and from any other Nation, Government or Monarchy, and that this be done announcing its reasons to the world.
2. That Catholicism be the only religion, with none others tolerated.
3. That its priests be supported only by the full amount of the tithe and the first harvests, and that the people shall not pay more obligations other than those of their faith and offerings.
4. That the religious dogma shall be maintained by the Church hierarchy, composed of the Pope, the bishops, and the priests, because every plant, which my heavenly Father has not planted, shall be rooted up . . . Matthew 15:13.
5. That Sovereignty springs directly from the people, who only wish to place it in the Supreme National Congress of America, composed of representatives from all of the provinces in equal number.
6. That the Legislative, Executive, and Judiciary powers be divided into branches that will execute those powers.
7. Elected terms shall be for four years, with turnover of the oldest representatives so that the newly elected can take their place.
8. Compensation for the elected representatives shall be an adequate but not excessive sum, and it shall not for now exceed 8,000 pesos.
9. That public posts be held only by Americans.
10. That foreigners not be allowed to enter, with the exception of skilled artisans capable of teaching their trades and of good reputation.
11. Since States change customs, the Fatherland will not be fully free and ours unless the Government is reformed, beating back tyranny and replacing

---

José María Morelos, "Sentiments of the Nation," 1813. Translated by Jerry Dávila.

it with liberalism, and equally expelling from our soil the Spanish enemy, who has declared himself against our Fatherland.

12. Because just law is above every man, so must be those laws that are issued by our Congress, requiring steadiness and patriotism, moderating opulence and indigence, and so improving the lot of the poor by improving their customs, helping them leave behind ignorance, rapaciousness and theft.

13. That general law applies to everyone, without exception for privileged groups; and such privileges only be held in relation to their public function.

14. That laws be written by committees composed of many knowledgeable men, so that they can be drafted with greater effectiveness, and that these men be relieved of some responsibilities in order to meet this task.

15. That slavery is banned forever, along with caste distinctions, with all being equal. The only thing that will distinguish one American from another is vice or virtue.

16. That our ports be opened to [the ships of] friendly foreign nations, but that foreign nations may not enter the land no matter how much they are allies, and only specified ports will be open, with disembarkation in all others prohibited. A ten percent or other tariff applied to foreign merchandise.

17. That the property of all will be safeguarded and the home respected as a sacred sanctuary, with penalties for violating these.

18. The new laws shall not allow torture.

19. Constitutional Law will establish December 12 to observe a celebration, in all of the pueblos, dedicated to the Patron of our Liberty, Holy Mary of Guadalupe, and that every pueblo shall make monthly devotions to her.

20. That no foreign troops, or those of any other kingdom, may set on our land. If they come as allies, they cannot be in the location of the Suprema Junta (National Assembly).

21. That there be no military incursions outside of the limits of the Kingdom, especially overseas; but missions intended to bring the faith to our brothers in the hinterlands are not excluded by this.

22. That the array of tributes, taxes, and fees that smother us shall be ended. In its place, each individual shall be taxed five percent of their seeds, produce, or other goods, which will be lighter and not oppress as much as the sales tax, the tobacco monopoly, and tribute, because with this light contribution and the good management of the property confiscated from the enemy, it will be possible to bear the cost of the war and the salaries of the officials.

Chilpancingo, 14 September 1813. Signed, José María Morelos

23. That we honor September 16 every year as the anniversary of the day in which the voice of Independence was raised and our holy Liberty began, because it was on that day that the voices of the Nation demanded their rights, with sword in hand in order to be heard; remembering always the merit of the great hero, Don Miguel Hidalgo, and his companion, Don Ignacio Allende.

READING AND DISCUSSION QUESTIONS

1. Who is the "enemy" according to this document, and what measures does it envision to ensure freedom from the enemy?

2. What elements of this document make it a liberal declaration? Are there elements that are more conservative? How would you explain the mixture of ideas it represents?

3. Do you see any potential for conflict between the religious monopoly vested in the Catholic Church and the sovereignty of the people as represented by the national congress? How do you think Morelos would respond to such a concern?

▪ COMPARATIVE QUESTIONS ▪

1. Compare and contrast the three declarations excerpted in this chapter: the Declaration of the Rights of Man, the Declaration of the Rights of Woman, and the Sentiments of the Nation. How does each document describe past problems, and how does each present a vision of a new world? What values do all three embrace, and where do the documents diverge?

2. What is the role of violence in each of this chapter's documents? According to each, when is violence justified in order to bring about positive social change? Which documents do not address the problem of violence?

3. Which is the most radical of these documents? Which is the most conservative? Explain.

4. To what extent do these documents present a "universal" vision of humankind? To what extent do they focus on forms of human difference, such as gender, racial, and economic differences? How would you account for each document's emphasis on universalism or difference?

23

The Revolution in Energy and Industry

1760–1850

The Industrial Revolution, though less visibly dramatic than the bloody political and social revolutions taking place in Europe and the Americas, did more to transform human societies around the world than any single development since the beginning of agriculture. Changes in farming, manufacturing, and domestic and foreign trade—first in Britain, and then in Europe, Japan, and the United States—resulted in unprecedented economic growth. At the same time, shifts in social relations revealed obvious and disturbing inequalities between prosperous business owners and their often-abused workers. In the following documents, politicians, workers, and intellectuals address some of the social effects of rapid modernization. Whether seeking protection for women and children in the workplace, demanding universal male suffrage, analyzing the challenges of a rapidly increasing population, or outlining the international effects of industrialization, these texts show ways in which people tried to understand and navigate their changing social and economic worlds.

VIEWPOINTS

The Realities of Manufacturing

In the earliest phases of industrialization, entire families often worked together in the same factory, with children working side by side with their parents. Over time, however, changes in factory design and machinery led to new labor patterns that took the supervision and control of child workers out of the hands of parents. As familial connections and control broke down, public concern about the potential for the abuse of child laborers, particularly young girls and women, intensified. The documents included in this feature focus on the impact of industrialization on workers in general and on working-class families in particular. As you read them, ask yourself how industrialization changed the lives of Britain's laboring classes. How and why did the British government seek to exert greater control over factory conditions and the composition of the industrial labor force?

23-1 | A Mill Owner Describes the Human Costs of Industrialization

ROBERT OWEN, From *Observations on the Effect of the Manufacturing System* (1815)

Robert Owen (1771–1858), a British socialist from a coal-rich area of Wales, first gained fame through his management of a cotton mill in New Lanark, Scotland. As part owner, Owen incorporated philanthropy with capitalism, and his concern for working conditions, education, and workers' lives helped establish New Lanark's international reputation as a model industrial community. Beginning in 1815, Owen lobbied the British Parliament for legislation to protect British workers, but the many concessions made to industrialists in the 1819 law left him disappointed. Owen penned his *Observations* in 1815; although he would not develop utopian socialist ideals until later, his interest in public welfare and his distrust of naked capitalism are evident here.

Those who were engaged in the trade, manufactures, and commerce of this country thirty or forty years ago, formed but a very insignificant portion of the knowledge, wealth, influence, or population of the Empire.

Prior to that period, Britain was essentially agricultural. But, from that time to the present, the home and foreign trade have increased in a manner so rapid and extraordinary as to have raised commerce to an importance, which it never previously attained in any country possessing so much political power and influence. This change has been owing chiefly to the mechanical inventions which introduced the cotton trade into this country, and to the cultivation of the cotton-tree in America. The wants, which this trade created for the various materials requisite to forward its multiplied operations, caused an extraordinary demand for almost all the manufactures previously established, and, of course, for human labor. The numerous fanciful and useful fabrics manufactured from cotton soon became objects of desire in Europe and America: and the consequent extension of the British foreign trade was such as to astonish and confound the most enlightened statesmen both at home and abroad.

Robert Owen, *Observations on the Effect of the Manufacturing System: With Hints for the Improvement of Those Parts of It Which Are Most Injurious to Health and Morals* (London: R. and A. Taylor, 1817), pp. 3–6.

The immediate effects of this manufacturing phenomenon were a rapid increase of the wealth, industry, population and political influence of the British empire; and by the aid of which it has been enabled to contend for five-and-twenty years against the most formidable military and *immoral* power that the world perhaps ever contained.[1]

These important results, however, great as they really are, have not been obtained without accompanying evils of such a magnitude as to raise a doubt whether the latter do not preponderate over the former.

Hitherto, legislators have appeared to regard manufactures only in one point of view, as a source of national wealth. The other mighty consequences, which proceed from extended manufactures, *when left to their natural progress*, have never yet engaged the attention of any legislature. Yet the political and moral effects to which we allude, well deserve to occupy the best faculties of the greatest and the wisest statesmen.

The general diffusion of manufactures throughout a country generates a new character in its inhabitants; and as this character is formed upon a principle quite unfavorable to individual or general happiness, it will produce the most lamentable and permanent evils, unless its tendency be counteracted by legislative interference and direction.

The manufacturing system has already so far extended its influence over the British empire, as to effect an essential change in the general character of the mass of the people. This alteration is still in rapid progress; and ere long, the comparatively happy simplicity of the agricultural peasant will be wholly lost amongst us: It is even now scarcely any where to be found, without a mixture of those habits, which are the offspring of trade, manufactures, and commerce.

The acquisition of wealth, and the desire which it naturally creates for a continued increase, have introduced a fondness for essentially injurious luxuries among a numerous class of individuals, who formerly never thought of them, and they have also generated a disposition which strongly impels its possessors to sacrifice the best feelings of human nature to this love of accumulation. To succeed in this career, the industry of the lower orders from whose labor this wealth is now drawn, has been carried by new competitors striving against those of longer standing, to a point of real oppression, reducing them by successive changes, as the spirit of competition increased, and the ease of acquiring wealth diminished, to a state more wretched than can be imagined by those who have not attentively observed the changes as they have gradually occurred. In consequence, they are at present in a situation infinitely more degraded and miserable than they were before the introduction of these manufactories, upon the success of which their bare subsistence now depends.

---

[1]**the most formidable . . . contained:** Owen is referring to revolutionary and Napoleonic France.

READING AND DISCUSSION QUESTIONS

1. What is the principal product that characterizes industry for Owen? How does Owen situate British industry in the larger context of international relations?

2. According to Owen, what is the chief cause of the increased misery of the working classes? Who is gaining from the labor they are providing?

3. What, in Owen's view, has been the attitude of government toward industry? What is government's implicit responsibility?

23-2 | Child Labor in Industrial Britain

SADLER COMMITTEE AND ASHLEY COMMISSION, *Testimonies Before Parliamentary Committees on Working Conditions in England* (1832, 1842)

The Industrial Revolution depended on men, women, and children working under harsh and often deadly conditions. Troubled by the social changes wrought by Britain's rapid industrialization, politician Michael Sadler (1780–1835) formed the Committee on the Labour of Children in the Mills and Factories of the United Kingdom. The committee's 1832 report shocked the public and mobilized support for labor reform. In 1840, another labor reform advocate, Lord Ashley (1801–1885), established the Children's Employment Commission. Its 1842 report shed light on the practice of child labor in coal mines, or "collieries." Both of these reports prompted legislation and raised public awareness of the human cost of the Industrial Revolution.

Testimony Before the Sadler Committee, 1832[2]

Elizabeth Bentley, Called in; and Examined

What age are you? — Twenty-three. . . .

What time did you begin to work at a factory? — When I was six years old. . . .

What kind of mill is it? — Flax-mill. . . .

What was your business in that mill? — I was a little doffer.[3]

What were your hours of labor in that mill? — From 5 in the morning till 9 at night, when they were thronged [busy].

For how long a time together have you worked that excessive length of time? — For about half a year.

What were your usual hours of labor when you were not so thronged? — From 6 in the morning till 7 at night.

What time was allowed for your meals? — Forty minutes at noon.

Had you any time to get your breakfast or drinking? — No, we got it as we could.

John Bowditch, ed., *Voices of the Industrial Revolution* (Ann Arbor: University of Michigan Press, 1961), pp. 82–90.

[2]**Testimony . . . 1832:** Michael Sadler first proposed a ten-hour workday in 1831; his bill was rejected by Parliament but prompted the formation of this investigative committee.

[3]**doffer:** A young child whose job was to clean the machinery.

And when your work was bad, you had hardly any time to eat it at all? — No; we were obliged to leave it or take it home, and when we did not take it, the overlooker took it, and gave it to his pigs.

Do you consider doffing a laborious employment? — Yes.

Explain what it is you had to do. — When the frames are full, they have to stop the frames, and take the flyers off, and take the full bobbins off, and carry them to the roller; and then put empty ones on, and set the frames on again.

Does that keep you constantly on your feet? — Yes, there are so many frames and they run so quick.

Your labor is very excessive? — Yes; you have not time for anything.

Suppose you flagged a little, or were too late, what would they do? —Strap us.

Are they in the habit of strapping those who are last in doffing? — Yes.

Constantly? — Yes.

Girls as well as boys? — Yes.

Have you ever been strapped? — Yes.

Severely? — Yes.

Could you eat your food well in that factory? — No, indeed, I had not much to eat, and the little I had I could not eat it, my appetite was so poor, and being covered with dust; and it was no use to take it home, I could not eat it, and the overlooker took it, and gave it to the pigs. . . .

Did you live far from the mill? — Yes, two miles.

Had you a clock? — No, we had not.

Supposing you had not been in time enough in the morning at the mills, what would have been the consequence? — We should have been quartered.

What do you mean by that? — If we were a quarter of an hour too late, they would take off half an hour; we only got a penny an hour, and they would take a halfpenny more. . . .

Were you generally there in time? — Yes, my mother has been up at 4 o'clock in the morning, and at 2 o'clock in the morning; the colliers used to go to their work about 3 or 4 o'clock, and when she heard them stirring she has got up out of her warm bed, and gone out and asked them the time, and I have sometimes been at Hunslet Car at 2 o'clock in the morning, when it was streaming down with rain, and we have had to stay till the mill was opened. . . .

Testimony Before the Ashley Commission on the Conditions in Mines, 1842[4]

Edward Potter

I am a coal viewer, and the manager of the South Hetton colliery. We have about 400 bound people (contract laborers), and in addition our bank people (foremen), men and boys about 700. In the pits 427 men and boys; of these, 290 men. . . .

---

[4]**Testimony . . . 1842:** This testimony led to the Mines Act of 1842, which prohibited boys under the age of ten and women from working in the mines.

Of the children in the pits we have none under eight, and only three so young. We are constantly beset by parents coming making application to take children under the age, and they are very anxious and very dissatisfied if we do not take the children; and there have been cases in times of brisk trade, when the parents have threatened to leave the colliery, and go elsewhere if we did not comply. At every successive binding, which takes place yearly, constant attempts are made to get the boys engaged to work to which they are not competent from their years. In point of fact, we would rather not have boys until nine years of age complete. If younger than that, they are apt to fall asleep and get hurt; some get killed. It is no interest to the company to take any boys under nine. . . .

Hannah Richardson

I've one child that works in the pit; he's going on ten. He is down from 6 to 8. . . . He's not much tired with the work, it's only the confinement that tires him. He likes it pretty well, for he'd rather be in the pit than to go to school. There is not much difference in his health since he went into the pit. He was at school before, and can read pretty well, but can't write. He is used pretty well; I never hear him complain. I've another son in the pit, 17 years old. . . . He went into the pit at eight years old. It's not hurt his health nor his appetite, for he's a good size. It would hurt us if children were prevented from working till 11 or 12 years old, because we've not jobs enough to live now as it is. . . .

Mr. George Armitage

I am now a teacher at Hoyland school; I was a collier at Silkstone until I was 22 years old and worked in the pit above 10 years. . . . I hardly know how to reprobate the practice sufficiently of girls working in pits; nothing can be worse. I have no doubt that debauchery is carried on, for which there is every opportunity; for the girls go constantly, when hurrying, to the men, who work often alone in the bank-faces apart from every one. I think it scarcely possible for girls to remain modest who are in pits, regularly mixing with such company and hearing such language as they do — it is next to impossible. I dare venture to say that many of the wives who come from pits know nothing of sewing or any household duty, such as women ought to know — they lose all disposition to learn such things; they are rendered unfit for learning them also by being overworked and not being trained to the habit of it. I have worked in pits for above 10 years, where girls were constantly employed, and I can safely say it is an abominable system; indecent language is quite common. I think, if girls were trained properly, as girls ought to be, that there would be no more difficulty in finding suitable employment for them than in other places. Many a collier spends in drink what he has shut up a young child the whole week to earn in a dark cold corner as a trapper. The education of the children is universally bad. They are generally ignorant of common facts in Christian history and principles, and, indeed, in almost everything else. Little can be learned merely on Sundays, and they are too tired as well as indisposed to go to night schools. . . .

The Rev. Robert Willan, Curate of St. Mary's, Barnsley

I have been resident here as chief minister for 22 years. I think the morals of the working classes here are in an appalling state. . . . The ill manners and conduct of the weavers are daily presented to view in the streets, but the colliers work under ground and are less seen, and we have less means of knowing. . . . The master-sin among the youths is that of gambling; the boys may be seen playing at pitch-and-toss on the Sabbath and on week-days; they are seen doing this in all directions. The next besetting sin is promiscuous sexual intercourse; this may be much induced by the manner in which they sleep—men, women, and children often sleeping in one bed-room. I have known a family of father and mother and 12 children, some of them up-grown, sleeping on a kind of sacking and straw bed, reaching from one side of the room to the other, along the floor; they were an English family. Sexual intercourse begins very young. This and gambling pave the way; then drinking ensues, and this is the vortex which draws in every other sin.

Thomas Wilson, Esq., Owner of Three Collieries

I object on general principles to government interference in the conduct of any trade, and I am satisfied that in the mines it would be productive of the greatest injury and injustice. The art of mining is not so perfectly understood as to admit of the way in which a colliery shall be conducted being dictated by any person, however experienced, with such certainty as would warrant an interference with the management of private business. I should also most decidedly object to placing collieries under the present provisions of the Factory Act[5] with respect to the education of children employed therein. First, because, if it is contended that coal-owners, as employers of children, are bound to attend to their education, this obligation extends equally to all other employers, and therefore it is unjust to single out one class only; secondly, because, if the legislature asserts a right to interfere to secure education, it is bound to make that interference general; and thirdly, because the mining population is in this neighborhood so intermixed with other classes, and is in such small bodies in any one place, that it would be impossible to provide separate schools for them.

READING AND DISCUSSION QUESTIONS

1. How do these testimonies present the realities of child labor? Give specific examples.

2. Both reports make particular note of the gender of workers. What is the effect of calling attention to female labor? Describe the attitudes toward gender differences conveyed in these reports.

3. Summarize the arguments presented in the Ashley Commission report for and against the regulation of female and child labor in mines. How is the issue of education used in each argument?

---

[5]**Factory Act:** The Factory Act of 1833 restricted the workday to eight hours for children between the ages of nine and fourteen and twelve hours for those between fourteen and eighteen.

VIEWPOINTS COMPARATIVE QUESTIONS

1. How might Owen have explained the harsh conditions described by the witnesses before the Sadler Committee and the Ashley Commission? How might the Reverend Robert Willan have explained those conditions?

2. What light do these two documents shed on the social consequences of industrialization? How did industrialization change both work and family life?

23-3 | Britain Forces the Ottoman Empire to Make Economic Concessions

The Treaty of Balta-Liman (August 16, 1838)

The British Industrial Revolution led to increased demands for overseas markets. In 1838, the United Kingdom signed a treaty with the Ottoman Empire at Balta-Liman, near Istanbul. The treaty responded to complaints by British merchants that their goods were subject to a high tariff or other taxes when shipped into or across Egypt. Egypt, nominally a territory of the Ottoman Empire but virtually independent under the rule of Muhammad Ali (or Mehmet Ali), had embarked on its own efforts to industrialize, including high tariffs and state monopolies of important industrial sectors. These excerpts from the treaty show how the United Kingdom's demands and the Ottoman Empire's acquiescence helped destroy Egypt's industries by flooding its markets with cheap British goods.

Article I

All rights, privileges, and immunities which have been conferred on the subjects or ships of Great Britain by the existing Capitulations and Treaties, are confirmed now and for ever, except in as far as they may be specifically altered by the present Convention: and it is moreover expressly stipulated, that all rights, privileges, or immunities which the Sublime Porte[6] now grants, or may hereafter grant, to the ships and subjects of any other foreign Power, or which it may suffer the ships and subjects of any other foreign Power to enjoy, shall be equally granted to, and exercised and enjoyed by, the subjects and ships of Great Britain.

Article II

The subjects of Her Britannic Majesty, or their agents, shall be permitted to purchase at all places in the Ottoman Dominions (whether for the purposes of internal trade or exportation) all articles, without any exception whatsoever, the produce, growth,

---

Convention of Commerce and Navigation Between Her Majesty and the Sultan of the Ottoman Empire (London: J. Harrison and Son, 1839), pp. 3–6.

[6]**Sublime Porte:** Literally, the gate of the sultan's palace; the term refers to the sultan and his sovereignty.

or manufacture of the said Dominions; and the Sublime Porte formally engages to abolish all monopolies of agricultural produce, or of any other articles whatsoever, as well as all *Permits* from the local Governors, either for the purchase of any article, or for its removal from one place to another when purchased; and any attempt to compel the subjects of Her Britannic Majesty to receive such *Permits* from the local Governors, shall be considered as an infraction of Treaties, and the Sublime Porte shall immediately punish with severity any Vizirs [ministers] and other officers who shall have been guilty of such misconduct, and render full justice to British subjects for all injuries or losses which they may duly prove themselves to have suffered. . . .

Additional Articles

Certain difficulties having arisen between the Ambassador of Her Britannic Majesty and the Plenipotentiaries of the Sublime Porte, in fixing the new conditions which should regulate the commerce in British goods imported into the Turkish Dominions, or passing through the same in transit, it is agreed between His Excellency the British Ambassador and the Plenipotentiaries of the Sublime Porte, that the present Convention should receive their signatures, without the articles which have reference to the above-mentioned subjects forming part of the body of the said Convention.

But at the same time it is also agreed, — the following Articles having been consented to by the Turkish Government, — that they shall be submitted to the approbation of Her Majesty's Government, and should they be approved and accepted by Her Majesty's Government, they shall then form an integral part of the Treaty now concluded.

The Articles in question are the following:

Article I

All articles being the growth, produce, or manufacture of the United Kingdom of Great Britain and Ireland and its dependencies, and all merchandise, of whatsoever description, embarked in British vessels, and being the property of British subjects, or being brought over land, or by sea, from other countries by the same, shall be admitted, as heretofore, into all parts of the Ottoman Dominions, without exception, on the payment of three per cent. duty, calculated upon the value of such articles.

And in lieu of all other and interior duties, whether levied on the purchaser or seller, to which these articles are at present subject, it is agreed that the importer, after receiving his goods, shall pay, if he sells them at the place of reception, or if he sends them thence to be sold elsewhere in the interior of the Turkish Empire, one fixed duty of two per cent.; after which such goods may be sold and resold in the interior, or exported, without any further duty whatsoever being levied or demanded on them.

But all goods that have paid the three per cent. import duty at one port, shall be sent to another free of any further duty, and it is only, when sold there or transmitted thence into the interior, that the second duty shall be paid.

It is always understood that Her Majesty's Government do not pretend, either by this Article or any other in the present Treaty, to stipulate for more than the plain and fair construction of the terms employed; nor to preclude, in any manner, the Ottoman Government from the exercise of its rights of internal administration, where the exercise of those rights does not evidently infringe upon the privileges accorded by ancient Treaties, or the present Treaty, to British merchandise or British subjects.

Article II

All foreign goods brought into Turkey from other countries, shall be freely purchased and traded in, in any manner, by the subjects of Her Britannic Majesty or the agents of the same, at any place in the Ottoman Dominions; and if such foreign goods have paid no other duty than the duty paid on importation, then the British subject or his agent shall be able to purchase such foreign goods on paying the extra duty of two per cent., which he will have to pay on the sale of his own imported goods, or on their transmission for sale into the interior; and after that such foreign goods shall be resold in the interior, or exported, without further duty; or should such foreign goods have already paid the amount of the two duties (*i.e.* the import duty and the one fixed interior duty), then they shall be purchased by the British subject or his agent, and afterwards resold or exported, without being ever submitted to any further duty.

Article III

No charge whatsoever shall be made upon British goods, — (such being the growth, produce, or manufacture of the United Kingdom or its dependencies, or the growth, produce, or manufacture of any foreign country, and charged in British vessels and belonging to British subjects) — passing through the straits of the Dardanelles, of the Bosphorus, and of the Black Sea, whether such goods shall pass through those straits in the ships that brought them, or are transshipped in those straits, or, destined to be sold elsewhere, are landed with a view to their being transferred to other vessels (and thus to proceed on their voyage) within a reasonable time. All merchandise imported into Turkey for the purpose of being transmitted to other countries, or which, remaining in the hands of the importer, shall be transmitted by him for sale to other countries, shall only pay the duty of three per cent. paid on importation, and no other duty whatsoever.

READING AND DISCUSSION QUESTIONS

1. The first article stipulates that any future concession to any other foreign power will be matched by a concession to Great Britain. This is known as a "most-favored nation clause." What does this clause tell you about this treaty? What does it tell you about international relations between the Ottoman Empire and other powers at this point in history?

2. What is the significance of eliminating Ottoman monopolies on any particular item? What is the significance of establishing lowered tariffs and shipping duties?

3. Does this treaty benefit both parties equally? Explain. If it provides benefit primarily to one party, then why might the other have signed it?

23-4 | The Role of Working-Class Women

FLORA TRISTAN, *The Workers' Union* (1843)

In response to the harsh conditions of industrial life, working people formed labor unions in the first decades of the nineteenth century to make claims for higher wages, improved safety, and hourly limits to the workday. Although they challenged the dominance of capitalists and business owners, labor unions generally did not question prevailing gender norms. They tended to be organized by men to support skilled male labor, often with the goal of eliminating competition from women and children. In France, Flora Tristan (1804–1844) became frustrated with this situation. The passage below is from her book, *The Workers' Union*, in which she advocated for the creation of a union for both male and female workers, and pioneered the idea that the advancement of the working class as a whole was impossible without improving the situation of women.

Notice that in all the trades engaged in by men and women, the woman worker gets *only half* what a man does for a day's work, or, if she does piecework, her rate is less than half. Not being able to imagine such a flagrant injustice, the first thought to strike us is this: because of his muscular strength, man doubtless does *double* the work of woman. Well, readers, just the contrary happens. In all the trades where skill and finger dexterity are necessary, women do almost *twice* as much work as men. . . . What is happening? For example, in printing, in *setting* [type] (to tell the truth they make many errors, but that is from their lack of education); in cotton or silk spinning mills, to *fasten the* threads; in a word, in all the trades where a certain lightness of touch is needed, women excel. A printer said to me one day with a *naïveté* completely characteristic: "Oh, they are paid a half less, it is true, since they work more quickly than men; they would earn too much if they were paid the same." Yes, they are paid, not according to the work they do, but because of their *low* cost, a result of the privations they impose on themselves. Workers, you have not foreseen the disastrous consequences that would result for you from a similar injustice done to the detriment of your mothers, sisters, wives, and daughters. What is happening? The manufacturers, seeing the women laborers work *more quickly* and *at half price*, day by day dismiss men from their workshops and replace them with women. Consequently the man crosses his arms and dies of hunger on the pavement! That is what the heads of factories in England have done. Once started in this direction, women will be dismissed in order to replace them with *twelve-year-old children*. A saving of *half the wages*! Finally one gets to the point of using only *seven- and eight-year-old children*. Overlook one injustice and you are sure to get thousands more.

The result of this is that the husband at the very least treats his wife with much disdain. . . . After the bitter chagrins caused by the husband, next comes the pregnancies, the illnesses, the lack of work, and the poverty. . . . Add to all that the incessant irritation caused by four or five crying children, unruly, tiresome, who turn round and round the mother, and all that in a small laborer's room where there is

Flora Tristan, *Utopian Feminist: Her Travel Diaries and Personal Crusade*, trans. Doris and Paul Beik, pp. 116, 118–19. Copyright © 1993 by Indiana University Press. Used with permission.

no place to stir. Oh! One would have to be an angel descended on earth not to be irritated, not become brutal and ill-natured in such a situation. However, in such a family milieu, what becomes of the children? They see their father only evenings and Sundays. This father, always in a state of irritation or of drunkenness, speaks to them only in anger, and they get only insults and blows from him; hearing their mother's continual complaints about him, they dislike and scorn him. As for their mother, they fear her, obey her, but do not love her; for man is so made that he cannot love those who mistreat him. And what a great tragedy it is for a child not to be able to love his mother! . . .

Among the unfortunates who people the houses of prostitution, and those who lament in prison, how many there are who can say: "If we had had a mother *capable of raising us*, we certainly would not be here."

I repeat, the woman is everything in the life of the worker. As mother, she influences him during his infancy; it is from her and only from her that he draws the first notions of that science so important to acquire, the science of life, that which teaches us to live befittingly toward ourselves and toward others, according to the milieu in which fate has placed us. . . . As wife, she influences him for three-fourths of his life. Finally, as a daughter she influences him in his old age. . . .

. . . It follows from this situation that it would be of the greatest importance from the point of view of the *intellectual, moral,* and *material* betterment of the working class for the women of the people to receive from their infancy a rational, solid education, suitable for developing all their good, natural bents, in order that they might become skillful workers in their trade, good mothers of families, capable of raising and guiding their children and of being for then . . . *natural free-of-charge school-mistresses,* and in order, too, that they might serve as *moralizing agents* for the men over whom they have influence from birth to death. . . .

I demand rights for women because I am convinced that *all the ills of the world come from this forgetfulness and scorn that until now have been inflicted on the natural and imprescriptible rights of the female.* I demand rights for women because that is the *only way that their education will be attended to* and because on the education of women depends that of men in general, and *particularly of the men of the people.* . . . All the ills of the working class are summed up by these two words: poverty and ignorance, ignorance and poverty. But to get out of this labyrinth, I see only one way: *to start by educating women, because women are entrusted with raising the children, male and female.*

READING AND DISCUSSION QUESTIONS

1. According to Tristan, why are women workers paid only half as much as men, and what "disastrous consequences" does she foresee from this injustice? Who do you think her intended audience was for this warning?

2. How do the challenges of working-class life affect the family and relations among family members? What possible outcomes of unhappy family life does she foresee?

3. Why does Tristan believe that educating women is the key to reversing the ills of the working class? Do you think this is a radical or conservative belief? What assumptions about women's role in the family and in the workforce lie behind this belief?

23-5 | Spreading Stories of the Industrial Revolution
James Watt, c. 1890 (ca. 1890)

Stories about the heroic inventors of the Industrial Revolution were appealing to both European and non-European audiences. In the late nineteenth century, the Japanese Ministry of Education sponsored a series of woodblock prints depicting key moments of innovation as part of a government propaganda effort to import Western science and industrial technology to Japan. This one shows a young James Watt observing steam from a kettle over a coal stove, with his aunt watching in the background. According to a story told by Watt's son, the origins of the steam engine lay in this episode, as a twelve-year-old James Watt sat in the kitchen with his aunt watching a boiling kettle. The steam from the boiling water caused the lid to rattle; when he held the lid down tightly, the steam escaped through the spout, but when he removed his hand, the lid began to rattle again. Watt spent an hour observing and repeating this phenomenon, leading his aunt to scold him for wasting time, as explained by the Japanese characters written on the wall.

Photo 12/Getty Images

READING AND DISCUSSION QUESTIONS

1. Why would the Japanese Ministry of Education choose this image as a means to inspire technological progress in Japan?

2. How have the creators of this image made it accessible to a Japanese audience? What elements of the image do you think would have remained foreign, and possibly exciting, to a Japanese viewer?

3. How does this image help reinforce the idea that the Industrial Revolution was the creation of heroic men? What impression of women's role in the Industrial Revolution does this woodblock suggest?

▪ COMPARATIVE QUESTIONS ▪

1. The prevailing political doctrine in the nineteenth century was that of *laissez faire*, meaning that governments should allow the economy to function independently without government oversight or interference. What evidence do you see in these documents for the practice of *laissez faire*? What evidence do you see that governments, in Britain or elsewhere, intervened to promote or regulate industrial development?

2. How would Flora Tristan react to the testimony before the parliamentary committees in Document 23-2? What elements of the testimony support her views, and what elements might challenge them? How do you think the various individuals who testified would respond to her ideas?

3. Compare and contrast the methods of disseminating industrialization beyond Britain's borders as presented by the Treaty of Balta-Liman and the Japanese woodblock print. What conclusions can you draw about how British economic superiority may have been perceived by people outside of Britain?

4. What assumptions and arguments do these documents make about who belongs in the workforce and what kinds of work they should do? How do these ideas compare with your own expectations and experiences of who performs what jobs in the workforce?

24

Ideologies of Change in Europe
1815–1914

Following the defeat of Napoleon and his imperial aspirations, a period of ideological development promised to transform the economic and political foundations of Europe. Born in part out of calls for national mobilization in revolutionary France, nationalism gained strength as cultural groups began to seek their own political identity as nation-states. While nationalist rhetoric in Europe often emphasized language, territory, or ethnicity as unifying principles, other movements coalesced around shared identities of gender or social class. In many cases, nationalism, socialism, and other ideologies led to uprisings, revolutions, and wars. In most cases, nationalist movements strengthened states through standardized culture, language, and history as they created both internal solidarity and external threats. Some nationalist movements fought unsuccessfully for recognition, and socialism threatened new nation-states and their nationalist ideologies with a universal call to recognize and respond to the social divisions wrought by the Industrial Revolution.

24-1 | Marx and Engels Predict the Coming of a New Social Order

KARL MARX AND FRIEDRICH ENGELS, From *The Communist Manifesto* (1848)

Published in 1848, *The Communist Manifesto* was commissioned by the Communist League, an early socialist organization that advocated for workers' rights and societal reforms. Party members Karl Marx (1818–1883) and Friedrich Engels (1820–1895) set forth the group's

Karl Marx and Friedrich Engels, "The Communist Manifesto," in *The Essential Works of Marxism*, ed. Arthur P. Mendel (New York: Bantam, 1961), pp. 13–17, 19, 23, 40–44.

analysis of social conditions under capitalism, their historical basis, and the roles of the bourgeoisie (middle-class property holders) and the proletariat (urban workers) in social change. Written in German, the document was translated into English in 1850 but received little attention. In later years, however, Marx's writings spurred great debate in England and around the world.

A specter is haunting Europe—the specter of communism. All the powers of old Europe have entered into a holy alliance to exorcise this specter: Pope and Czar, Metternich and Guizot,[1] French Radicals and German police-spies. . . .

Communism is already acknowledged by all European powers to be itself a power.

It is high time that Communists should openly, in the face of the whole world, publish their views, their aims, their tendencies, and meet this nursery tale of the specter of communism with a Manifesto of the party itself. . . .

The history of all hitherto existing society is the history of class struggles. . . .

Modern industry has established the world market, for which the discovery of America paved the way. This market has given an immense development to commerce, to navigation, to communication by land. This development has, in its turn, reacted on the extension of industry; and in proportion as industry, commerce, navigation, railways extended, in the same proportion the bourgeoisie developed, increased its capital, and pushed into the background every class handed down from the Middle Ages. . . .

The bourgeoisie, historically, has played a most revolutionary part.

The bourgeoisie, wherever it has got the upper hand, has put an end to all feudal, patriarchal, idyllic relations. It has pitilessly torn asunder the motley feudal ties that bound man to his "natural superiors," and has left remaining no other nexus between man and man than naked self-interest, than callous "cash payment." It has drowned the most heavenly ecstasies of religious fervor, of chivalrous enthusiasm, of philistine sentimentalism, in the icy water of egotistical calculation. It has resolved personal worth into exchange value, and in place of the numberless indefeasible chartered freedoms, has set up that single, unconscionable freedom—Free Trade. In a word, for exploitation, veiled by religious and political illusions, it has substituted naked, shameless, direct, brutal exploitation.

The bourgeoisie has stripped of its halo every occupation hitherto honored and looked up to with reverent awe. It has converted the physician, the lawyer, the priest, the poet, and the man of science into its paid wage-laborers.

The bourgeoisie has torn away from the family its sentimental veil and has reduced the family relation to a mere money relation. . . .

The bourgeoisie has subjected the country to the rule of the towns. It has created enormous cities, greatly increased the urban population as compared

---

[1]**Metternich and Guizot:** Prince Klemens von Metternich (1773–1859) was foreign minister and chancellor of the Austrian Empire (1809–1848); François Guizot (1787–1874) was a French politician who served as prime minister from 1847 to 1848.

with the rural, and thus rescued a considerable part of the population from the idiocy of rural life. . . .

The bourgeoisie, during its rule of scarcely one hundred years, has created more massive and more colossal productive forces than have all preceding generations together. . . .

But not only has the bourgeoisie forged the weapons that bring death to itself; it has also called into existence the men who are to wield those weapons — the modern working class — the proletariat.

In proportion as the bourgeoisie, i.e., capital, develops, in the same proportion the proletariat, the modern working class, develops — a class of laborers, who live only so long as they find work, and who find work only so long as their labor increases capital. These laborers, who must sell themselves piecemeal, are a commodity, like every other article of commerce, and are consequently exposed to all the vicissitudes of competition, to all the fluctuations of the market. . . .

Of all the classes that stand face to face with the bourgeoisie today, the proletariat alone is a really revolutionary class. The other classes decay and finally disappear in the face of modern industry; the proletariat is its special and essential product. . . .

The socialist and communist systems properly so called, those of Saint-Simon, Fourier, Owen[2] and others, spring into existence in the early undeveloped period, described above, of the struggle between proletariat and bourgeoisie. . . .

Such fantastic pictures of future society, painted at a time when the proletariat is still in a very undeveloped state and has but a fantastic conception of its own position, correspond with the first instinctive yearnings of that class for a general reconstruction of society.

But these socialist and communist publications contain also a critical element. They attack every principle of existing society. . . .

The Communists fight for the attainment of the immediate aims, for the enforcement of the momentary interests of the working class; but in the movement of the present, they also represent and take care of the future of that movement. . . .

The Communists turn their attention chiefly to Germany, because that country is on the eve of a bourgeois revolution that is bound to be carried out under more advanced conditions of European civilization, and with a much more developed proletariat, than that of England was in the seventeenth, and of France in the eighteenth century, and because the bourgeois revolution in Germany will be but the prelude to an immediately following proletarian revolution.

---

[2]**Saint-Simon, Fourier, Owen:** French utopian socialists Henri de Saint-Simon (1760–1825) and Charles Fourier (1772–1837) and Welsh utopian socialist Robert Owen (1771–1858) believed that capitalists and workers could overcome their antagonism and work cooperatively for the common good.

In short, the Communists everywhere support every revolutionary movement against the existing social and political order of things.

In all these movements they bring to the fore, as the leading question in each, the property question, no matter what its degree of development at the time.

Finally, they labor everywhere for the union and agreement of the democratic parties of all countries.

The Communists disdain to conceal their views and aims. They openly declare that their ends can be attained only by the forcible overthrow of all existing social conditions. Let the ruling classes tremble at a Communistic revolution. The proletarians have nothing to lose but their chains. They have a world to win.

WORKING MEN OF ALL COUNTRIES, UNITE!

READING AND DISCUSSION QUESTIONS

1. Evaluate the actions of the bourgeoisie described by Marx and Engels. Which actions seem positive, and which seem negative?

2. What do Engels and Marx mean when they say that the bourgeoisie "has played a most revolutionary part" in history?

3. According to Marx and Engels, what is the purpose of their manifesto? How successful was it in achieving that purpose?

VIEWPOINTS

Peoples Without Nations

European nationalism came in many forms and drew on a variety of intellectual and cultural traditions. Nonetheless, all nationalists agreed on one thing: to achieve its historical potential, a people needed a nation, a defined geographic space in which to live and develop. For French and British nationalists, this imperative created no real obstacle to the fulfillment of the nationalist dream since the people they identified as "French" or "British" were already concentrated within the boundaries of autonomous states. For other European nationalists, however, the situation was not as straightforward. In the early nineteenth century, Johann Gottlieb Fichte (Document 24-2) dreamed of a Germany "of Germans" and "for Germans"; however, not only were ethnic German populations scattered across central and eastern Europe, but there was no unified German nation at that time in which they could gather. At the end of the nineteenth century, Zionists like Max Nordau (Document 24-3) faced an even more difficult challenge. Convinced that Jews would never be accepted as full citizens of European nations, and at the same time committed to the notion that the full development of the Jewish people could only take place within a nation, Zionists had to look further back in history and outside of Europe for a potential solution to their dilemma. As you read these excerpts from the writings of Fichte and Nordau, look for areas of agreement between the two authors. What assumptions do both men make about the importance of a nation to the development of a people?

24-2 | Fichte Imagines a Future Germany

JOHANN GOTTLIEB FICHTE, *Address to the German Nation* (1808)

Johann Gottlieb Fichte (1762–1814) was a German philosopher who wrote and studied widely but is perhaps best known for his contributions to political theory. During the Napoleonic Wars in the early nineteenth century, Fichte fled Berlin and the French forces attacking Prussia. Returning in 1807, he was disheartened to find French troops and a dispirited greater German public in the city. The anti-imperial (anti-French) sentiment of the day found form in Fichte's celebration of German identity, which fostered German pride through an exaggerated litany of German accomplishments and virtues. His speeches (1807–1808) were published in 1808, inspiring citizens of German states to help fight and defeat Napoleon and laying the foundation for German nationalism.

Time is taking giant strides with us more than with any other age since the history of the world began. . . . At some point self-seeking has destroyed itself, because by its own complete development it has lost its self and the independence of that self; and since it would not voluntarily set itself any other aim but self, an external power has forced upon it another and a foreign purpose. He who has once undertaken to interpret his own age must make his interpretation keep pace with the progress of that age, if progress there be. It is, therefore, my duty to acknowledge as past what has ceased to be the present, before the same audience to whom I characterized it as the present.

. . . Whatever has lost its independence has at the same time lost its power to influence the course of events and to determine these events by its own will. If it remain in this state its age, and itself with the age, are conditioned in their development by that alien power which governs its fate. From now onwards it has no longer any time of its own, but counts its years by the events and epochs of alien nations and kingdoms. From this state, in which all its past world is removed from its independent influence and in its present world only the merit of obedience remains to it, it could raise itself only on condition that a new world should arise for it, the creation of which would begin, and its development fill, a new epoch of its own in history. . . . Now if, for a race which has lost its former self, its

Johann Gottlieb Fichte, *Addresses to the German Nation*, trans. R. F. Jones and G. H. Turnbull (Chicago: Open Court Publishing, 1922), pp. 2–4.

former age and world, such a world should be created as the means of producing a new self and a new age, a thorough interpretation of such a possible age would have to give an account of the world thus created.

Now for my part I maintain that there is such a world, and it is the aim of these addresses to show you its existence and its true owner, to bring before your eyes a living picture of it, and to indicate the means of creating it. . . .

I speak for Germans simply, of Germans simply, not recognizing, but setting aside completely and rejecting, all the dissociating distinctions which for centuries unhappy events have caused in this single nation. You, gentlemen, are indeed to my outward eye the first and immediate representatives who bring before my mind the beloved national characteristics, and are the visible spark at which the flame of my address is kindled. But my spirit gathers round it the educated part of the whole German nation, from all the lands in which they are scattered. It thinks of and considers our common position and relations; it longs that part of the living force, with which these addresses may chance to grip you, may also remain in and breathe from the dumb printed page which alone will come to the eyes of the absent, and may in all places kindle German hearts to decision and action. Only of Germans and simply for Germans, I said. In due course we shall show that any other mark of unity or any other national bond either never had truth and meaning or, if it had, that owing to our present position these bonds of union have been destroyed and torn from us and can never recur; it is only by means of the common characteristic of being German that we can avert the downfall of our nation which is threatened by its fusion with foreign peoples, and win back again an individuality that is self-supporting and quite incapable of any dependence upon others. With our perception of the truth of this statement its apparent conflict (feared now, perhaps, by many) with other duties and with matters that are considered sacred will completely vanish.

Therefore, as I speak only of Germans in general, I shall proclaim that many things concern us which do not apply in the first instance to those assembled here, just as I shall pronounce as the concern of all Germans other things which apply in the first place only to us. In the spirit, of which these addresses are the expression, I perceive that organic unity in which no member regards the fate of another as the fate of a stranger. I behold that unity (which shall and must arise if we are not to perish altogether) already achieved, completed, and existing.

READING AND DISCUSSION QUESTIONS

1. In 1808, there were more than two dozen German states, most of which had yielded to Napoleonic control in 1806. What does Fichte mean when he talks about "the whole German nation"?

2. What is the tone of Fichte's address? Who is his intended audience? What is the purpose of his address?

3. What does Fichte mean when he speaks of the "organic unity" that exists between Germans?

24-3 | Nordau Calls on Jews to Forge Their Own Nation

MAX NORDAU, *On Zionism* (1905)

Max Nordau (1849–1923) cofounded, with Theodor Herzl, the World Zionist Organization in 1897. His first work, *Die Conventionellen Lügen der Kulturmenschheit* (*The Conventional Lies of Civilization*), published in 1883, critiqued modern society for its failure to relate to humanity's "natural" characteristics. His *Entartung* (*Degeneration*) of 1893 drew even more directly on his training as a physician by lamenting the effects of civilization on the healthy physiques of modern humans. Nordau saw Zionism as a means to combat the "degeneration" he identified in modern society. Excerpted here is his 1905 definition of Zionism.

The generations that were under the influence of the Mendelssohnian rhetoric and enlightenment — of reform and assimilation — were followed in the last twenty years of the 19th century by a new generation which strove to secure for the Zionist question a different position from the traditional one. These new Jews shrug their shoulders at the talk of Rabbis and writers about a "Mission of Judaism" that has been in vogue these hundred years.

The Mission is said to consist in this, that the Jews must always live in dispersion among the nations in order to be unto them teachers and models of morality and to educate them gradually to a pure rationalism, to a universal brotherhood of man, and to an ideal cosmopolitanism. They declare this Mission to be a piece of presumption or folly. More modern and practical in their attitude, they demand for the Jewish people only the right to live and to develop in accordance with its own powers to the natural limits of its type. They have found, however, that this is impossible in a state of dispersion, as under such circumstances prejudice, hatred, contempt ever pursue and oppress them, and either inhibit their development or else tend to reduce them to an ethnic mimicry. Thus, instead of their being originals worthy of their existence, this striving at imitation will mold them into mediocre or wretched copies of foreign models. They are therefore working systematically to make the Jewish people once again a normal people, which shall live on its own soil and discharge all the economic, spiritual, moral and political functions of a civilized people. . . .

This goal is not to be attained immediately. It lies in a near or a more distant future. It is an ideal, a wish, a hope, just as Messianic Zionism was and is. But the new Zionism, which is called political, is distinguished from the old religious Messianic Zionism in this, that it repudiates all mysticism, and does not rely upon the return to Palestine to be accomplished by a miracle, but is resolved to bring it about through its own efforts. . . .

The new Zionism has partly arisen out of the inner impulses of Jewry, out of the enthusiasm of modern educated Jews for their history and martyrology, out of the awakened consciousness of their racial fitness, out of their ambition to preserve the ancient stock to as distant a future as possible and to follow up the worthy deeds of ancestors with worthy deeds of descendants. . . .

Max Nordau, "Zionism," from the English Zionist Federation, *Zionism, Its History and Its Aims*, trans. Israel Cohen (London: English Zionist Federation, 1905), pp. 3–20.

But it is also partly the effect of two influences that have come from without: first, the national idea that has dominated European thought and feeling for half a century and determined international politics; secondly, Anti-Semitism, under which the Jews of all countries have to suffer more or less. . . .

The national idea has educated all nations to self-consciousness; it has taught them to feel that their peculiarities are so many valuable factors, and it has inspired them with the passionate wish for independence. It could not fail to exert a deep influence upon educated Jews. It stimulated them to reflect about themselves, to feel once again what they had unlearned, and to demand for themselves the normal destinies of a people. This task of re-discovering their national individuality, although not free from pain, was lightened for them by the attitude of the nations who isolated them as a foreign element and did not hesitate to emphasize the real and imagined contrasts, or rather differences, existing between them and the Jews. . . .

The national idea has, in its extravagances, deteriorated in different directions. It has been distorted into Chauvinism, transformed into an imbecile hatred of foreigners, besotted into grotesque self-deification. Jewish nationalism is quite secure from these self-caricatures. The Jewish nationalist does not suffer from vanity; on the contrary, he feels that he must put forth unremitting effort to render the name of Jew a name of honor. He discreetly recognizes the good qualities of other nations, and eagerly strives to acquire them so far as they harmonize with his natural powers. He knows what terrible injuries have been wrought upon his originally proud and upright character by centuries of slavery and denial of rights, and he endeavors to heal them by strenuous self-education. But while Jewish nationalism is secure from distortion, it, moreover, is a natural phase of the process of development from barbarian self-seeking individualism to the status of noble manhood and altruism, a phase the justification and necessity of which can be denied only by him who knows nothing of the laws of organic evolution and is utterly void of historical sense. . . .

Anti-Semitism has likewise taught many educated Jews how to find the way back to their people. It has had the effect of a severe ordeal, which the weak cannot withstand, but from which the strong step forth stronger, or rather with a keener self-consciousness. It is not correct to say that Zionism is merely a gesture of defiance or an act of despair in the face of Anti-Semitism. Doubtless many an educated Jew has been constrained only through Anti-Semitism to attach himself again to Judaism, and he would again fall away if his Christian compatriots would welcome him as a friend. But in the case of most Zionists, Anti-Semitism was only a stimulus causing them to reflect upon their relation to the nations, and their reflection has led them to results that must remain for them a permanent intellectual and spiritual possession, even if Anti-Semitism were to vanish completely from the world. . . .

Let it be clearly understood. The Zionism that has hitherto been analyzed is that of the free and educated Jews, the Jewish élite. The uneducated multitude that cling to old traditions are Zionistic without much reflection, out of sentiment, out of instinct, out of affliction and longing. They suffer too grievously from the misery of life, from the hatred of the nations, from legal restrictions and social proscriptions. They feel that they cannot hope for any permanent improvement of their position so long as they must live as a helpless minority in the midst of evil-disposed majorities. They want to be a people, to renew their youth in intimate touch with Mother Earth, and to become master of their own fate. A certain proportion of this Zionistic multitude are not altogether free from mystical tendencies. They allow Messianic reminiscences to flit through their Zionism, which they transfuse with religious emotions. They are quite clear about the goal, the national re-union, but not about the ways to attain it. Yet upon them, too, has been borne the necessity of putting forth their own efforts, and a vast difference exists between their organized activity with its voluntary labors and the prayerful passivity of the purely religious Messianist.

READING AND DISCUSSION QUESTIONS

1. How does Nordau differentiate between ancient and contemporary Zionism? For whom does he seem to be defining Zionism?

2. According to Nordau, what role does evolution play in Zionism?

3. Does Nordau's Zionism seem like nationalism to you? Why or why not?

VIEWPOINTS COMPARATIVE QUESTIONS

1. Why did Fichte think it was so important for each people to have its own nation? Did Nordau agree? Why?

2. How did the success of Fichte's nationalist vision help bring about the conditions that gave rise to Nordau's Zionism?

24-4 | Embodying the French Nation

EUGÈNE DELACROIX, *Liberty Leading the People* (1830)

Marianne, a female figure representing liberty and reason, became a central element in French political iconography during the French Revolution. From that point forward, French artists have used Marianne to connect the political events of their day to France's revolutionary legacy, drawing on this powerful symbol of the promise of the Revolution to give meaning to their own struggles. The work of French artist Eugène Delacroix (1798–1863) provides an example of this phenomenon. In 1830, with France once again convulsed by revolutionary upheaval, Delacroix placed Marianne in the thick of the Parisian street fighting, leading a crowd of revolutionaries forward over their fallen comrades, pointing the way toward the realization of France's national destiny.

Bettmann/Getty Images

READING AND DISCUSSION QUESTIONS

1. How might we interpret the fact that liberty is portrayed as a young woman? What significance might we attach to the fact that her dress is torn, revealing her breasts?

2. What does Delacroix's painting suggest about the place of the French Revolution in French national identity in the early nineteenth century?

24-5 | Survival of the Fittest in Human Society

HERBERT SPENCER, *Social Statistics* (1850)

Herbert Spencer (1820–1903) was an English intellectual whose work focused on philosophy and social theory. Spencer was one of the earliest champions of what would later be called "Social Darwinism" — the idea that the very struggle for survival that characterized life in the natural world also applied to human societies. Indeed, Spencer coined the phrase "survival of the fittest," later adopted by Charles Darwin, to describe the

Herbert Spencer, *Social Statics: The Conditions Essential to Human Happiness Specified, and the First of Them Developed* (London: John Chapman, 1851), pp. 311–312, 322–323.

evolutionary process. The following excerpt comes from his first major work, *Social Statics: The Conditions Essential to Human Happiness* (1851), which attracted relatively little attention on publication but contains many of the ideas that would make Spencer one of the best-known and most influential British intellectuals during the 1870s and 1880s. This passage is from the chapter "Poor-Laws," in which he criticizes those who called for providing charitable support to the poor.

In common with its other assumptions of secondary offices, the assumption by a government of the office of Reliever-general to the poor, is necessarily forbidden by the principle that a government cannot rightly do anything more than protect. In demanding from a citizen contributions for the mitigation of distress — contributions not needed [for] the due administration of men's rights — the state is, as we have seen, reversing its function, and diminishing that liberty to exercise the faculties which it was instituted to maintain. Possibly . . . some will assert that by satisfying the wants of the pauper, a government is in reality extending his liberty to exercise his faculties, inasmuch as it is giving him something without which the exercise of them is impossible. . . . But this statement of the case implies a confounding of two widely different things. To enforce the fundamental law — to take care that every man has freedom to do all that he wills, provided he infringes not the equal freedom of any other man — this is the special purpose for which the civil power exists. Now insuring to each the right to pursue within the specified limits the objects of his desires without let or hindrance, is quite a separate thing from insuring him satisfaction. Of two individuals, one may use his liberty of action successfully — may achieve the gratifications he seeks after, or accumulate what is equivalent to many of them — property; whilst the other, having like privileges, may fail to do so. But with these results the state has no concern. . . .

Pervading all nature we may see at work a stern discipline, which is a little cruel that it may be very kind. That state of universal warfare maintained throughout the lower creation, to the great perplexity of many worthy people, is at bottom the most merciful provision which the circumstances admit of. It is much better that the ruminant animal, when deprived by age of the vigour which made its existence a pleasure, should be killed by some beast of prey, than that it should linger out a life made painful by infirmities, and eventually die of starvation. By the destruction of all such, not only is existence ended before it becomes burdensome, but room is made for a younger generation capable of the fullest enjoyment; and moreover, out of the very act of substitution happiness is derived for a tribe of predatory creatures. Note further, that their carnivorous enemies not only remove from herbivorous herds individuals past their prime, but also weed out the sickly, the malformed, and the least fleet or powerful. By the aid of which purifying process, as well as by the fighting, so universal in the pairing season, all vitiation [weakening] of the race through the multiplication of its inferior samples is prevented; and the [maintenance] of a constitution completely adapted to surrounding conditions, and therefore most productive of happiness, is ensured.

The development of the higher creation is a progress towards a form of being capable of a happiness undiminished by these drawbacks. It is in the human race that the consummation is to be accomplished. Civilization is the last stage of its accomplishment. And the ideal man is the man in whom all the conditions of that accomplishment are fulfilled. Meanwhile the well-being of existing humanity, and the unfolding of it into this ultimate perfection, are both secured by that same beneficent, though severe discipline, to which the animate creation at large is subject: a discipline which is pitiless in the working out of good: a felicity-pursuing law which never swerves for the avoidance of partial and temporary suffering. The poverty of the incapable, the distresses that come upon the imprudent, the starvation of the idle, and those shoulderings aside of the weak by the strong, which leave so many "in shallows and miseries," are the decrees of a large, farseeing benevolence. It seems hard that an unskillfulness which with all its efforts he cannot overcome should entail hunger upon the artisan. It seems hard that a laborer incapacitated by [sickness] from competing with his stronger fellows, should have to bear the resulting privations. It seems hard that widows and orphans should be left to struggle for life or death. Nevertheless, when regarded not separately, but in connection with the interests of universal humanity, these harsh fatalities are seen to be full of the highest beneficence — the same beneficence which brings to early graves the children of diseased parents, and singles out the low-spirited, the intemperate, and the debilitated as the victims of an epidemic.

READING AND DISCUSSION QUESTIONS

1. What, according to Spencer, is the "fundamental law"? Why does he believe this law is not consistent with "satisfying the wants of the pauper"?

2. On what grounds could Spencer argue that the death of "the children of diseased parents" was in the "interests of universal humanity" and "full of the highest beneficence for mankind"? Why does he believe relief work for the poor would hurt humanity rather than help it?

3. What lessons does Spencer draw from the natural world to support his arguments? Do you think it makes sense to understand human society through the example of other animals?

■ COMPARATIVE QUESTIONS ■

1. National identity was a major theme of the nineteenth century. How does each document in this chapter either encourage or discourage national identity?

2. Fichte and Nordau speak about the unity of the German and Jewish nations, respectively. Compare and contrast the way that each author defines national unity and presents it as a motivating factor.

3. Compare and contrast Marx and Engels's and Spencer's diagnosis of social and economic inequality and their proposed solutions. Is there any issue on which they agreed?

4. When Spencer refers to the "ideal man" and Nordau speaks of the "Jewish nationalist," do you think they are referring to humans in general, or specifically to men? Is their intended audience men, or both men and women? What should we make of Delacroix's *Liberty Leading the People* in this context?

5. What social or political problem is defined in each document? What are the different ways in which each document presents a crisis, and what kind of language or imagery is used to motivate the intended audience?

25

Africa, the Ottoman Empire, and the New Imperialism
1800–1914

The rise of industrial economies in Europe drove European nations to expand their empires in Africa and Asia. In search of markets, resources, and occasionally adventure, Europeans gained control of an increasingly large part of the globe through commerce and colonization. At the same time, states like the Ottoman Empire mixed western European notions of civilization with their own cultures to develop alternative visions of a "modern society." The documents in this chapter present different perspectives on the global progress of modernization and westernization: from the Ottoman Empire's government as it sought to draw on modern Western ideas to reform and strengthen its state, from a leading voice of British imperialism, from an African who fought and then submitted to British colonial rule, and from Africans who endured terrible abuses in the Belgian Congo. All of the documents offer insight on how non-Western peoples adapted and endured as nationalism, progress, and empire changed their worlds.

25-1 | Ottoman Reform from the Top Down
SULTAN ABDUL MEJID, *Imperial Rescript* (1856)

Building on the work of previous rulers to enact military and administrative reforms, many of which were inspired by modern Western institutions, Sultan Abdul Mejid or Abdülmecid (r. 1839–1861) instituted a period of "reorganization," or *Tanzimat*, in the aging Ottoman Empire. Various non-Turkish groups had been pulling away from Ottoman rule since the early 1800s, and large-scale violence against non-Muslim subjects was not uncommon. In this imperial rescript, or official proclamation, the sultan affirms his policy of "Ottomanism," or equal treatment of all citizens without regard to race, language, or religion. Ottomanism may

E. A. Van Dyck, *Report upon the Capitulations of the Ottoman Empire Since the Year 1150*, pt. 1 (Washington, D.C.: U.S. Government Printing Office, 1881, 1882), pp. 106–108.

be seen as a doomed and even hypocritical attempt to reassert central authority; however, the rescript represented real reform in Ottoman society.

Let it be done as herein set forth. . . . It being now my desire to renew and enlarge still more the new Institutions ordained with the view of establishing a state of things conformable with the dignity of my Empire and . . . by the kind and friendly assistance of the Great Powers, my noble Allies.[1] . . . The guarantees promised on our part by the Hatti-Humaïoun of Gülhané,[2] and in conformity with the Tanzimat, . . . are today confirmed and consolidated, and efficacious measures shall be taken in order that they may have their full and entire effect.

All the privileges and spiritual immunities granted by my ancestors from time immemorial, and at subsequent dates, to all Christian communities or other non-Muslim persuasions established in my empire, under my protection, shall be confirmed and maintained.

Every Christian or other non-Muslim community shall be bound within a fixed period, and with the concurrence of a commission composed . . . of members of its own body, to proceed with my high approbation and under the inspection of my Sublime Porte,[3] to examine into its actual immunities and privileges, and to discuss and submit to my Sublime Porte the reforms required by the progress of civilization and of the age. The powers conceded to the Christian Patriarchs and Bishops[4] by the Sultan Mehmed II[5] and his successors, shall be made to harmonize with the new position which my generous and beneficent intentions ensure to these communities. . . . The ecclesiastical dues, of whatever sort of nature they be, shall be abolished and replaced by fixed revenues of the Patriarchs and heads of communities. . . . In the towns, small boroughs, and villages, where the whole population is of the same religion, no obstacle shall be offered to the repair, according to their original plan, of buildings set apart for religious worship, for schools, for hospitals, and for cemeteries. . . .

Every distinction or designation tending to make any class whatever of the subjects of my Empire inferior to another class, on account of their religion, language, or race, shall be forever effaced from Administrative Protocol. The laws shall be put in force against the use of any injurious or offensive term, either among private individuals or on the part of the authorities. . . .

As all forms of religion are and shall be freely professed in my dominions, no subject of my Empire shall be hindered in the exercise of the religion that he

---

[1]**the Great Powers, my noble Allies:** During the Crimean War (1853–1856), the Ottoman Empire fought with Great Britain and France against Russia.

[2]**The guarantees . . . Gülhané:** The Noble Rescript of 1839, also written by Sultan Abdul Mejid, guaranteed personal security, a fair tax system, controlled military conscriptions, and full rights to citizens regardless of faith.

[3]**Sublime Porte:** The term refers to the sultan and his sovereignty.

[4]**Christian Patriarchs and Bishops:** Ruling officials of the Greek and Armenian churches in the Ottoman Empire.

[5]**Sultan Mehmed II:** Ottoman ruler from 1451 to 1481.

professes. . . . No one shall be compelled to change their religion . . . and . . . all the subjects of my Empire, without distinction of nationality, shall be admissible to public employments. . . . All the subjects of my Empire, without distinction, shall be received into the civil and military schools of the government. . . . Moreover, every community is authorized to establish public schools of science, art, and industry. . . .

All commercial, correctional, and criminal suits between Muslims and Christian or other non-Muslim subjects, or between Christian or other non-Muslims of different sects, shall be referred to Mixed Tribunals. The proceedings of these Tribunals shall be public; the parties shall be confronted, and shall produce their witnesses, whose testimony shall be received, without distinction, upon an oath taken according to the religious law of each sect. . . .

Penal, correctional, and commercial laws, and rules of procedure for the Mixed Tribunals, shall be drawn up as soon as possible, and formed into a code. . . . Proceedings shall be taken, for the reform of the penitentiary system. . . .

The organization of the police . . . shall be revised in such a manner as to give to all the peaceable subjects of my Empire the strongest guarantees for the safety both of their persons and property. . . . Christian subjects, and those of other non-Muslim sects, . . . shall, as well as Muslims, be subject to the obligations of the Law of Recruitment [for military service]. The principle of obtaining substitutes, or of purchasing exemption, shall be admitted.

Proceedings shall be taken for a reform in the constitution of the Provincial and Communal Councils, in order to ensure fairness in the choice of the deputies of the Muslim, Christian, and other communities, and freedom of voting in the Councils. . . .

As the laws regulating the purchase, sale, and disposal of real property are common to all the subjects of my Empire, it shall be lawful for foreigners to possess landed property in my dominions. . . .

The taxes are to be levied under the same denomination from all the subjects of my Empire, without distinction of class or of religion. The most prompt and energetic means for remedying the abuses in collecting the taxes, and especially the tithes, shall be considered. The system of direct collection shall gradually, and as soon as possible, be substituted for the plan of farming,[6] in all the branches of the revenues of the state.

A special law having been already passed, which declares that the budget of the revenue and the expenditure of the state shall be drawn up and made known every year, the said law shall be most scrupulously observed. . . .

The heads of each community and a delegate, designated by my Sublime Porte, shall be summoned to take part in the deliberations of the Supreme Council of Justice on all occasions which might interest the generality of the subjects of my Empire. . . .

---

[6]**farming:** Tax farming, in which the government contracted with private financiers who collected taxes for a profit.

Steps shall be taken for the formation of banks and other similar institutions, so as to effect a reform in the monetary and financial system, as well as to create funds to be employed in augmenting the sources of the material wealth of my Empire.

Everything that can impede commerce or agriculture shall be abolished. To accomplish these objects means shall be sought to profit by science, the art, and the funds of Europe, and thus gradually to execute them.

READING AND DISCUSSION QUESTIONS

1. What specific measures does the sultan take to ensure religious and ethnic equality? What do these measures imply about life in the Ottoman Empire before the rescript was issued?

2. The sultan is careful to extend military service to people of all religious and ethnic backgrounds. How does this right compare to rights regarding public employment, education, taxation, and real estate?

3. The rescript mentions communities of Christian and non-Muslim people and villages or small areas where all people share a common religion. What does this imply about the integration of different religious groups in Ottoman society?

4. In explaining the purpose of his rescript, the sultan refers to the "dignity" of his empire and mentions the Ottoman Empire's relationship with European "Great Powers." How do you think the ideas of religious equality, social reform, and international relations and the dignity of the empire work together?

VIEWPOINTS

The Colonial Encounter in Africa

The scramble for Africa brought almost all of the continent under European colonial rule in only a few short decades. Against industrialized European adversaries with overwhelming technological advantages, African forces could offer little sustained military resistance. This does not mean, however, that conquest and colonization brought African resistance to an end. Instead, resistance took on new forms as the European powers settled into the difficult task of governing their new colonies. British businessman and financier Cecil Rhodes (Document 25-2) may have imagined that African peoples would simply disappear, washed away by a tidal wave of racially superior "Anglo-Saxon" settlers, but they did not. The European presence had a profound impact on African society and culture, but it was a complex one, forged out of cross-cultural interactions and the ongoing efforts of Africans to regain control of their lives and destinies. As you read the documents included in this feature, think about the African reaction to colonization. Why did African peoples never fully accept the legitimacy and permanence of colonial rule?

25-2 | Cecil Rhodes Dreams of Global Domination

CECIL RHODES, From *Confession of Faith* (ca. 1877)

Perhaps no single man exemplified European colonial exploitation of the African continent more than Cecil Rhodes (1853–1902). He was sent as a child from England to South Africa—then the British Cape Colony—for his health, and there he amassed a fortune by controlling diamond production. He entered politics in the Cape Colony and quickly parlayed his wealth and political influence into expanded colonial control of South African territories, one of which (comprising present-day Zambia and Zimbabwe) was named Rhodesia in his honor. Rhodes sent the following text to British journalist William Thomas Stead as representative of his thoughts on empire and race; it has survived as a marker of European pride and global ambitions in the late nineteenth century.

It often strikes a man to inquire what is the chief good in life; to one the thought comes that it is a happy marriage, to another great wealth, and as each seizes on his idea, for that he more or less works for the rest of his existence. To myself thinking over the same question the wish came to render myself useful to my country. I then asked myself how could I and after reviewing the various methods I have felt that at the present day we are actually limiting our children and perhaps bringing into the world half the human beings we might owing to the lack of country for them to inhabit that if we had retained America there would at this moment be millions more of English living. I contend that we are the finest race in the world and that the more of the world we inhabit the better it is for the human race, just fancy those parts that are at present inhabited by the most despicable specimens of human beings what an alteration there would be if they were brought under Anglo-Saxon influence, look again at the extra employment a new country added to our dominions gives. I contend that every acre added to our territory means in the future birth to some more of the English race who otherwise would not be brought into existence. Added to this the absorption of the greater portion of the world under our rule simply means the end of all wars, at this moment had we not lost America I believe we could have stopped the Russian-Turkish war[7] by merely refusing money and supplies. Having these ideas what scheme could we think of to forward this object. I look into

---

John Flint, *Cecil Rhodes* (New York: Hachette, 1974), appendix.

[7]**Russian-Turkish war:** This 1870s conflict between the Ottoman Empire and Russia was spurred in part by various ethnic or religious nationalisms in Ottoman territories.

history and I read the story of the Jesuits[8] I see what they were able to do in a bad cause and I might say under bad leaders.

In the present day I become a member in the Masonic order[9] I see the wealth and power they possess the influence they hold and I think over their ceremonies and I wonder that a large body of men can devote themselves to what at times appear the most ridiculous and absurd rites without an object and without an end.

The idea gleaming and dancing before one's eyes like a will-of-the-wisp at last frames itself into a plan. Why should we not form a secret society with but one object the furtherance of the British Empire and the bringing of the whole uncivilized world under British rule for the recovery of the United States for the making the Anglo-Saxon race but one Empire. What a dream, but yet it is probable, it is possible. I once heard it argued by a fellow in my own college, I am sorry to own it by an Englishman, that it was a good thing for us that we have lost the United States. There are some subjects on which there can be no arguments, and to an Englishman this is one of them, but even from an American's point of view just picture what they have lost, look at their government, are not the frauds that yearly come before the public view a disgrace to any country and especially theirs which is the finest in the world. Would they have occurred had they remained under English rule great as they have become how infinitely greater they would have been with the softening and elevating influences of English rule, think of those countless 000's of Englishmen that during the last 100 years would have crossed the Atlantic and settled and populated the United States. Would they have not made without any prejudice a finer country of it than the low class Irish and German emigrants? All this we have lost and that country loses owing to whom? Owing to two or three ignorant pig-headed statesmen of the last century, at their door lies the blame. Do you ever feel mad? Do you ever feel murderous? I think I do with those men. I bring facts to prove my assertion. Does an English father when his sons wish to emigrate ever think of suggesting emigration to a country under another flag, never — it would seem a disgrace to suggest such a thing I think that we all think that poverty is better under our own flag than wealth under a foreign one.

Put your mind into another train of thought. Fancy Australia discovered and colonized under the French flag, what would it mean merely several millions of English unborn that at present exist we learn from the past and to form our future. We learn from having lost to cling to what we possess. We know the size of the world we know the total extent. Africa is still lying ready for us it is our duty to take it. It is our duty to seize every opportunity of acquiring more

---

[8]**the Jesuits:** The Society of Jesus, or the Jesuits, was founded in 1534 as a missionary arm of the Roman Catholic Church and in partial response to the Protestant Reformation. Rhodes seems to be voicing anti-Catholic sentiments in his assessment of the "bad cause" and "bad leaders" of the Jesuits.

[9]**Masonic order:** A male fraternal organization largely centered in Great Britain, northwest Europe, and the United States.

territory and we should keep this one idea steadily before our eyes that more territory simply means more of the Anglo-Saxon race more of the best the most human, most honorable race the world possesses.

READING AND DISCUSSION QUESTIONS

1. How is race a part of Rhodes's justification for empire? What does British society possess that he most admires?

2. What are the different races that Rhodes mentions? How do they relate to one another?

3. What is the purpose of the secret society that Rhodes proposes?

25-3 | A Firsthand Account of Imperial Conquest

NDANSI KUMALO, *On the British Incursion in Zimbabwe* (1932)

Ndansi Kumalo was a member of the Ndebele people who lived in what is now Zimbabwe, where the Ndebele had settled after years of struggle with Zulu and Dutch forces. The Ndebele sovereign, Lobengula, negotiated with the new wave of British colonizers intent on access to the region's mineral resources, but tensions mounted and conflict broke out in the 1890s. Kumalo, a witness to the British incursion, was hired to play the role of Lobengula in a 1932 British film about the life of colonizer Cecil Rhodes (see Document 25-2). While filming in England, Kumalo met the African scholar Margery Perham, who recorded the following firsthand account of British colonization.

We were terribly upset and very angry at the coming of the white men, for Lobengula . . . was under her . . . [the Queen's] protection and it was quite unjustified that white men should come with force into our country.[10] . . . Lobengula had no war in his heart: he had always protected the white men and been good to them. If he had meant war, would he have sent our regiments far away to the north at this moment? As far as I know the trouble began in this way. Gandani, a chief who was sent out, reported that some of the Mashona[11] had taken the king's cattle; some regiments were detailed to follow and recover them. They followed the Mashona to Ziminto's people. Gandani had strict instructions not to molest the white people established in certain parts and to confine himself to

---

Margery Perham, ed., *Ten Africans* (London: Faber and Faber, 1936). Originally published by Faber and Faber Ltd. in 1936. Used by permission of the Trustees of the Will of the Late Dame Margery Perham.

[10]**under her . . . our country:** In an 1888 agreement Lobengula made with Cecil Rhodes, the British government guaranteed that there would be no incursion of English settlers on Ndebele land and that Lobengula's authority would continue. Unhappy with Lobengula's concessions, many Ndebele warriors began to press for war against the Europeans.

[11]**the Mashona:** A people who raised livestock and were ruled by the Ndebele.

the people who had taken the cattle. The commander was given a letter which he had to produce to the Europeans and tell them what the object of the party was. But the members of the party were restless and went without reporting to the white people and killed a lot of Mashonas. The pioneers were very angry and said, "You have trespassed into our part." They went with the letter, but only after they had killed some people, and the white men said, "You have done wrong, you should have brought the letter first and then we should have given you permission to follow the cattle." The commander received orders from the white people to get out, and up to a certain point which he could not possibly reach in the time allowed. A force followed them up and they defended themselves. When the pioneers turned out there was a fight at Shangani and at Bembezi. . . .

The next news was that the white people had entered Bulawayo; the King's kraal [stockade] had been burnt down and the King had fled. Of the cattle very few were recovered; most fell into the hands of the white people. Only a very small portion were found and brought to Shangani where the King was, and we went there to give him any assistance we could. . . . Three of our leaders mounted their horses and followed up the King and he wanted to know where his cattle were; they said they had fallen into the hands of the whites, only a few were left. He said, "Go back and bring them along." But they did not go back again; the white forces had occupied Bulawayo and they went into the Matoppos [hills]. Then the white people came to where we were living and sent word round that all chiefs and warriors should go into Bulawayo and discuss peace, for the King had gone and they wanted to make peace. . . . The white people said, "Now that your King has deserted you, we occupy your country. Do you submit to us?" What could we do? "If you are sincere, come back and bring in all your arms, guns, and spears." We did so. . . .

So we surrendered to the white people and were told to go back to our homes and live our usual lives and attend to our crops. But the white men sent native police who did abominable things; they were cruel and assaulted a lot of our people and helped themselves to our cattle and goats. These policemen were not our own people; anybody was made a policeman. We were treated like slaves. They came and were overbearing and we were ordered to carry their clothes and bundles. They interfered with our wives and our daughters and molested them. In fact, the treatment we received was intolerable. We thought it best to fight and die rather than bear it. How the rebellion started I do not know; there was no organization, it was like a fire that suddenly flames up. We had been flogged by native police and then they rubbed salt water in the wounds. There was much bitterness because so many of our cattle were branded and taken away from us; we had no property, nothing we could call our own. We said, "It is no good living under such conditions; death would be better—let us fight." Our King gone, we had submitted to the white people and they ill-treated us until we became desperate and tried to make an end of it all. We knew that we had very little chance because their weapons were so much superior to ours.

But we meant to fight to the last, feeling that even if we could not beat them we might at least kill a few of them and so have some sort of revenge.

I fought in the rebellion. We used to look out for valleys where the white men were likely to approach. We took cover behind rocks and trees and tried to ambush them. We were forced by the nature of our weapons not to expose ourselves. I had a gun, a breech-loader [rear-loading gun]. They — the white men — fought us with big guns and Maxims [early machine guns] and rifles.

I remember a fight in the Matoppos when we charged the white men. There were some hundreds of us; the white men also were as many. We charged them at close quarters: we thought we had a good chance to kill them but the Maxims were too much for us. We drove them off at the first charge, but they returned and formed up again. We made a second charge, but they were too strong for us. I cannot say how many white people were killed, but we think it was quite a lot. . . . Many of our people were killed in this fight: I saw four of my cousins shot. One was shot in the jaw and the whole of his face was blown away — like this — and he died. One was hit between the eyes; another here, in the shoulder; another had part of his ear shot off. We made many charges but each time we were beaten off, until at last the white men packed up and retreated. But for the Maxims, it would have been different. . . .

So peace was made. Many of our people had been killed, and now we began to die of starvation; and then came the rinderpest [an infectious cow disease] and the cattle that were still left to us perished. We could not help thinking that all these dreadful things were brought by the white people. We struggled, and the Government helped us with grain; and by degrees we managed to get crops and pulled through. Our cattle were practically wiped out, but a few were left and from them we slowly bred up our herds again. We were offered work in the mines and farms to earn money and so were able to buy back some cattle. At first, of course, we were not used to going out to work, but advice was given that the chief should advise the young people to go out to work, and gradually they went. At first we received a good price for our cattle and sheep and goats. Then the tax came. It was 10s.[12] a year. Soon the Government said, "That is too little, you must contribute more; you must pay £1." We did so. Then those who took more than one wife were taxed; 10s. for each additional wife. The tax is heavy, but that is not all. We are also taxed for our dogs; 5s. for a dog. Then we were told we were living on private land; the owners wanted rent in addition to the Government tax; some 10s. some £1, some £2 a year. . . .

Would I like to have the old days back? Well, the white men have brought some good things. For a start, they brought us European implements — plows; we can buy European clothes, which are an advance. The Government has arranged for education and through that, when our children grow up, they may rise in status. We want them to be educated and civilized and make better citizens. Even in our own time there were troubles, there was much fighting and

---

[12]**10s.:** Ten shillings.

many innocent people were killed. It is infinitely better to have peace instead of war, and our treatment generally by the officials is better than it was at first. But, under the white people, we still have our troubles. Economic conditions are telling on us very severely. We are on land where the rainfall is scanty, and things will not grow well. In our own time we could pick our own country, but now all the best land has been taken by the white people. We get hardly any price for our cattle; we find it hard to meet our money obligations. If we have crops to spare we get very little for them; we find it difficult to make ends meet and wages are very low. When I view the position, I see that our rainfall has diminished, we have suffered drought and have poor crops and we do not see any hope of improvement, but all the same our taxes do not diminish. We see no prosperous days ahead of us. There is one thing we think an injustice. When we have plenty of grain the prices are very low, but the moment we are short of grain and we have to buy from Europeans at once the price is high. If when we have hard times and find it difficult to meet our obligations some of these burdens were taken off us it would gladden our hearts. As it is, if we do raise anything, it is never our own: all, or most of it, goes back in taxation. We can never save any money. If we could, we could help ourselves: we could build ourselves better houses; we could buy modern means of traveling about, a cart, or donkeys or mules.

As to my own life, I have had twelve wives altogether, five died and seven are alive. I have twenty-six children alive, five have died. Of my sons five are married and are all at work farming; three young children go to school. I hope the younger children will all go to school. I think it is a good thing to go to school.

There are five schools in our district. Quite a number of people are Christians, but I am too old to change my ways. In our religion we believe that when anybody dies the spirit remains and we often make offerings to the spirits to keep them good-tempered. But now the making of offerings is dying out rapidly, for every member of the family should be present, but the children are Christians and refuse to come, so the spirit-worship is dying out. A good many of our children go to the mines in the Union, for the wages are better there. Unfortunately a large number do not come back at all. And some send money to their people—others do not. Some men have even deserted their families, their wives, and children. If they cannot go by train they walk long distances.

READING AND DISCUSSION QUESTIONS

1. What reasons does Kumalo give for rebelling against British colonial forces? What caused the initial violence, and what was the outcome?

2. If the Ndebele leader Gandani had delivered the letter to the British and not acted in haste, do you think the British pioneers would have responded as violently as they did? What gives you that impression?

3. What is Kumalo's opinion of British colonial influence in Africa? Cite examples to support your answer.

25-4 | The Law as a Form of Resistance

JOHN MENSAH SARBAH, *Fanti Customary Law* (1897)

John Mensah Sarbah (1864–1910) was born in the Gold Coast, a British colony in West Africa that would become the nation Ghana upon gaining independence in 1957. As one of the Gold Coast's African elite, Sarbah studied law in England and passed the bar in 1887. He dedicated his life to using his legal training to protect the rights of his people and to resist British domination. It was in this context that he wrote *Fanti Customary Law*, an introduction to the laws and customs of one of the Gold Coast's most important ethnic groups. Sarbah believed that for laws to be effective they had to reflect local conditions, social norms, and experiences. Thus, if the British wanted to administer genuine justice in the Gold Coast, they had to be familiar with local customs and traditions. As you read this excerpt, think about the implications of Sarbah's argument. How might it have been used to support calls for the Gold Coast's independence?

Words which cause or produce any injury to the reputation of another are called defamatory, and, if false, are actionable. False defamatory words, when spoken, constitute slander. Where a person has been found guilty for using slanderous words, he is bound to retract his words publicly, in addition to paying a small fine by way of compensation to the aggrieved party. Words imputing witchcraft, adultery, immoral conduct, crime, and all words which sound to the disreputation of a person of whom they are spoken are actionable. The native custom is more in accordance with natural justice, equity, and good conscience than the English law, which has been denounced by many a learned judge. Says Lord Chancellor Campbell, in *Lynch* v. *Knight and Wife*, "I may lament the unsatisfactory state of our law, according to which the imputation by words, however gross, on an occasion however public, upon the chastity of a modest matron or a pure virgin is not actionable, without proof that it has actually produced special temporal damage to her." Instead of the word "unsatisfactory" I should substitute the word "barbarous," said Lord Brougham on the same occasion.

An effective way of punishing a person guilty of slander of serious consequences, is to make him walk through the town or village carrying a heavy stone in front of an officer of the Court, who, at convenient halting-places, beats a gong; the guilty slanderer is compelled to recant his base falsehoods, and to confess his disgraceful behavior, amid the sneers and jeers of the multitude. The heavy stone so carried is called *oturbiba*.

READING AND DISCUSSION QUESTIONS

1. Why did Sarbah believe that the Fanti approach to slander was superior to the British approach?

2. What does the punishment that Sarbah described suggest about the nature of Fanti society?

3. In what ways was Sarbah's publication of Fanti customs, traditions, and laws an anti-imperialist act?

John Mensah Sarbah, *Fanti Customary Law* (London: William Clowes and Sons, 1897), pp. 93–94.

VIEWPOINTS COMPARATIVE QUESTIONS

1. How might Kumalo and Sarbah have responded to Rhodes's claim that the world would be a better place if it were inhabited solely by the "Anglo-Saxon race"?

2. What aspects of British culture did Kumalo and Sarbah value? Why did both believe that their people would be better off if the British left?

25-5 | The Brutality of Colonial Rule

ROGER CASEMENT AND DAVID ENGOHAHE, *Victims of Belgian Congo Atrocities* (ca. 1904–1905)

In 1903, the British consul Roger Casement investigated abuses in the Congo Free State for the British government. The Congo Free State was the private holding of King Leopold II of Belgium from 1885 to 1908, and under Leopold's control the extraction of rubber led to gross human rights abuses. Casement's report led to a public outcry in Europe. The report, upheld by an independent commission in 1905 and verified through later research, detailed the mutilation and murder practiced by Leopold's representatives to ensure rubber production. Here, an excerpt from Casement's report shows the testimony of eyewitness David Engohahe—a member of the Bolia ethnicity—detailing the violence employed to ensure the continued profits from rubber cultivation. The photographs of three residents of the Congo show the human cost of the atrocities Engohahe describes.

At the time the district headquarters of the Basengele[13] was at Mbongo.[14] When the rubber was prepared you took it to Mbongo. . . . The State man[15] would stretch [the lengths of rubber] . . . out, and if they split he would reject them and throw them to one side. At the end of the count, if the rubber was bad, out of a village complement of 25 men he might shoot 5, out of 30, perhaps 10; and perhaps 20 out of 50. It was dreadful persecution. He then sent the rest of the men back to the forest to collect more rubber to make up the quota. . . . He forbad us to harvest the things in our own gardens so much so that our immediate forefathers did not eat manioc.[16] He forbad us the palm nuts in our own trees, and the plantains and all the garden produce, and sugar cane. It was all kept for his soldiers and his followers. . . . Many fled and some were mutilated. I myself saw a man at Likange who had had both his hands cut off. Sometimes

---

Roger Anstey, "The Congo Rubber Atrocities: A Case Study," *African Historical Studies*, 4:1 (1971): 72.

[13]**Basengele:** A Bantu-language ethnic group.
[14]**Mbongo:** Near present-day Isoko, Democratic Republic of the Congo.
[15]**State man:** A representative of Leopold.
[16]**manioc:** A popular West African root crop, also called cassava.

they cut them at the wrist, sometimes farther up . . . with a machete. Also there is a Muboma[17] . . . who has a long scar across the back of his neck. There is another man called Botei at Ihanga with the same sort of scar, where they wounded him maliciously, expecting him to die. They didn't cut his head off, they didn't get to the bone, but expected him to bleed to death. It was sheer cruelty; the State treated us abominably.

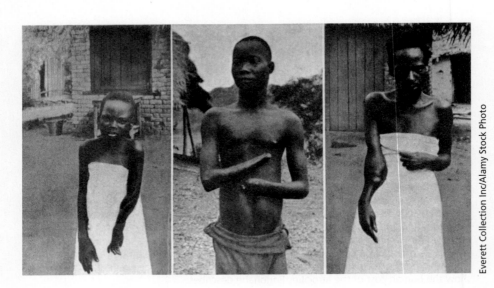

Everett Collection Inc/Alamy Stock Photo

READING AND DISCUSSION QUESTIONS

1. How does Engohahe connect the production of rubber to the presence or absence of subsistence agriculture?

2. How does the system of labor described here compare or contrast with your impression of slavery in the Americas?

3. Engohahe describes Leopold's representative as "the State man," but Leopold operated the territory as his own private holding rather than as a colony of Belgium. How might Leopold's relationship to the territory change your impression of the abuses described here?

4. What is the effect of the photographs? Do they look posed or natural? What might have been the purpose of these photographs?

---

[17]**Muboma:** An ethnic group.

▪ COMPARATIVE QUESTIONS ▪

1. Most of the documents in this chapter are written from a non-Western point of view; two, however, present a European view of non-Europeans. How do the photographs and Rhodes's "Confession" each present Africans? What is the role of Africans in each document?

2. Each of these documents deals in some way with the intersection of non-Western cultures and modern (if not Western) ideas and influences. How does each present the idea of modernization? What is the influence of the modern world in each case?

3. Consider the 1856 Ottoman rescript on equality and Rhodes's 1877 "Confession." How does each present the idea of managing diverse populations?

4. Taken together, what do the documents in this chapter tell you about the nature of colonial rule in the late nineteenth and early twentieth centuries? What do they reveal about the motives behind the New Imperialism?

26

Asia and the Pacific in the Era of Imperialism
1800–1914

Though not colonized as directly or thoroughly as Africa, Asia was heavily influenced by the imperial aspirations of Western industrial societies. British colonial rule directly reshaped the Indian economy and Indian culture, forcibly incorporating many Indians into the British-dominated world economy. In East Asia, treaties gave multiple Western powers—and Japan—economic, political, and military control over key areas of China. Spared the full brunt of Western attention, Japan incorporated Western ideas as it pushed to become an industrial power in its own right. But in every case, Asian nations wrestled with the presence of Westerners and Western ideas as well as their own domestic transformations. The documents in this chapter reflect the broad range of strategies that Asians used to appropriate or contest the new framework of international power as they understood it.

26-1 | A Chinese Official Denounces the British Opium Trade
LIN ZEXU, *From a Letter to Queen Victoria* (1839)

Lin Zexu (1785–1850) was a Confucian scholar-bureaucrat tapped by the Daoguang Emperor in 1838 to stop the illegal importation of opium by Great Britain and other foreign powers. In 1839, he arrived in Guangzhou and, after increasingly hostile negotiations, seized and destroyed more than 2 million pounds of raw opium from British warehouses. This action, viewed as heroic by Chinese, ignited the first Opium War (1839–1842). Lin wrote to Queen Victoria, pleading with her to stop the British opium trade. Although his letter was never conveyed to the queen, it was published in Guangdong and later in Britain, where it aroused both outrage and sympathy.

It is only our high and mighty emperor, who alike supports and cherishes those of the Inner Land [China], and those from beyond the seas—who looks upon all

The Chinese Repository, 20 vols. (Japan: Canton Press, 1840), 8:497–593.

mankind with equal benevolence—who, if a source of profit exists anywhere, diffuses it over the whole world—who, if the tree of evil takes root anywhere, plucks it up for the benefit of all nations:—who, in a word, hath implanted in his breast that heart (by which beneficent nature herself) governs the heavens and the earth! You, the queen of your honorable nation, sit upon a throne occupied through successive generations by predecessors, all of whom have been styled respectful and obedient. Looking over the public documents accompanying the tribute sent (by your predecessors) on various occasions, we find the following:—"All the people of my (i.e. the king of England's) country, arriving at the Central Land for purposes of trade, have to feel grateful to the great emperor for the most perfect justice, for the kindest treatment," and other words to that effect. Delighted did we feel that the kings of your honorable nation so clearly understood the great principles of propriety, and were so deeply grateful for the heavenly goodness (of our emperor):—therefore, it was that we of the heavenly dynasty nourished and cherished your people from afar, and bestowed upon them redoubled proofs of our urbanity and kindness. It is merely from these circumstances, that your country—deriving immense advantage from its commercial intercourse with us, which has endured now two hundred years—has become the rich and flourishing kingdom that it is said to be!

But, during the commercial intercourse which has existed so long, among the numerous foreign merchants resorting hither, are wheat and tares, good and bad; and of these latter are some, who, by means of introducing opium by stealth, have seduced our Chinese people, and caused every province of the land to overflow with that poison. These then know merely to advantage themselves, they care not about injuring others! This is a principle which heaven's Providence repugnates; and which mankind conjointly look upon with abhorrence! Moreover, the great emperor hearing of it, actually quivered with indignation, and especially dispatched me, the commissioner, to Canton, that in conjunction with the viceroy and lieut.-governor of the province, means might be taken for its suppression! . . .

We find that your country is distant from us about sixty or seventy thousand [Chinese] miles, that your foreign ships come hither striving the one with the other for our trade, and for the simple reason of their strong desire to reap a profit. Now, out of the wealth of our Inner Land, if we take a part to bestow upon foreigners from afar, it follows, that the immense wealth which the said foreigners amass, ought properly speaking to be portion of our own native Chinese people. By what principle of reason then, should these foreigners send in return a poisonous drug, which involves in destruction those very natives of China? Without meaning to say that the foreigners harbor such destructive intentions in their hearts, we yet positively assert that from their inordinate thirst after gain, they are perfectly careless about the injuries they inflict upon us! And such being the case, we should like to ask what has become of that conscience which heaven has implanted in the breasts of all men?

We have heard that in your own country opium is prohibited with the utmost strictness and severity:—this is a strong proof that you know full well how hurtful it is to mankind. Since then you do not permit it to injure your own country, you ought not to have the injurious drug transferred to another country, and above all others, how much less to the Inner Land! Of the products which China exports to your foreign countries, there is not one which is not beneficial to mankind in some shape or other. There are those which serve for food, those which are useful, and those which are calculated for re-sale;—but all are beneficial. Has China (we should like to ask) ever yet sent forth a noxious article from its soil? Not to speak of our tea and rhubarb, things which your foreign countries could not exist a single day without, if we of the Central Land were to grudge you what is beneficial, and not to compassionate [pity] your wants, then wherewithal could you foreigners manage to exist? And further, as regards your woolens, camlets, and longells [all woolen, woven fabrics], were it not that you get supplied with our native raw silk, you could not get these manufactured! If China were to grudge you those things which yield a profit, how could you foreigners scheme after any profit at all? Our other articles of food, such as sugar, ginger, cinnamon, &c., and our other articles for use, such as silk piece-goods, chinaware, &c., are all so many necessaries of life to you; how can we reckon up their number! On the other hand, the things that come from your foreign countries are only calculated to make presents of, or serve for mere amusement. It is quite the same to us if we have them, or if we have them not. If then these are of no material consequence to us of the Inner Land, what difficulty would there be in prohibiting and shutting our market against them? It is only that our heavenly dynasty most freely permits you to take off her tea, silk, and other commodities, and convey them for consumption everywhere, without the slightest stint or grudge, for no other reason, but that where a profit exists, we wish that it be diffused abroad for the benefit of all the earth!

. . . Now we have always heard that your highness possesses a most kind and benevolent heart, surely then you are incapable of doing or causing to be done unto another, that which you should not wish another to do unto you! We have at the same time heard that your ships which come to Canton do each and every of them carry a document granted by your highness' self, on which are written these words "you shall not be permitted to carry contraband goods"; this shows that the laws of your highness are in their origin both distinct and severe, and we can only suppose that because the ships coming here have been very numerous, due attention has not been given to search and examine; and for this reason it is that we now address you this public document, that you may clearly know how stern and severe are the laws of the central dynasty, and most certainly you will cause that they be not again rashly violated!

Moreover, we have heard that in London the metropolis where you dwell, as also in Scotland, Ireland, and other such places, no opium whatever is produced. It is only in sundry parts of your colonial kingdom of Hindostan, such as Bengal, Madras, Bombay, Patna, Malwa, Benares, Malacca, and other places where the very hills are covered with the opium plant, where tanks are made for the preparing of the drug; month by month, and year by year, the volume of the poison increases, its unclean stench ascends upwards, until heaven itself grows angry, and the very gods thereat get indignant! You, the queen of the said honorable nation, ought immediately to have the plant in those parts plucked up by the very root! Cause the land there to be hoed up afresh, sow in its stead the five grains, and if any man dare again to plant in these grounds a single poppy, visit his crime with the most severe punishment. By a truly benevolent system of government such as this, will you indeed reap advantage, and do away with a source of evil. Heaven must support you, and the gods will crown you with felicity! This will get for yourself the blessing of long life, and from this will proceed the security and stability of your descendants! . . .

Suppose the subject of another country were to come to England to trade, he would certainly be required to comply with the laws of England, then how much more does this apply to us of the celestial empire! Now it is a fixed statute of this empire, that any native Chinese who sells opium is punishable with death, and even he who merely smokes it, must not less die. Pause and reflect for a moment: if you foreigners did not bring the opium hither, where should our Chinese people get it to re-sell? It is you foreigners who involve our simple natives in the pit of death, and are they alone to be permitted to escape alive? If so much as one of those deprive one of our people of his life, he must forfeit his life in requital for that which he has taken: — how much more does this apply to him who by means of opium destroys his fellow-men? Does the havoc which he commits stop with a single life? Therefore it is that those foreigners who now import opium into the Central Land are condemned to be beheaded and strangled by the new statute, and this explains what we said at the beginning about plucking up the tree of evil, wherever it takes root, for the benefit of all nations.

We further find that during the second month of this present year, the superintendent of your honorable country, Elliot, viewing the law in relation to the prohibiting of opium as excessively severe, duly petitioned us, begging for "an extension of the term already limited, say five months for Hindostan and the different parts of India, and ten for England, after which they would obey and act in conformity with the new statute," and other words to the same effect. Now we, the high commissioner and colleagues, upon making a duly prepared memorial to the great emperor, have to feel grateful for his extraordinary goodness, for his redoubled compassion. Any one who within the next year and a half may by mistake bring opium to this country, if he will but voluntarily come forward, and deliver up the entire quantity, he shall be absolved from all punishment for his crime. If, however, the appointed term shall have expired, and there are still persons who continue to bring it, then such shall be accounted as knowingly violating the laws, and shall most assuredly be put to death! On no account shall we show mercy or clemency! This then may be called truly the extreme of benevolence, and the very perfection of justice!

Our celestial empire rules over ten thousand kingdoms! Most surely do we possess a measure of godlike majesty which ye cannot fathom! Still we cannot bear to slay or exterminate without previous warning, and it is for this reason that we now clearly make known to you the fixed laws of our land. If the foreign merchants of your said honorable nation desire to continue their commercial intercourse, they then must tremblingly obey our recorded statutes, they must cut off for ever the source from which the opium flows, and on no account make an experiment of our laws in their own persons! Let then your highness punish those of your subjects who may be criminal, do not endeavor to screen or conceal them, and thus you will secure peace and quietness to your possessions, thus will you more than ever display a proper sense of respect and obedience, and thus may we unitedly enjoy the common blessings of peace and happiness. What greater joy! What more complete felicity than this!

Let your highness immediately, upon the receipt of this communication, inform us promptly of the state of matters, and of the measures you are pursuing utterly to put a stop to the opium evil. Please let your reply be speedy. Do not on any account make excuses or procrastinate. A most important communication.

P. S. We annex an abstract of the new law, now about to be put in force. "Any foreigner or foreigners bringing opium to the Central Land, with design to sell the same, the principals shall most assuredly be decapitated, and the accessories strangled;—and all property (found on board the same ship) shall be confiscated. The space of a year and a half is granted, within the which, if any one bringing opium by mistake, shall voluntarily step forward and deliver it up, he shall be absolved from all consequences of his crime."

READING AND DISCUSSION QUESTIONS

1. Describe the tone of Lin's letter. What language or phrases establish his understanding of the relationship between China and Great Britain?
2. According to Lin, what should motivate Queen Victoria to halt the opium trade? How will she be rewarded?
3. What does Lin say about trade between China and the world? How do you imagine a British trader would respond to Lin's assertions?

26-2 | A Woodblock Print Depicts Japan's Modernization

Illustration of the Opening of Azuma Bridge in Tokyo (1887)

During the Meiji period (1868–1912) Japan undertook major efforts to modernize its government and economy along Western lines, seeing that as a necessary step to becoming militarily strong. Transportation and communication systems were seen as vital, and in the 1870s Japan introduced steamships, railways, and a telegraph system. Artists often celebrated these achievements in colorful woodblock prints, printed in large numbers to make them relatively affordable. Looking at the print on the next page (composed of three sheets of paper, measuring 14 by 28 inches altogether), think about the artist's choice of subject and what those who viewed the print would have found interesting or appealing.

The Metropolitan Museum of Art, New York/Gift of Lincoln Kirstein, 1959/www.metmuseum.org

READING AND DISCUSSION QUESTIONS

1. What are people doing in this print? How are they dressed?
2. What means of transportation do you see depicted?
3. Is there anything particularly modern about the bridge itself?

VIEWPOINTS

Reactions to Imperialism and Modernity

Most Western proponents of imperialism had little doubt that the conquest and colonization of Africa and Asia were a moral undertaking. Starting with the assumption that their own societies represented the pinnacle of human achievement, that they were citizens of the most "civilized" nations the world had ever seen, they argued that the West had a right, even a duty, to rule. The "backwards" peoples of the world could only benefit from Western guidance. Westerners were likened to firm but fair teachers, patiently pointing unruly and unpromising students in the direction of progress and morality. Not surprisingly, many non-Western critics of imperialism rejected such analogies, pointing out both the defects in Western societies and the value of their own traditions and accomplishments. But Asian countries did not all respond in the same ways. The three documents below were all written in the early years of the twentieth century by major leaders in Japan, India, and China. As you read these documents, focus on their understandings of the West. What is deemed good and what is not? What claims do they make about their own societies? What can explain the differences in their viewpoints?

26-3 | Japan Embraces the West

OKUMA SHIGENOBU, *Fifty Years of New Japan* (1910)

Okuma Shigenobu (1838–1922), active in the Meiji Restoration in Japan, became a leading political figure in the new government. He served briefly as prime minister in 1898 and afterward became president of Waseda University. The following passage is from a book that he edited, first published in 1910.

By comparing the Japan of fifty years ago with the Japan of to-day, it will be seen that she has gained considerably in the extent of her territory, as well as in her population, which now numbers nearly fifty millions. Her Government has become constitutional not only in name, but in fact, and her national education has attained to a high degree of excellence. In commerce and industry, the emblems of peace, she has also made rapid strides, until her import and export trades together amounted in 1907 to the enormous sum of 926,000,000 yen (£94,877,000), an increase of 84,000,000 yen (£8,606,000) on the previous year. Her general progress, during the short space of half a century, has been so sudden and swift that it presents a spectacle rare in the history of the world. This leap forward is the result of the stimulus which the country received on coming into contact with the civilization of Europe and America, and may well, in its broad sense, be regarded as a boon conferred by foreign intercourse. Foreign intercourse it was that animated the national consciousness of our people, who under the feudal system lived localized and disunited, and foreign intercourse it is that has enabled Japan to stand up as a world-Power. We possess today a powerful army and navy, but it was after Western models that we laid their foundations by establishing a system of conscription, in pursuance of the principle 'all our sons are soldiers,' by promoting military education, and by encouraging the manufacture of arms and the art of ship building. We have reorganized the systems of central and local administration, and effected reforms in the educational system of the empire. All this is nothing but the result of adopting the superior features of Western institutions. That Japan has been enabled to do so is a boon conferred on her by foreign intercourse, and it may be said that the nation has succeeded in this grand metamorphosis through the promptings and the influence of foreign civilization.

I take it that the Japanese people, as a race, possess the trait of broad-mindedness, little tainted by prejudice against things foreign, and ready to admire, aspire after, and assimilate good points in others. To keep the country's doors wide open and to be abreast of the world's progress is a national principle to which Japan has attached the greatest importance from its earliest days. During the twenty-five centuries of her history, only two and a half centuries

Fifty Years of New Japan, compiled by Count Shigēnobu Okuma, english version ed. by Marcus B. Huish, 2d ed. (London: Smith, Elder & Co., 1910), pp. 554–558. From HathiTrust digital library.

found her pursuing a policy of seclusion, and this was therefore a mere incident in her career. It is due to this principle that the moment there came a break in that narrow-minded policy the channel steadily widened for foreign intercourse, and the people, taking advantage of the opportunity to get into touch with Western civilization in all spheres of activity, cemented a national union and set out as one entity on the road to progress and development.

Soon after the Restoration the nation began to feel keenly the necessity of codifying her laws. For this there were two reasons. The first arose out of the country's foreign relations. In other words, the nation had so far advanced in knowledge that it could no longer bear the humiliation of remaining tied to the ex-territorial treaties, which had been entered into with the nations in Europe and America when the Tokugawa Shogunate reopened the country to foreign inter-course fifty years ago, in the days when we had as yet but scant knowledge of international usages. The signing of the treaties was the result of a misconception on our part, but thereby the Western Powers secured to themselves the right of ex-territoriality, and Japan came to be rated on the same level as China, Turkey, or Persia. It was therefore only natural that, as we obtained better information and awoke to the real aspect of affairs, we came to cherish an irrepressible desire for the revision of the treaties and to have the country placed in a position of equality. But prior to this being accomplished, we felt that it was only reasonable that we should prove that we had attained to a tolerable stage of civilization, and hence arose the urgent necessity to bring the laws of the land to a condition of efficiency.

The second reason had its origin in domestic matters. With the restoration of the de facto power of administration to the Imperial Government, the feudal system fell to pieces, and the incongruous laws and usages hitherto obtaining in the various semi-regal fiefs were useless for purposes of general application; in short, legal uniformity for the whole country became indispensable. At the same time, with their eyes opened to the trend of affairs abroad, our statesmen recognized the value of written codes of law, while their own conception of legal justice attained to a higher phase of development. Yet again, after a constitution had been given to the nation, establishing the great principle of government by law, the people could not be subject any longer to the arbitrary rule of a few officials. Thus it was only in the order of things that there should arise a desire to see good and just laws codified, and competent courts established to administer real justice, and to formulate a system whereby the rights and wrongs of the hundred-and-one acts of life should be determined, and everyone (native or foreigner) be brought under the equal control of the same laws. Hence not a day was to be lost in the compilation of codes of law, and consequently steps were at once taken to study the laws of France, Germany, England, and other countries, the result being the enactment of complete codes, comparing not unfavourably with those of the countries senior to us in modern civilization. This done, England, first of all, agreed to the revision of the old treaties, and she was followed by the United States, Germany, France, and others. Thus a thoroughly satisfactory solution of the difiicult problems which had vexed the nation for a quarter of a century, from the day of the grand restoration of Imperial administration, was effected. It was a success due to the national awakening, which, in its turn, had arisen out of the stimulus received from foreign civilization, culminating in the replacement of old defective statutes by comparatively perfect codes of law. But it is necessary to acknowledge that foreign intercourse primarily prompted this turn of affairs.

At the same time that these efforts were made to gain a position of equality with Western countries, a system of local autonomy was established, accompanied by efforts to arouse and encourage the spirit of local self-government. This again was an attempt to follow the example of advanced countries, and therefore a result of foreign intercourse. Innumerable, indeed, are the other instances in which our people derived benefit from the introduction from outside of material civilization. Improvements of our armaments is one of them, for it was the acquisition of accurate implements of war, which Western sciences taught us to make and use, that enabled us to face successfully national emergencies and achieve world-wide feats of glory. Although endowed with an intense spirit of patriotism, our people could not have issued victorious from modern warfare had they been without the weapons which Western science had invented. One may recall in this connection the Taiko's Korean expedition of 1592–98. Soldier of rare genius as he was, his weapons of war were not superior to those of his adversaries, and his memorable seven-years' campaign not only failed to accomplish any lasting results, but so exasperated certain critics that they preferred against him the charge of having tarnished the glory of the martial profession. From this it will be seen (and the fact is worthy of more attention than a passing notice) that we of to-day have been thoughtful enough to thoroughly reform our armaments and create an army with systematic training, by drawing liberally on the material progress of Western countries.

READING AND DISCUSSION QUESTIONS

1. What elements of Western institutions did Okuma see as positive?
2. What did the Japanese gain by adopting Western practices?
3. What did Okuma view as strong traits of the Japanese?

26-4 | Gandhi Rejects British "Civilization"

MOHANDAS GANDHI, *Indian Home Rule* (1909)

In his seminal 1909 pamphlet entitled "Indian Home Rule," Mohandas Gandhi (1869–1948) introduced the world to the key ideas that would inform the rest of his career as an activist for Indian independence. In the pamphlet, Gandhi rejected political violence and made the case for passive resistance. He also took direct aim at the claims of British imperialists that they were bringing civilization to India. In the excerpt included below, Gandhi contrasted European civilization with the "true civilization" of India. As you read it, think about the values Gandhi associated with each society. Why did he reject European civilization? What did he value most in his own civilization?

Homer A. Jack, ed., *The Gandhi Reader* (Bloomington: Indiana University Press, 1956), pp. 105–109. Copyright © 1956 by The Navajivan Trust. Used with permission.

Civilization

READER: . . . Now will you tell me something of what you have read and thought of this civilization?

EDITOR: Let us first consider what state of things is described by the word "civilization." Its true test lies in the fact that people living in it make bodily welfare the object of life. We will take some examples. The people of Europe today live in better-built houses than they did a hundred years ago. This is considered an emblem of civilization, and this is also a matter to promote bodily happiness. Formerly, they wore skins, and used spears as their weapons. Now, they wear long trousers, and, for embellishing their bodies, they wear a variety of clothing, and, instead of spears, they carry with them revolvers containing five or more chambers. If people of a certain country, who have hitherto not been in the habit of wearing much clothing, boots, etc., adopt European clothing, they are supposed to have become civilized out of savagery. Formerly, in Europe, people plowed their lands mainly by manual labor. Now, one man can plow a vast tract by means of steam engines and can thus amass great wealth. This is called a sign of civilization. Formerly, only a few men wrote valuable books. Now, anybody writes and prints anything he likes and poisons people's minds. Formerly, men traveled in wagons. Now, they fly through the air in trains at the rate of four hundred and more miles per day. This is considered the height of civilization. It has been stated that, as men progress, they shall be able to travel in airships and reach any part of the world in a few hours. Men will not need the use of their hands and feet. They will press a button, and they will have their clothing by their side. They will press another button, and they will have their newspaper. A third, and a motor-car will be in waiting for them. They will have a variety of delicately dished up food. Everything will be done by machinery. Formerly, when people wanted to fight with one another, they measured between them their bodily strength; now it is possible to take away thousands of lives by one man working behind a gun from a hill. This is civilization. Formerly, men worked in the open air only as much as they liked. Now thousands of workmen meet together and for the sake of maintenance work in factories or mines. Their condition is worse than that of beasts. They are obliged to work, at the risk of their lives, at most dangerous occupations, for the sake of millionaires. Formerly, men were made slaves under physical compulsion. Now they are enslaved by temptation of money and of the luxuries that money can buy. There are now diseases of which people never dreamt before, and an army of doctors is engaged in finding out their cures, and so hospitals have increased. This is a test of civilization. Formerly, special messengers were required and much expense was incurred in order to send letters; today, anyone can abuse his fellow by means of a letter for one penny. True, at the same cost, one can send one's thanks also. Formerly, people had two or three meals consisting of home-made bread and vegetables; now, they require something to eat every two hours so that they have hardly leisure for anything else. What more need I say? All this you can ascertain from several authoritative books. These are all true tests of civilization. And if anyone speaks to the contrary, know that he is ignorant. This civilization takes note neither of morality nor of religion. Its votaries calmly state that their business is not to teach religion. Some even consider it to be a superstitious growth. Others put on the cloak of religion, and prate about morality. Even a child can understand that in all I have described above there can be no inducement to morality. Civilization seeks to increase bodily comforts, and it fails miserably even in doing so.

This civilization is irreligion, and it has taken such a hold on the people in Europe that those who are in it appear to be half mad. They lack real physical strength or courage. They keep up their energy by intoxication. They can hardly be happy in solitude. Women, who should be the queens of households, wander in the streets or they slave away in factories. For the sake of a pittance, half a million women in England alone are laboring under trying circumstances in factories or similar institutions. This awful fact is one of the causes of the daily growing suffragette movement.

This civilization is such that one has only to be patient and it will be self-destroyed. According to the teaching of Mahomed this would be considered a Satanic Civilization. Hinduism calls it the Black Age. I cannot give you an adequate conception of it. It is eating into the vitals of the English nation. It must be shunned. Parliaments are really emblems of slavery. If you will sufficiently think over this, you will entertain the same opinion and cease to blame the English. They rather deserve our sympathy. They are a shrewd nation and I therefore believe that they will cast off the evil. They are enterprising and industrious, and their mode of thought is not inherently immoral. Neither are they bad at heart. I therefore respect them. Civilization is not an incurable disease, but it should never be forgotten that the English people are at present afflicted by it.

What Is True Civilization?

READER: You have denounced railways, lawyers and doctors. I can see that you will discard all machinery. What, then, is civilization?

EDITOR: The answer to that question is not difficult. I believe that the civilization India has evolved is not to be beaten in the world. Nothing can equal the seeds sown by our ancestors. Rome went, Greece shared the same fate; the might of the Pharaohs was broken; Japan has become westernized; of China nothing can be said; but India is still, somehow or other, sound at the foundation. The people of Europe learn their lessons from the writings of the men of Greece or Rome, which exist no longer in their former glory. In trying to learn from them, the Europeans imagine that they will avoid the mistakes of Greece and Rome. Such is their pitiable condition. In the midst of all this India remains immovable and that is her glory. It is a charge against India that her people are so uncivilized, ignorant, and solid, that it is not possible to induce them to adopt any changes. It is a charge really against our merit. What we have tested and found true on the anvil of experience, we dare not change. Many thrust their advice upon India, and she remains steady. This is her beauty: it is the sheet-anchor of our hope.

Civilization is that mode of conduct which points out to man the path of duty. Performance of duty and observance of morality are convertible terms. To observe morality is to attain mastery over our mind and our passions. So doing, we know ourselves. The Gujarati equivalent for civilization means "good conduct."

If this definition be correct, then India, as so many writers have shown, has nothing to learn from anybody else, and this is as it should be. We notice that the mind is a restless bird; the more it gets the more it wants, and still remains unsatisfied. The more we indulge our passions, the more unbridled they become. Our ancestors, therefore, set a limit to our indulgences. They saw that happiness was largely a mental condition. A man is not necessarily happy because he is rich, or unhappy because he is poor. The rich are often seen to be unhappy, the poor to be happy. Millions will always remain poor. Observing all this, our ancestors dissuaded us from luxuries and pleasures. We have managed with the same kind of plow as existed thousands of years ago. We have retained the same kind of cottages that we had in former times and our indigenous education remains the same as before. We have had no system of life-corroding competition. Each followed his own occupation or trade and charged a regulation wage. It was not that we did not know how to invent machinery, but our forefathers knew that, if we set our hearts after such things, we would become slaves and lose our moral fiber. They, therefore, after due deliberation decided that we should only do what we could with our hands and feet. They saw that our real happiness and health consisted in a proper use of our hands and feet. They further reasoned that large cities were a snare and a useless encumbrance and that people would not be happy in them, that there would be gangs of thieves and robbers, prostitution and vice flourishing in them and that poor men would be robbed by rich men. They were, therefore, satisfied with small villages. They saw that kings and their swords were inferior to the sword of ethics, and they, therefore, held the sovereigns of the earth to be inferior to the Rishis and the Fakirs.[1] A nation with a constitution like this is fitter to teach others than to learn from others. This nation had courts, lawyers and doctors, but they were all within bounds. Everybody knew that these professions were not particularly superior; moreover, these vakils and vaids[2] did not rob people; they were considered people's

---

[1] **the Rishis and the Fakirs:** Seers and holy men.
[2] **vakils and vaids:** Doctors of Indian medicine.

dependents, not their masters. Justice was tolerably fair. The ordinary rule was to avoid courts. There were no touts to lure people into them. This evil, too, was noticeable only in and around capitals. The common people lived independently and followed their agricultural occupation. They enjoyed true Home Rule. . . .

Now you see what I consider to be real civilization. Those who want to change conditions such as I have described are enemies of the country and are sinners.

READING AND DISCUSSION QUESTIONS

1. What evils did Gandhi associate with industrialization? Why did he believe that economic progress had little to do with social and moral progress?
2. How did Gandhi define "true civilization"? In his view, what marked Indian civilization as truly great?

26-5 | Sun Yatsen Calls on China to Take Its Rightful Place in the World

SUN YATSEN, *On the Three People's Principles and the Future of the Chinese People* (1906)

Trained as a Western physician in Hong Kong, Sun Yatsen (1866–1925) studied and traveled extensively and became an important revolutionary during the final years of the Qing Dynasty (1644–1912). While in exile after a failed coup, he formed the Tongmenghui revolutionary organization and won support among Chinese expatriates through his "Three Principles of the People," presented in this excerpt from a 1906 speech in Tokyo. Although the 1911 revolution occurred in his absence, he was selected as provisional president of the new Republic of China, a post he occupied for less than three months. However, his legacy as founder of the Guomindang (Nationalist Party) and his position as an iconic figure of Chinese modernity remain strong.

Let us pause to consider for a moment: Where is the nation? Where is the political power? Actually, we are already a people without a nation! The population of the globe is only one billion, several hundred million; we Han,[3] being 400 million, comprise one-fourth of that population.

Our nation is the most populous, most ancient, and most civilized in the world, yet today we are a lost nation. Isn't that enormously bizarre? The African

---

Prescriptions for Saving China: Selected Writings of Sun Yat-sen, ed. Julie Lee Wei, Ramon H. Myers, and Donald G. Gillin (Palo Alto, Calif.: Hoover Institution Press, 1994). Translation copyright © 1994 by the Board of Trustees of the Leland Stanford Junior University. Reprinted with permission of the publisher, Hoover Institution Press.

[3]**Han:** The Chinese people.

nation of the Transvaal has a population of only 200,000, yet when Britain tried to destroy it, the fighting lasted three years.[4] The Philippines have a population of only several million, but when America tried to subdue it, hostilities persisted for several years.[5] Is it possible that the Han will gladly be a lost nation?

We Han are now swiftly being caught up in a tidal wave of nationalist revolution, yet the Manchus continue to discriminate against the Han. They boast that their forefathers conquered the Han because of their superior unity and military strength and that they intend to retain these qualities so as to dominate the Han forever. . . . Certainly, once we Han unite, our power will be thousands of times greater than theirs, and the success of the nationalist revolution will be assured.

As for the Principle of Democracy, it is the foundation of the political revolution. . . . For several thousand years China has been a monarchical autocracy, a type of political system intolerable to those living in freedom and equality. A nationalist revolution is not itself sufficient to get rid of such a system. Think for a moment: When the founder of the Ming dynasty expelled the Mongols and restored Chinese rule, the nationalist revolution triumphed, but his political system was only too similar to those of the Han, Tang, and Song dynasties.[6] Consequently, after another three hundred years, foreigners again began to invade China. This is the result of the inadequacy of the political system, so that a political revolution is an absolute necessity. . . . The aim of the political revolution is to create a constitutional, democratic political system. . . .

* * *

Now, let me begin by discussing the origins of the Principle of the People's Livelihood, a principle that began to flourish only in the latter part of the nineteenth century. . . . As civilization advanced, people relied less on physical labor and more on natural forces, since electricity and steam could accomplish things a thousand times faster than human physical strength. For example, in antiquity a single man tilling the land could harvest at best enough grain to feed a few people, notwithstanding his toil and trouble. Now, however, as a result of the development of scientific agriculture, one man can grow more than enough to feed a thousand people because he can use machinery instead of his limbs, with a consequent increase in efficiency. . . .

In view of this, everyone in Europe and America should be living in a state of plenty and happiness undreamed of in antiquity. If we look around, however, we see that conditions in those countries are precisely the opposite. Statistically, Britain's wealth has increased more than several thousandfold over the previous

---

[4]**The African nation . . . three years:** A reference to the South African War (1899–1902).

[5]**The Philippines . . . several years:** Between 1899 and 1901, Filipinos fought against the United States after the United States took over the Philippines from Spain at the end of the Spanish-American War.

[6]**When the founder . . . dynasties:** The Ming Dynasty ruled from 1368 to 1644 C.E.; the Han (206 B.C.E.–220 C.E.), Tang (618–907 C.E.), and Song (960–1279 C.E.) were earlier Chinese dynasties.

generation, yet poverty of the people has also increased several thousandfold over the previous generation. Moreover, the rich are extremely few, and the poor extremely numerous. This is because the power of human labor is no match for the power of capital. In antiquity, agriculture and industry depended completely on human labor; but now, with the development of natural forces that human labor cannot match, agriculture and industry have fallen completely into the hands of capitalists. The greater the amount of capital, the more abundant the resources that can be utilized. Unable to compete, the poor have naturally been reduced to destitution. . . .

Indeed, this constitutes a lesson for China. . . . Civilization yields both good and bad fruits, and we should embrace the good and reject the bad. In the countries of Europe and America, the rich monopolize the good fruits of civilization, while the poor suffer from its evil fruits. . . . Our current revolution will create a nation that not only belongs to the citizenry but is socially responsible. Certainly, there will be nothing comparable to it in Europe or America.

Why have Europe and America failed to solve their social problems? Because they have not solved their land problem. Generally speaking, wherever civilization is advanced, the price of land increases with each passing day. . . . In China capitalists have not yet emerged, so that for several thousand years there has been no increase in land prices. . . . After the revolution, however, conditions in China will be different. For example, land prices in Hong Kong and Shanghai are currently as much as several hundred times higher than those in the interior. This increment is the result of the advance of civilization and the development of communications. It is inevitable that, as the entire nation advances, land prices everywhere will rise accordingly. . . . Fifty years ago, land along the banks of the Huangpu River in Shanghai was worth up to a million dollars a *mou* [1.5 acres]. This is evidence of the clearest sort, from which we can see that in the future the rich will get richer every day, and the poor poorer. . . . Consequently, we must come up with a solution now. . . .

With respect to a solution, although the socialists have different opinions, the procedure I most favor is land valuation. For example, if a landlord has land worth 1,000 dollars, its price can be set at 1,000 or even 2,000 dollars. Perhaps in the future, after communications have been developed, the value of his land will rise to 10,000 dollars; the owner should receive 2,000, which entails a profit and no loss, and the 8,000 increment will go to the state. Such an arrangement will greatly benefit both the state and the people's livelihood. Naturally, it will also eliminate the shortcomings that have permitted a few rich people to monopolize wealth. This is the simplest, most convenient, and most feasible method. . . .

Once we adopt this method, the more civilization advances, the greater the wealth of the nation, and then we can be sure our financial problems will not become difficult to handle. After the excessive taxes of the present have been abolished, the price of consumer goods will gradually fall and the people will become increasingly prosperous. We will forever abolish the vicious taxation policies that have prevailed for several thousand years. . . . After China's social revolution is accomplished, private individuals will never again have to pay taxes. The collection of land revenues alone will make China the richest nation on earth. . . .

Obviously, . . . it is necessary to give considerable attention to what the constitution of the Republic of China should be. . . . The British constitution embodies the so-called separation of powers into executive, legislative, and judicial, all mutually independent. . . . The Frenchman[7] later embraced the British system and melded it with his own ideals to create his own school of thought. The American constitution was based on Montesquieu's theories but went further in clearly demarcating the separation of powers. . . . As to the future constitution of the Republic of China, I propose that we introduce a new principle, that of the "five separate powers."

Under this system, there will be two other powers in addition to the three powers just discussed. One is the examination power. . . . American officials are either elected or appointed. . . .

With respect to elections, those endowed with eloquence ingratiated themselves with the public and won elections, while those who had learning and ideals but lacked eloquence were ignored. Consequently, members of America's House of Representatives have often been foolish and ignorant people who have made its history quite ridiculous. As for appointees, they all come and go with the president. The Democratic and Republican parties have consistently taken turns holding power, and whenever a president is replaced, cabinet members and other officials, comprising no fewer than 60,000–70,000 people, including the postmaster general, are also replaced. As a result, the corruption and laxity of American politics are unparalleled among the nations of the world. . . . Therefore, the future constitution of the Republic of China must provide for an independent branch expressly responsible for civil service examinations. Furthermore, all officials, however high their rank, must undergo examinations in order to determine their qualifications. Whether elected or appointed, officials must pass those examinations before assuming office. This procedure will eliminate such evils as blind obedience, electoral abuses, and favoritism. . . .

The other power is the supervisory power, responsible for monitoring matters involving impeachment. For reasons that should be evident to all, such a branch is indispensable to any nation. The future constitution of the Republic of China must provide for an independent branch. Since ancient times, China had a supervisory organization, the Censorate,[8] to monitor the traditional social order. Inasmuch as it was merely a servant of the monarchy, however, it was ineffectual. . . .

With this added to the four powers already discussed, there will be five separate powers. That constitution will form the basis of the sound government of a nation that belongs to its own race, to its own citizens, and to its own society.

---

[7]**the Frenchman:** Montesquieu (1689–1755), a French political philosopher who argued that individual freedom is safest when the three powers of government—the judicial, executive, and legislative—are kept separate in a state.

[8]**the Censorate:** A unique feature of Chinese government during the Ming and Qing eras. Also called the Board of Censors, it was responsible for reviewing the conduct of officials and reporting any offenses to the emperor.

This will be the greatest good fortune for our 400 million Han people. I presume that you gentlemen are willing to undertake and complete this task. It is my greatest hope.

READING AND DISCUSSION QUESTIONS

1. Sun presents his first principle only indirectly in the first three paragraphs of this speech. Describe what you think that principle is, based on your reading of the speech.
2. Sun mentions the Han and the Manchu. Why do you think he uses ethnic groups to describe the situation in China?
3. What are Sun's second and third principles? What distinction does he make between the third principle and socialism?
4. How does Sun invoke Western countries to strengthen the argument for his three principles?

VIEWPOINTS COMPARATIVE QUESTIONS

1. Was there anything on which Okuma, Gandhi, and Sun would have agreed?
2. How did each author understand imperialism?
3. How might a Western imperialist have responded to these documents? What counter-arguments might such a person have made in response?

■ COMPARATIVE QUESTIONS ■

1. The documents in this chapter show different ways that Asian cultures engaged with Western modernity. Describe some of those forms of engagement.
2. Several of the documents deal with the question of violence, either impending or ongoing. How does the position (or positions) taken in each document show a tolerance of or distaste for violence? How is violence justified, and why? How and why is it condemned?

The Americas in the Age of Liberalism
1810–1917

During the nineteenth century, rebellions and revolutions overturned long-established patterns of European colonial rule throughout the Americas. The newly independent countries focused on nation building and economic development. They struggled to establish systems of government and new trade patterns and to address issues of land management, urbanization, and regional and ethnic differences. As a result, internal unrest, civil war, and wars between neighboring countries were common across the Americas. The century also saw the gradual consolidation of national territory at the expense of indigenous populations who had resisted colonial powers. Throughout the Americas, African slavery was slowly abolished, sometimes violently as in the case of the United States. With national territory consolidated, economies stabilized, and slavery abolished, the Americas received swelling numbers of immigrants, particularly from Europe, Russia, the Middle East, South Asia, and East Asia.

27-1 | Bolívar Identifies the Challenges Latin America Faces
SIMÓN BOLÍVAR, *Jamaica Letter* (1815)

Simón Bolívar (1783–1830), the son of a wealthy colonial family whose ancestors had been in Venezuela since the sixteenth century, was educated in both Enlightenment ideals and military science. He rose to prominence during the 1810s, when American rebels took advantage of Napoleon's occupation of Spain and formed independent states in former Spanish colonies. Despite early revolutionary successes that earned him the title of *El Libertador*, or "the Liberator," Bolívar fled to Jamaica and then Haiti in 1815. Returning to Venezuela with

Guillermo A. Sherwell, *Simón Bolívar, El Libertador* (Washington, D.C.: Byron S. Adams, 1921), pp. 89–92.

Haitian support the following year, he launched the campaign that would liberate much of Latin America from Spanish rule. Bolívar's goals of freedom and equality were compromised in their execution by Latin American political and economic interests, and Bolívar died disenchanted with the "ungovernable" continent. His famous Jamaica Letter outlines his grievances and hopes for American independence.

Europe itself, . . . by reasons of wholesome policies, should have prepared and carried out the plan of American independence, not only because it is so required for the balance of the world, but because this is a legitimate and safe means of obtaining commercial posts on the other side of the ocean. . . .

I consider the actual state of America as when, after the collapse of the Roman Empire, each member constituted a political system in conformity with its interests and position, but with this great difference: that these scattered members reestablished the old nationalities with the alterations required by circumstances or events. But we, who scarcely keep a vestige of things of the past, and who, on the other hand, are not Indians nor Europeans, but a mixture of the legitimate owners of the country and the usurping Spaniards; in short, we, being Americans by birth and with rights equal to those of Europe, have to dispute these rights with the men of the country, and to maintain ourselves against the possession of the invaders. Thus, we find ourselves in the most extraordinary and complicated predicament. . . .

Americans, under the Spanish system now in vigor, have in society no other place than that of serfs fit for work, and, at the most, that of simple consumers; and even this is limited by absurd restrictions, such as prohibition of the cultivation of European products; the monopoly of certain goods in the hands of the king; the prevention of the establishment in America of factories not possessed by Spain; the exclusive privileges of trade, even regarding the necessities of life; the obstacles placed in the way of the American provinces so that they may not deal with each other, nor have understandings, nor trade. In short, do you want to know what was our lot? The fields, in which to cultivate indigo, cochineal,[1] coffee, sugar cane, cocoa, cotton; the solitary plains, to breed cattle; the deserts, to hunt the wild beasts; the bosom of the earth, to extract gold, with which that avaricious country was never satisfied.

We were never viceroys or governors except by very extraordinary reasons; archbishops and bishops, seldom; ambassadors, never; military men, only as subordinates; nobles, without privileges; lastly, we were neither magistrates nor financiers, and hardly merchants. All this we had to accept in direct opposition to our institutions.

The Americans have risen suddenly and without previous preparation and without previous knowledge and, what is more deplorable, without experience in public affairs, to assume in the world the eminent dignity of legislators, magistrates, administrators of the public treasury, diplomats, generals and all the supreme and subordinate authorities which form the hierarchy of an organized state.

---

[1]**cochineal:** An insect from which valuable (and exportable) carmine dye is derived.

The events of the mainland have proved that perfectly representative institutions do not agree with our character, habits, and present state of enlightenment.... So long as our fellow citizens do not acquire the talents and the political virtues which distinguish our brothers of the North, who have a system of government altogether popular in character, I am very much afraid these institutions might lead to our ruin instead of aiding us....

I desire more than anybody else to see the formation in America of the greatest nation in the world, not so much as to its extension and wealth as to its glory and freedom.

READING AND DISCUSSION QUESTIONS

1. As Bolívar describes it, what is the advantage of American independence for Europe?

2. How did Europe (especially Spain) treat its American holdings, according to Bolívar?

3. What are the problems that Bolívar predicts for American self-governance? What kind of a system does he propose?

27-2 | Mary Seacole Reflects on Race and Class in the Americas

MARY SEACOLE, *Wonderful Adventures of Mrs. Seacole in Many Lands* (1857)

Mary Seacole was born in Jamaica in 1805, the daughter of a Scottish soldier and a local Jamaican Creole woman. She learned folk medical treatment from her mother, who ran a boarding house, and gradually took to running hotels and working as a nurse. During the Crimean War she volunteered to go to the Crimea to treat wounded soldiers. Shortly afterward, in 1857, she wrote an autobiography, an excerpt of which follows.

I was born in the town of Kingston, in the island of Jamaica, some time in the present century.... I am a Creole, and have good Scotch blood coursing in my veins. My father was a soldier, of an old Scotch family; and to him I often trace my affection for a camp-life, and my sympathy with what I have heard my friends call "the pomp, pride, and circumstance of glorious war." Many people have also traced to my Scotch blood that energy and activity which are not always found in the Creole race, and which have carried me to so many varied scenes: and perhaps they are right. I have often heard the term "lazy Creole" applied to my country people; but I am sure I do not know what it is to be indolent....

Mary Seacole, *Wonderful Adventures of Mrs. Seacole in Many Lands* (London: Blackwood, 1857), pp. 1–17.

My mother kept a boarding-house in Kingston, and was, like very many of the Creole women, an admirable doctress; in high repute with the officers of both services, and their wives, who were from time to time stationed at Kingston. It was very natural that I should inherit her tastes; and so I had from early youth a yearning for medical knowledge and practice which has never deserted me. . . .

[After returning to Kingston from a trip in 1825], I nursed my old indulgent patroness in her last long illness. After she died, in my arms, I went to my mother's house, where I stayed, making myself useful in a variety of ways, and learning a great deal of Creole medicinal art, until I couldn't find courage to say "no" to a certain arrangement timidly proposed by Mr. Seacole, but married him, and took him down to Black River, where we established a store. Poor man! He was very delicate; and before I undertook the charge of him, several doctors had expressed most unfavorable opinions of his health. I kept him alive by kind nursing and attention as long as I could; but at last he grew so ill that we left Black River, and returned to my mother's house at Kingston.

Within a month of our arrival there he died. This was my first great trouble, and I felt it bitterly. For days I never stirred — lost to all that passed around me in a dull stupor of despair. If you had told me that the time would soon come when I should remember this sorrow calmly, I should not have believed it possible: and yet it was so. I do not think that we hot-blooded Creoles sorrow less for showing it so impetuously; but I do think that the sharp edge of our grief wears down sooner than theirs who preserve an outward demeanor of calmness, and nurse their woe secretly in their hearts. . . .

In the year 1850, the cholera swept over the island of Jamaica with terrible force. . . . While the cholera raged, I had but too many opportunities of watching its nature, and from a Dr. B—, who was then lodging in my house, received many hints as to its treatment which I afterwards found invaluable.

Early in the same year my brother had left Kingston for the Isthmus of Panama, then the great high-road to and from golden California, where he had established a considerable store and hotel. Ever since he had done so, I had found some difficulty in checking my reviving disposition to roam, and at last persuading myself that I might be of use to him (he was far from strong), I resigned my house into the hands of a cousin, and made arrangements to journey to Chagres. . . .

All my readers must know — a glance at the map will show it to those who do not — that between North America and the envied shores of California stretches a little neck of land, insignificant-looking enough on the map, dividing the Atlantic from the Pacific. By crossing this, the travellers from America avoided a long, weary, and dangerous sea voyage round Cape Horn, or an almost impossible journey by land.

But that journey across the Isthmus, insignificant in distance as it was, was by no means an easy one. It seemed as if nature had determined to throw every conceivable obstacle in the way of those who should seek to join the two great oceans of the world. . . .

When, after passing Chagres, an old-world, tumble-down town, for about seven miles, the steamer reached Navy Bay, I thought I had never seen a more luckless, dreary spot. . . . It seemed as capital a nursery for ague and fever as Death could hit upon anywhere, and those on board the steamer who knew it confirmed my opinion. As we arrived a steady down-pour of rain was falling from an inky sky; the white men who met us on the wharf appeared ghostly and wraith-like, and the very negroes seemed pale and wan. The news which met us did not tempt me to lose any time in getting up the country to my brother. According to all accounts, fever and ague, with some minor diseases, especially dropsy, were having it all their own way at Navy Bay, and, although I only stayed one night in the place, my medicine chest was called into requisition. But the sufferers wanted remedies which I could not give them—warmth, nourishment, and fresh air. Beneath leaky tents, damp huts, and even under broken railway wagons, I saw men dying from sheer exhaustion. Indeed, I was very glad when, with the morning, the crowd, as the Yankees called the bands of pilgrims to and from California, made ready to ascend to Panama. . . .

It was not so easy to hire a boat as I had been led to expect. The large crowd had made the boatmen somewhat exorbitant in their demands. . . . There were several reasons why I should engage one for my own exclusive use, instead of sharing one with some of my traveling companions. In the first place, my luggage was somewhat bulky; and, in the second place, my experience of travel had not failed to teach me that Americans (even from the Northern States) are always uncomfortable in the company of colored people, and very often show this feeling in stronger ways than by sour looks and rude words. I think, if I have a little prejudice against our cousins across the Atlantic—and I do confess to a little—it is not unreasonable. I have a few shades of deeper brown upon my skin which shows me related—and I am proud of the relationship—to those poor mortals whom you once held enslaved, and whose bodies America still owns. And having this bond, and knowing what slavery is; having seen with my eyes and heard with my ears proof positive enough of its horrors—let others affect to doubt them if they will—is it surprising that I should be some-what impatient of the airs of superiority which many Americans have endeavored to assume over me? Mind, I am not speaking of all. I have met with some delightful exceptions.

READING AND DISCUSSION QUESTIONS

1. How does Mary Seacole understand race?

2. How does she understand disease? What health problems does she see as most serious?

3. How does Seacole describe geography and the environment?

VIEWPOINTS

Female Abolitionists Make the Case Against Slavery

From the abolitionist movement's beginnings in the eighteenth century, women played important roles in the fight against slavery. Despite discrimination from male abolitionists and social prohibitions against female activism, female abolitionists were in the forefront of the movement, writing antislavery literature, participating in abolitionist organizations, and speaking out against the evils of slavery. For many, participation in the abolitionist movement inspired an equally strong commitment to the cause of women's rights. It is no coincidence that the 1840s saw both the intensification of the struggle over slavery and the organization of the Seneca Falls women's rights convention. This feature includes excerpts from the writings of two of the most important female abolitionists: Angelina Grimke and Harriet Beecher Stowe. As you read them, ask yourself how their antislavery activism might have been shaped by their gender. What differences between Grimke and Stowe do you note in this context?

27-3 | Angelina Grimke Explains the Fundamental Principle of Abolitionism

ANGELINA GRIMKE, *Letters to Catharine E. Beecher* (1838)

Angelina Grimke (1805–1879) was the daughter of a prominent South Carolina slave owner. From a young age, Grimke demonstrated a strong will and the courage of her convictions. Her personal religious journey brought her into contact with antislavery activists, and she joined the movement, leaving her family and moving to Philadelphia in 1829 to pursue her new calling. In 1837, she and her sister Sarah became the first women to conduct a speaking tour on behalf of the American Anti-Slavery Society, scandalizing traditionalists by appearing before mixed-gender audiences. The excerpt included here was written by Grimke in response to a book by Catharine E. Beecher, the daughter of a prominent minister and an opponent of slavery. While Grimke wanted an immediate end to slavery through any means short of violence, Beecher was in favor of gradual emancipation through persuasion and compromise. As you read Grimke's letter, ask yourself why her argument was incompatible with Beecher's approach. What connection can you make between Grimke's position on slavery and her willingness to transgress conventional social mores?

Angelina Grimke, *Letters to Catharine E. Beecher* (Boston: Isaac Knapp, 1838), pp. 4–5.

The great fundamental principle of Abolitionists is, that man cannot rightfully hold his fellow man as property. Therefore, we affirm, that *every slaveholder is a man-stealer*. We do so, for the following reasons: to steal a man is to rob him of himself. It matters not whether this be done in Guinea, or Carolina; a man is a *man*, and as a man he has *inalienable* rights, among which is the right to personal *liberty*. Now if every man has an *inalienable* right to personal liberty, it follows, that he cannot rightfully be reduced to slavery. But I find in these United States, 2,250,000 men, women and children, robbed of that to which they have an *inalienable* right. How comes this to pass? Where millions are plundered, are there no *plunderers*? If, then, the slaves have been robbed of their liberty, *who* has robbed them? Not the man who stole their forefathers from Africa, but he who now holds them in bondage; no matter *how* they came into his possession, whether he inherited them, or bought them, or seized them at their birth on his own plantation. The only difference I can see between the original man-stealer, who caught the African in his native country, and the American slaveholder, is, that the former committed *one* act of robbery, while the other perpetrates the same crime *continually*. Slaveholding is the perpetrating of acts, all of the same kind, in a *series*, the first of which is technically called man-stealing. The *first* act robbed the man of himself; and the same state of mind that prompted *that act, keeps up the series*, having *taken* his all from him: it *keeps* his all from him, not only *refusing* to *restore*, but still robbing him of all he gets, and as fast as he gets it. Slaveholding, then, is *the constant or habitual perpetration of the act of man-stealing. To make* a slave is *man-stealing — the* act *itself —* to *hold* him such is man-stealing — the *habit*, the *permanent* state, made up of *individual* acts. In other words — to *begin* to hold a slave is man-stealing — to *keep on* holding him is merely a *repetition* of the first act — a doing the same identical thing *all the time.* A series of the same acts continued for a length of time is a *habit — a permanent state*. And the *first* of this series of the *same* acts that make up this *habit* or state is just like all the rest.

If every slave has a right to freedom, then surely the man who withholds that right from him to-day is a man-stealer, though he may not be the first person who has robbed him of it. Hence we find that Wesley says — "Men-*buyers* are *exactly on a level* with men-*stealers*." And again — "Much less is it possible that any child of man should ever be *born a slave*." Hear also Jonathan Edwards — "To hold a man in a state of slavery, is to be *every day guilty* of robbing him of his liberty, or of *man-stealing*." And Grotius says — "Those are men-stealers who abduct, *keep*, sell or buy *slaves* or freemen."

READING AND DISCUSSION QUESTIONS

1. According to Grimke, what is the fundamental principle of abolitionism?

2. Why does Grimke make no distinction between slave owners and those who participated in the slave trade?

3. What connections can you make between this letter and Grimke's uncompromising approach to the fight against slavery?

27-4 | A Slave Dealer Explains His Craft

HARRIET BEECHER STOWE, From *Uncle Tom's Cabin* (1852)

The 1852 publication of *Uncle Tom's Cabin* by Harriet Beecher Stowe (1811–1896) was a pivotal event in the American abolitionist movement. An instant success, the novel appealed to the sentimentalism of the mid-nineteenth-century reading public, humanizing the issue of slavery for many Northerners by presenting readers with sympathetic slave characters and then placing those characters in emotionally charged circumstances. The opening scene of the novel provides a good example of Stowe's approach. In it, Mr. Shelby, a slave owner, and Mr. Haley, a slave trader, negotiate the possible sale of a young boy and his mother. The boy, Harry, is innocent and charming; the mother, Eliza, beautiful, sincere, and virtuous. As the scene develops, an implicit contrast is created between the absence of feeling displayed by the slave trader and the depth of emotion the reader imagines the mother and child will experience if their parting comes to pass. As you read this excerpt, place yourself in the position of a nineteenth-century reader. How might such a reader have responded to the scene? Why?

"Hurrah! bravo! what a young 'un!" said Haley; "that chap's a case, I'll promise. Tell you what," said he, suddenly clapping his hand on Mr. Shelby's shoulder, "fling in that chap, and I'll settle the business — I will. Come, now, if that ain't doing the thing up about the rightest."

At this moment, the door was pushed gently open, and a young quadroon woman, apparently about twenty-five, entered the room.

There needed only a glance from the child to her, to identify her as its mother. There was the same rich, full, dark eye, with its long lashes; the same ripples of silky black hair. The brown of her complexion gave way on the cheek to a perceptible flush, which deepened as she saw the gaze of the strange man fixed upon her in bold and undisguised admiration. Her dress was of the neatest possible fit, and set off to advantage her finely-molded shape. A delicately formed hand, and a trim foot and ankle, were items of appearance that did not escape the quick eye of the trader, well used to run up at a glance the points of a fine female article.

"Well, Eliza?" said her master, as she stopped and looked hesitatingly at him.

"I was looking for Harry, please, sir;" and the boy bounded toward her, showing his spoils, which he had gathered in the skirt of his robe.

"Well, take him away, then," said Mr. Shelby; and hastily she withdrew, carrying the child on her arm.

"By Jupiter!" said the trader, turning to him in admiration, "there's an article now! You might make your fortune on that ar gal in Orleans, any day. I've seen over a thousand, in my day, paid down for gals not a bit handsomer."

"I don't want to make my fortune on her," said Mr. Shelby, drily; and, seeking to turn the conversation, he uncorked a bottle of fresh wine, and asked his companion's opinion of it.

Harriet Beecher Stowe, *Uncle Tom's Cabin* (London: John Cassell, 1852), pp. 3–5.

"Capital, sir—first chop!" said the trader; then turning, and slapping his hand familiarly on Shelby's shoulder, he added: "Come, how will you trade about the gal? what shall I say for her? what'll you take?"

"Mr. Haley, she is not to be sold," said Shelby; "my wife would not part with her for her weight in gold."

"Ay, ay, women always say such things, 'cause they ha'nt no sort of calculation. Just show 'em how many watches, feathers, and trinkets one's weight in gold would buy, and that alters the case, *I* reckon."

"I tell you, Haley, this must not be spoken of. I say no, and I mean no," said Shelby, decidedly.

"Well, you'll let me have the boy though?" said the trader; "you must own I've come down pretty handsomely for him."

"What on earth can you want with the child?" said Shelby.

"Why, I've got a friend that's going into this yer branch of the business— wants to buy up handsome boys to raise for the market. Fancy articles entirely—sell for waiters, and so on, to rich 'uns, that can pay for handsome 'uns. It sets off one of yer great places—a real handsome boy to open door, wait, and tend. They fetch a good sum; and this little devil is such a comical, musical concern, he's just the article."

"I would rather not sell him," said Mr. Shelby, thoughtfully; "the fact is, sir, I'm a humane man, and I hate to take the boy from his mother, sir."

"Oh, you do?—La! yes—something of that ar nature. I understand, perfectly. It is mighty onpleasant getting on with women sometimes. I al'ays hates these yer screechin,' screamin' times. They are *mighty* onpleasant; but, as I manages business, I generally avoids 'em, sir. Now, what if you get the girl off for a day, or a week, or so; then the thing's done quietly,—all over before she comes home. Your wife might get her some ear-rings, or a new gown, or some such truck, to make up with her."

"I'm afraid not."

"Lor bless ye, yes! These critters an't like white folks, you know; they gets over things, only manage right. Now, they say," said Haley, assuming a candid and confidential air, "that this kind o' trade is hardening to the feelings; but I never found it so. Fact is, I never could do things up the way some fellers manage the business. I've seen 'em as would pull a woman's child out of her arms, and set him up to sell, and she screechin' like mad all the time;—very bad policy—damages the article—makes 'em quite unfit for service sometimes. I knew a real handsome gal once, in Orleans, as was entirely ruined by this sort o' handling. The fellow that was trading for her didn't want her baby; and she was one of your real high sort, when her blood was up. I tell you, she squeezed up her child in her arms, and talked, and went on real awful. It kinder makes my blood run cold to think on't; and when they carried off the child, and locked her up, she jest went ravin' mad, and died in a week. Clear waste, sir, of a thousand dollars, just for want of management,—there's where 't is. It's always best to do the humane thing, sir; that's been *my* experience."

And the trader leaned back in his chair, and folded his arm, with an air of virtuous decision, apparently considering himself a second Wilberforce.[2]

The subject appeared to interest the gentleman deeply; for while Mr. Shelby was thoughtfully peeling an orange, Haley broke out afresh, with becoming diffidence, but as if actually driven by the force of truth to say a few words more.

"It don't look well, now, for a feller to be praisin' himself; but I say it jest because it's the truth. I believe I'm reckoned to bring in about the finest droves of niggers that is brought in—at least I've been told so; if I have once, I reckon I have a hundred times—all in good case—fat and likely, and I lose as few as any man in the business. And I lays it all to my management, sir; and humanity, sir, I may say, is the great pillar of *my* management."

Mr. Shelby did not know what to say, and so he said, "Indeed!"

"Now, I've been laughed at for my notions, sir, and I've been talked to. They an't pop'lar, and they an't common; but I stuck to 'em, sir; I've stuck to 'em, and realized well on 'em; yes, sir, they have paid their passage, I may say"; and the trader laughed at his joke.

There was something so piquant and original in these elucidations of humanity, that Mr. Shelby could not help laughing in company. Perhaps you laugh too, dear reader; but you know humanity comes out in a variety of strange forms now-a-days, and there is no end to the odd things that humane people will say and do.

READING AND DISCUSSION QUESTIONS

1. What does the scene suggest about Eliza's morals? How does her reaction to Mr. Haley's evident lust help establish her as a sympathetic character?

2. What importance should we attach to Mr. Shelby's references to his wife's opposition to the sale of the family's slaves? What do these references suggest about Stowe's views on the moral and emotional differences between men and women?

3. How would you explain the popularity of *Uncle Tom's Cabin*? Why might a nineteenth-century audience have found it so moving and persuasive?

VIEWPOINTS COMPARATIVE QUESTIONS

1. Compare and contrast Grimke's and Stowe's arguments against slavery. How might each have responded to the other's work?

2. How did each author appeal to the basic assumptions and beliefs of her audience? How did they seek to change those assumptions and beliefs?

---

[2]**Wilberforce:** William Wilberforce (1759–1833), British politician and antislavery activist.

27-5 | Argentina's Conquest and Displacement of Indigenous Peoples

JUAN MANUEL BLANES, *Military Occupation of the Black River During the Expedition of General Julio A. Roca* (1889)

Between 1878 and 1885, the government of Argentina conducted a devastating military campaign to seize indigenous lands in the northwest and south of Argentina. The campaign was called the Conquest of the Desert, implying that the areas that were conquered were simple wilderness. Uruguayan painter Juan Manuel Blanes (1830–1901) was commissioned by Argentina's newly created National Historical Museum to compose an educational painting about the military campaign. The main subject of the painting, General Julio Roca, had just served as president of Argentina from 1880 to 1886, and he would hold the presidency again between 1898 and 1904. Roca appears in the central foreground in the lighter coat.

Album/Alamy Stock Photo

READING AND DISCUSSION QUESTIONS

1. How are the soldiers depicted, and what does this representation convey about Argentina?

2. Where are indigenous peoples in this painting, and what does their placement tell us?

▪ COMPARATIVE QUESTIONS ▪

1. How might Seacole have commented on the difference between the Americas and Europe cited by Bolívar?

2. What light do the documents in this chapter shed on racial and economic inequality in the Americas? Which groups were in the best position to benefit from the opportunities the Americas presented? Which were in the worst position?

3. Compare and contrast Harriet Beecher Stowe's account of slavery with that of Olaudah Equiano (see Document 20-3). What techniques of persuasion did both authors employ?

28

World War and Revolution
1914–1929

World War I (1914–1918) changed the global balance of economic, military, and political power. Though the conflict started as a dispute between two small eastern European nations over a political assassination, a web of national alliances and long-suppressed hostilities over lost territory helped escalate it into four years of war that involved most major countries. The "Great War" led to a rise in Asian nationalism; the decline of Great Britain, France, and Germany as world powers; and the ascent of the United States as a global force. People everywhere seized opportunities created by the war to effect change, and Russia was transformed by a social revolution at home. At the end of the war, the victors redrew the world map.

28-1 | Life at Home and on the Battlefield
Correspondence of Evelyn and Fred Albright (1917)

Even for the millions of civilians fortunate enough to live far from the frontlines, the First World War presented dramatic interruptions to daily life at home. The correspondence of Evelyn and Fred Albright, two Canadian citizens, spanned the years from 1910 through 1917 and included over 550 letters. Fred, a lawyer, enlisted in 1916 and was sent to England for training in 1917. He shared vivid details of his overseas posting in letters to his wife. In letters back to her husband, Evelyn chronicled the challenges and triumphs of her life at home, including her work at Fred's law office. These excerpts show how the war touched lives far from Europe, capturing not only the Albrights' individual experiences but also their great love and, following Fred's death at the Second Battle of Passchendaele, Belgium, in late October 1917, Evelyn's grief.

An Echo in My Heart: The Letters of Elnora Evelyn (Kelly) Albright and Frederick Stanley Albright, comp. and ed. Lorna Brooks. www.echoinmyheart.ca. Letters and material pertaining to the Albright Collection are housed in The Archives and Research Collections Centre, Western University, London, ON, Canada.

Fred to Evelyn

France
Mon evening,
Oct. 1 1917

My darling wife, —

It is one of those beautiful clear evenings which have been our almost invariable portion since coming here. By daylight saving time, which still prevails with the army in France, it is 6.30 and a soft twilight haze has followed the setting of the sun. I went outside and stretched myself out on the bank, when before I started to write, I heard the distant hum of a German airplane and immediately after came the order "Get under cover," so we all hurried to our dugouts and now I am sitting at the entrance to the dugout which has been my home for the past 4 days and which we are leaving tonight for a while back of the lines.

We don't rush to cover from airplanes because of danger but because the aircraft are out for reconnaissance and the least movement on the ground is discernable. Naturally we don't want Heine[1] to know what positions we occupy. Of course he knows this and where most of the other trenches now held by us are, both because he can see them and because a large number of them were once occupied by him. But such matters are employed to conceal the guns, dispositions of troops etc. that Fritz[2] doesn't know where our strong points are, so on every available opportunity he sends over his airplanes for observation purposes, just as we do over Fritz's lines.

Later.

Since writing the above we had to put on our equipment and stand to, ready to move out. But as we have a wait of no one knows how long, I am back in the dugout writing by candle light. One has to snatch such odd moments if he would write at all. I haven't written any since last Friday. . . .

I haven't had any parcels from you since about a week prior to leaving Eng. I find that papers & boxes are sent up to the front line trenches however, when possible. Several of the fellows got parcels today. It really is wonderful to think that daily mail can be delivered even to the front line trenches. Yes—and hot tea and occasionally boiled rice or potatoes.

The grub here is remarkably good and there is no stint. Every night ration parties go out for the grub to the head of a narrow gauge railway about a mile away. Drinking water has to be carried rather farther. In some places it is almost impossible to get water for washing purposes at all but here we are unusually fortunate in having right at hand a spring well at the bottom of what Fritz had intended for a dugout before the water appeared.

---

[1]**Heine:** Slang for German.
[2]**Fritz:** Slang for German.

Wed. evening, Oct 3/17

Once again my abode has changed. On Monday night we came out of the line and while the battalion is still considered as being in support we are back 4 or 5 miles—quite beyond the range of all but the largest guns—and they rarely put a shell over this way except when firing at one of our captive balloons so we feel absolutely safe here.

Though freer from danger this place is in many respects less desirable than the line. There the grub is of the best & unstinted. Here we have a piece of bread a slice of bacon & tea for breakfast. Bully beef, bread jam & cheese for dinner & mulligan bread & tea for supper. There the quarters were much more commodious & comfortable. . . . The dugout from which I last wrote was about from 4 to 5 feet in height. The ceiling & walls were all carefully timbered and planked by Fritz and it was dry & quite comfortable. Of course there were lice—they are everywhere here—but they didn't trouble much. Most of the boys have already been attacked but as far as I know I am still free.

There were a few rats which we could plainly hear in the walls & ceiling but I never saw any inside. As for our present abode it is more a hut than a dugout for it is not really underground. Made of sandbags with a roof of loose sheets of corrugated iron it is situated on the side of a steep slope facing west. The floor is of chalk clay.

Rat holes in the sand bags abound and the rodents themselves can be seen scurrying all around at any time of day or night. The night before last when I was up for a visit to the latrine I saw 2 of the night cooks out on a rat hunting expedition. One wouldn't so much mind them outside, but when they play hide and seek around and over you while you are sleeping, and even nibble at one's toes, as they did the other night to the serj. maj. [sergeant major], they may truly be considered a pest.

Monday night I left a little bread & cheese in my mess tin for morning and as a result there are now 2 holes in the canvas cover and 2 distinct dents in the tin itself where Mr. Rat's teeth endeavored to punch a hole through the metal.

As for the mansion(?) itself—it is of such dimensions that when McKenzie, Edwards & I are in at night we have to put our packs & equipment outside. During the day we reverse the process. In plain figures, its inside dimensions are nearly 5' 10" long, 4½' wide & 3½' high—quite a snug little apartment for 3. Of course we sleep with our clothes on. We use our greatcoats for bedding, and the first night we each had a blanket over us but yesterday while we were out on a working party someone relieved us of 2 and now we have only 1 blanket for the 3 of us.

Fortunately the weather is mild, although the air becomes quite chilly before morning. However I always sleep warm. I haven't slept with my clothes off—I mean my outer clothes for 10 days. When we were in the line, of course we had to keep our puttees & boots on and wear our box respirators—and were supposed to keep all equipment on. In the front line everything is worn but in the support line where I was most of the fellows slept with their equipment off.

. . . I told you the night before we left the line we got back here about 3 a.m. had something to eat & got to bed about 3.30. Then 15 of us—among whom were McK. [McKenzie], Edwards & I had to get up at 6, breakfast at 6.30 & start at 7 on a working party. We marched back to within a mile of where we had been in the line—our work was under cover & needless to say we didn't work very hard. About 3.30 we quit & marched back—arriving here about 5.30. After supper I had a rub bath, & a shave and by the time I read your letter, & one from Don [Albright], I was ready for bed. Today we were on the same work and the same place.

It takes us about 2 hours each way going and coming, & the marching is all in trenches which wind and twist and turn. Nearly all the way the bottom is covered with trench matting—ie—a walk about 2 feet wide made of small slots laid crosswise on 2″ × 4″ scantling. This is a great boon in wet weather but makes hard walking in dry weather.

We have just been warned for the same working party tomorrow for which I am very glad. If we didn't go on the day party we'd be on a night one, and its nicer to work in the day and have the night for sleep. Don't worry about me darling. Though my time is full and I sometimes get tired, I'm hard as nails and never felt in better health in my life. I'm never too tired to sleep or rest and I'm sure I can hold up my end with the best of them.

Do you remember Mr. Lucas who was in the 191 & was with me at Sarcee? His son was killed last Thursday night. I wish you would see or phone Mrs. Lucas and assure her that her boy didn't suffer. He was killed instantaneously by a big shell which killed 1 other and wounded 2. This was the first night we were in the line. McKenzie helped to carry him out and he is buried near here in a little cemetery where the 50th now inter all their dead. If I get time I'll write the Lucases a short letter. Anyhow I know they would appreciate your telling them what I have just written.

Oh my darling, I am so glad you have been feeling better, and that you had a good visit at Beamsville. The other fellows have come in now and we must turn in so goodnight my own darling wife.

Your Ferd.[3]

Evelyn to Fred

Calgary,
Nov. 11 1917

Dearest Ferd: —

One year ago to-day was the Sunday when the gas was off. That was a memorable day, wasn't it? And to-day was so warm that I didn't even wear my little fur around my neck, much less carry my muff.

---

[3]**Ferd:** Fred's pet name, often used in their correspondence.

I took David to church this morning and Mr. and Mrs. Peters kindly brought us home. David kicked up a row, but I did not tell his parents as they would have felt very much humiliated, and I'm not sure that a spanking would have done him any good. I gave him a good talking to tonight when he was in bed. He needs a *very* firm hand, and he's just at a very saucy age.

Mr. Dagleish preached this morning about the halo on common things. It was a good enough sermon, freely interspersed with quotations from the poets, Ruskin, etc. I wonder why that stuff seems so academic to me now, whereas it used to appeal to me very much. The church was very well filled this morning and the music was good. Wilfred gave an Organ Recital yesterday afternoon, which I did not attend, but if he keeps them up all winter I hope to go often. . . .

Last night, in the night I woke up, and an utterable longing for you swept over me, and so dearest, I prayed for you, and then I went to sleep again. I had just received your letter telling me you were reading the 46th Psalm, the night we read the bad Russian news, and I read it and felt comforted. . . .

There are some things I'd like to tell Wray, yet I do not want to preach at him, and I can't say some of them without making him think we were discussing him at Beamsville, which as you very well know we were, so I had better keep my mouth shut.

Well dearie, I'll have a birthday this week. How funny you should think it was in October. . . .

Mr. Clarke told Miss Playter she was to get $40 after she had been there two months, the same as they gave me, but I was there 5 months before they gave me $40. And if she gets $40, then why shouldn't I get what Fitch, Roy and Bryenton have been getting? You don't think me mercenary, do you dear? Of course, I know I'm not worth very much to the office just now, but that's not my fault; I'll work if I get it to do.

I had a good story to tell you, but I've forgotten what it was. Maybe I'll remember it to tell you tomorrow. Goodnight dearest. I'm going up to get in bed now, and I'll write to my parents there. You seem far away tonight dearest. I wonder why. You are ever uppermost in my thoughts.

Your wife.

Evelyn to Fred, After His Death in Late October

Taber, Alta
Nov. 23, 1917

Dearest: —

It is not yet two weeks since I wrote my last letter to you, not two weeks since I read that awful telegram that told me you were gone from me.

I suppose it seems silly for me to write to you, but if you know, you'll understand, and nobody else need know. But it has come to me that time might dim your image and the knowledge of your dear companionship, and I cannot bear to think of that. Then too, my darling, oh my darling, I sometimes cannot believe that you are gone, and I go on pretending as I have ever since you went away last March, that you were coming home again. And if you should — why then you'd be glad of a link between the times. It is so easy, sweetheart, to lose myself in dreaming, for whenever hard unpleasant things have come, I have always made believe things were as I would have them. But in this case, the coming back to Earth is hard.

I think it has been like this, sweetheart. I could not, would not face the thought that you would not come back: I interpreted those psalms we read together, as meaning that you would be kept safe from accident, danger and death. When I knew that you were in the thick of things, I went calmly to sleep at night, believing that you were in God's hands and that He would keep you safe, for I could not, and do not yet believe that it is His will that any of you should fall. Some of the time, while I so calmly slept and went about my work, you were lying dead Dead! Oh my darling, as I have so often called you — the light of my life.

I have thought of late dear one, that I did not fully realize what it meant to you to go. I was so filled with my own grief, with the thought of my loneliness, and with the dread of what you would have to face, that I did not fully realize what it meant to you to give up all you did and to leave me, fearing that you might never come back. You have always said I wrote cheerful letters; I am glad if you thought they were, for I tried to make them so for you had enough to bear, without me making your lot harder.

The woman is coming up to sweep, so I'll stop. But my dear one, it almost seems as if you'll read this some day. Or is it that you are reading it over my shoulder as I write? In any case, you know I adore you, my sweetheart and my friend. Oh darling, I shall try to live on cheerfully and well, but it seems that I am like a tree, half killed my [sic] lightning. Such a tree, I suppose is not expected to give the shade of a whole one — but the question always comes, why should it have been marred and blighted? Do you know now?

Your wife, for wherever you are, my darling, I shall always be that.

READING AND DISCUSSION QUESTIONS

1. From the tone of their letters, how frequent do you imagine contact was between Fred and Evelyn? How might the frequency of contact affect the war experiences of those at the front and those at home?

2. What does the correspondence reveal about Evelyn's life without her husband? What had changed, and how had she adjusted to her new circumstances?

3. What is the role of religion in these letters? When is it mentioned, and how?

28-2 | War Brings Revolution to Russia

VLADIMIR ILYICH LENIN, *All Power to the Soviets!* (1917)

Vladimir Ilyich Ulyanov (1870–1924), better known by his nom de guerre Lenin, was a central intellectual and political force behind the uprisings that made up the Russian Revolution (1905–1917). Following years of exile and a triumphant return to Russia with the assistance of the German government, Lenin capitalized on the fall of the tsar by pushing for further revolution under the guidance of his Bolshevik faction of what would become the Russian Communist Party. In the months leading to the October 1917 revolution and Bolshevik power, Lenin took control of the popular newspaper *Pravda* (*Truth*) and used its editorial pages to powerful effect. The speech reproduced here demonstrates both the political infighting that marked the Russian Revolution and Lenin's relentless use of propaganda to outmaneuver his opponents.

"Drive nature out of the door and she will rush back through the window." It seems that the Socialist-Revolutionary and Menshevik parties[4] have to "learn" this simple truth time and again by their own experience. They under took to be "revolutionary democrats" and found themselves in the shoes of revolutionary democrats — they are now forced to draw the conclusions which every revolutionary democrat must draw.

Democracy is the rule of the majority. As long as the will of the majority was not clear, as long as it was possible to make it out to be unclear, at least with a grain of plausibility, the people were offered a counter-revolutionary bourgeois government disguised as "democratic." But this delay could not last long. During the several months that have passed since February 27[5] the will of the majority of the workers and peasants, of the overwhelming majority of the country's population, has become clear in more than a general sense. Their will has found expression in mass organizations — the Soviets of Workers', Soldiers' and Peasants' Deputies.

How, then, can anyone oppose the transfer of all power in the state to the Soviets? Such opposition means nothing but renouncing democracy! It means

---

"All Power to the Soviets!" *Pravda*, no. 99 (July 18, 1917). Republished in *Lenin Collected Works*, 45 vols. (Moscow: Progress, 1977), 25:155–156.

[4]**Socialist-Revolutionary and Menshevik parties:** Russian political factions during the Russian Revolutions. The Mensheviks, with the Bolsheviks, made up the Russian Marxist Party; the Mensheviks were more inclusive and favored more compromise than did their Bolshevik counterparts. They were banned by the Bolsheviks in 1921. The Socialist-Revolutionary Party emphasized rural peasants more than either wing of the Russian Marxists did; despite success at the polls, they were outmaneuvered by the Bolsheviks and largely dissolved.

[5]**February 27:** This date marked the initial revolution that toppled the Russian tsar and brought the provisional government to power.

no more no less than imposing on the people a government which *admittedly* can neither come into being nor hold its ground *democratically*, i.e., as a result of truly free, truly popular elections.

It is a fact, strange as it may seem at first sight, that the Socialist-Revolutionaries and Mensheviks have *forgotten* this perfectly simple, perfectly obvious and palpable truth. Their position is so false, and they are so badly confused and bewildered, that they are unable to "recover" this truth they have lost. Following the elections in Petrograd[6] and in Moscow, the convocation of the All-Russia Peasant Congress, and the Congress of Soviets,[7] the classes and parties throughout Russia have shown what they stand for so clearly and specifically that people who have not gone mad or deliberately got themselves into a mess simply cannot have any illusions on this score.

To tolerate the Cadet Ministers or the Cadet government or Cadet policies[8] means challenging democrats and democracy. This is the source of the political crises since February 27, and this also the source of the shakiness and vacillation of our government system. At every turn, daily and even hourly, appeals are being made to the people's revolutionary spirit and to their democracy on behalf of the most authoritative government institutions and congresses. Yet the government's policies in particular, are all departures from revolutionary principles, and breaches in democracy.

This sort of thing will not do.

It is inevitable that a situation like the present should show elements of instability now for one reason, now for another. And it is not exactly a clever policy of jib. Things are moving by fits and starts towards a point where power will be transferred to the Soviets, which is what our Party called for long ago.

READING AND DISCUSSION QUESTIONS

1. What is the main point of Lenin's speech, and how does he argue his point?

2. According to Lenin, who opposes his call for the transfer of power to the Soviets?

3. How does Lenin characterize those who are not directly in line with his thinking? To what end?

---

[6]**Petrograd:** Later Leningrad, and now St. Petersburg.

[7]**All-Russia Peasant Congress ... Congress of Soviets:** Meetings in 1918 that codified and strengthened Bolshevik control of the Russian government.

[8]**Cadet Ministers ... Cadet policies:** Members of the Constitutional Democratic (Konstitutionnaya Demokraticheskaya) Party prominent in the provisional government.

VIEWPOINTS

Competing Perspectives on the Treaty of Versailles

The 1919 Paris Peace Conference was contentious from the start. Even the victorious Allies disagreed among themselves about the shape of the postwar world and thus found no consensus on the peace terms. France, Britain, and the United States each had its own agenda and its own expectations. President Woodrow Wilson's vision of a permanent peace seemed to many in France a recipe for French isolation and decline. Britain was more interested in maintaining and expanding its overseas empire than it was in France's problems or Wilson's lofty principles. Asian, African, and the Middle Eastern delegates came to the conference hoping to share in Wilson's promise of self-determination, only to discover that, even before the war had ended, France and Britain had entered into secret agreements designed to perpetuate the imperialist system. Only Japan's delegation came away from the conference with any significant prize. The Versailles treaty transferred China's Shandong peninsula, Germany's prewar sphere of influence, from German to Japanese control, outraging the Chinese and worsening relations between the two Asian powers. Finally, Germany was forced to sit on the sidelines while the Allies reached compromises at its expense, ultimately producing a punitive treaty meant to prevent Germany from ever rejoining the ranks of the Great Powers.

28-3 | War and Peace from a Japanese Perspective

KONOE FUMIMARO, *Against a Pacifism Centered on England and America* (1918)

Konoe Fumimaro (1891–1945) held a range of political and diplomatic positions in modern Japan, including three terms as prime minister. As a member of the delegation to the Paris Peace Conference in 1918, Konoe argued for the inclusion of a "racial equality clause" in the charter of the League of Nations, a proposal that won majority support but was defeated through lack of support from Woodrow Wilson and active opposition from member states of the British Empire, such as Australia. Konoe's outspoken argument here, written before his departure for the Paris conference, foreshadows Japanese nationalist rhetoric against Anglo-British power during the Second World War.

William Theodore de Bary, Carol Gluck, and Arthur E. Tiedemann, eds., *Sources of Japanese Tradition*, 2 vols. (New York: Columbia University Press, 2006), 2:291–293. Copyright © 2006 Columbia University Press. Reprinted with permission of the publisher.

In my view, the European war has been a conflict between established powers and powers not yet established, a conflict between countries that found upholding the status quo convenient and countries that found overthrowing the status quo convenient. The countries that found upholding the status quo convenient clamored for peace, while the countries that found overthrowing the status quo convenient cried out for war. Pacifism does not always serve justice and humanism, and militarism does not always violate justice and humanism. All depends on the nature of the status quo. If the prewar status quo was the best possible and was consonant with justice and humanism, he who would destroy it is the enemy of justice and humanism; but if the status quo did not meet the criteria of justice and humanism, its destroyer is not necessarily the enemy of justice and humanism. By the same token, the pacifist countries that would uphold this status quo are not necessarily qualified to pride themselves on being the champions of justice and humanity.

Although England and America may have regarded Europe's prewar status as ideal, an impartial third party cannot acknowledge it to have been ideal in terms of justice and humanism. As the colonial history of England and France attests, they long ago occupied the less civilized regions of the world, made them into colonies, and had no scruples about monopolizing them for their own profit. Therefore not only Germany but all late-developing countries were in the position of having no land to seize and being unable to find any room for expansion. This state of affairs contravenes the principle of equal opportunity for all humanity, jeopardizes all nations' equal right to survival, and is a gross violation of justice and humanity. Germany's wish to overthrow this order was quite justified; the means it chose, however, were unfair and immoderate, and because they were based on militarism, with its emphasis on armed might, Germany received the world's opprobrium. Nevertheless, as a Japanese, I cannot help feeling deep sympathy for what Germany has to do.

. . . At the coming peace conference, in joining the League of Nations Japan must insist at the very least, that repudiation of economic imperialism and nondiscriminatory treatment of Orientals and Caucasians be agreed upon from the start. Militarism is not the only thing injurious to justice and humanism. Although the world has been saved from the smoke of gunpowder and the hail of bullets by Germany's defeat, military might is not all that threatens nations' equal right to survival. We must realize that there is invasion through money, conquest through wealth. Just as we repudiate military imperialism, so in the same spirit we should naturally repudiate economic imperialism, which seeks to profit by monopolizing enormous capital and abundant natural resources and suppressing other nations' free growth without recourse to arms. I cannot avoid grave misgivings as to how far economic imperialism can be repudiated at the coming peace conference, led as it is by England and America, which I fear will unsheathe the sword of their economic imperialism after the war.

If we cannot subdue this rampant economic imperialism at the peace conference, England and America, which have profited most from the war, will promptly unify the world under their economic dominance and will rule the world, using the League of Nations and arms limitations to fix the status quo that serves their purpose. How will other countries endure this? Deprived of arms to express their revulsion and indignation, they will have no choice but to follow England and America, bleating in their wake like a flock of meek sheep. England has lost no time in trumpeting a policy of self-sufficiency, and many are advocating that other countries be denied access to its colonies. Such are the contradictions between what England and America say and what they do. This, indeed, is why I am wary of those who glorify England and America. If such a policy is carried out, needless to say it would be a great economic blow to Japan. Japan is limited in territory, [is] poor in natural resources, and has a small population and thus a meager market for manufactured products. If England closed off its colonies, how would we be able to assure the nation's secure survival? In such a case, the need to ensure its survival would compel Japan to attempt to overthrow the status quo as Germany did before the war. If this is the fate awaiting all late-developing countries with little territory and no colonies, not only for the sake of Japan but for the sake of establishing the equal right to life of all nations of the world on the basis of justice and humanism, we must do away with economic imperialism and see that countries do not monopolize their colonies but accord other countries equal use of them both as markets for manufactured products and as suppliers of natural resources.

The next thing that the Japanese, especially, should insist upon is the elimination of discrimination between Caucasians and Orientals. There is no need to dwell on the fact that the United States, along with the English colonies of Australia and Canada, opens its doors to Caucasians but looks down on the Japanese and on Orientals in general and rejects them. This is something at which the Japanese have long chafed. Not only are Orientals barred from employment and forbidden to lease houses and farmland, but still worse, it is reported that in some places an Oriental wishing to spend the night at a hotel is required to have a Caucasian guarantor. This is a grave humanitarian problem that no defender of justice, Oriental or otherwise, should overlook.

At the coming peace conference, we must see that the English and Americans show deep remorse for their past sins and change their arrogant and insulting attitude, and we must insist, from the standpoint of justice and humanism, that they revise all laws that call for discriminatory treatment of Orientals, including of course rescinding immigration restrictions against Orientals. I believe that the coming peace conference will be the great test of whether the human race can bring itself to reconstruct a world based on justice and humanism. If Japan does not rashly endorse a pacifism centered on England and America but steadfastly asserts its position from the standpoint of justice and humanism in the true sense, it will long be celebrated in history as the champion of justice.

READING AND DISCUSSION QUESTIONS

1. What arguments did Konoe make against British and American pacifism? How did he describe the "status quo" supported by this pacifism?

2. Whom did Konoe blame for the war? Why did he sympathize with Germany?

3. What role did race play in Konoe's vision of the postwar world? What racial divisions did he employ? Why?

4. Do you think the transfer of China's Shandong peninsula from German to Japanese control represents the kind of outcomes Konoe wished for in the peace conference? Why or why not?

28-4 | Germany Protests the Terms of Peace

GERMAN DELEGATION TO THE PARIS PEACE CONFERENCE, *On the Conditions of Peace* (October 1919)

The Treaty of Versailles, signed at the 1919 Paris Peace Conference, formally brought World War I to an end and set the conditions for peace. Orchestrated by the Allied powers — the United States, Great Britain, and France — the treaty blamed the war on Germany and ordered it to pay $33 billion in reparations, cede all of its colonies, dismantle its air force, and greatly reduce other military operations. It also established the League of Nations as an international peacekeeping organization. Russia did not attend the conference, and Germany — the nation most impacted by the treaty — was not permitted to contribute to the negotiations. Fearing invasion, Germany ultimately signed the treaty despite continued protests.

Although President Wilson, in his speech of October 20th, 1916, has acknowledged that "no single fact caused the war, but that in the last analysis the whole European system is in a deeper sense responsible for the war, with its combination of alliances and understandings, a complicated texture of intrigues and espionage that unfailingly caught the whole family of nations in its meshes," . . . Germany is to acknowledge that Germany and her allies are responsible for all damages which the enemy Governments or their subjects have incurred by her and her allies' aggression. . . . Apart from the consideration that there is no incontestable legal foundation for the obligation for reparation imposed upon Germany, the amount of such compensation[9] is to be determined by a commission nominated solely by Germany's enemies, Germany taking no part. . . . The commission is plainly to have power to administer Germany like the estate of a bankrupt.

"Comments of the German Delegation to the Paris Peace Conference on the Conditions of Peace, Oct., 1919," in *International Conciliation*, no. 143 (October 1919).

[9]**amount of such compensation:** A reparations commission appointed by the peace conference determined the final sum to be $33 billion in 1921.

As there are innate rights of man, so there are innate rights of nations. The inalienable fundamental right of every state is the right of self-preservation and self-determination. With this fundamental right the demand here made upon Germany is incompatible. Germany must promise to pay an indemnity, the amount of which at present is not even stated. The German rivers are to be placed under the control of an international body upon which Germany's delegates are always to be but the smallest minority. Canals and railroads are to be built on German territory at the discretion of foreign authorities.

These few instances show that that is not the just peace we were promised, not the peace "the very principle of which," according to a word of President Wilson, "is equality and the common participation in a common benefit. . . ."

In such a peace the solidarity of human interests, which was to find its expression in a League of Nations, would have been respected. How often Germany has been given the promise that this League of Nations would unite the belligerents, conquerors as well as conquered, in a permanent system of common rights! . . .

But in contradiction to them, the Covenant of the League of Nations has been framed without the cooperation of Germany. Nay, still more. Germany does not even stand on the list of those States that have been invited to join the League of Nations. . . . What the treaty of peace proposes to establish, is rather a continuance of the present hostile coalition which does not deserve the name of "League of Nations." . . . The old political system based on force and with its tricks and rivalries will thus continue to thrive!

Again and again the enemies of Germany have assured the whole world that they did not aim at the destruction of Germany. . . .

In contradiction to this, the peace document shows that Germany's position as a world power is to be utterly destroyed. The Germans abroad are deprived of the possibility of keeping up their old relations in foreign countries and of regaining for Germany a share in world commerce, while their property, which has up to the present been confiscated and liquidated, is being used for reparation instead of being restored to them. . . .

In this war, a new fundamental law has arisen which the statesmen of all belligerent peoples have again and again acknowledged to be their aim: the right of self-determination. To make it possible for all nations to put this privilege into practice was intended to be one achievement of the war. . . .

Neither the treatment described above of the inhabitants of the Saar region[10] as accessories to the [coal] pits nor the public form of consulting the population in the districts of Eupen, Malmédy, and Prussian Moresnet[11] — which, moreover,

---

[10]**inhabitants of the Saar region:** After fifteen years, Saar inhabitants would vote in a plebiscite to decide if they would stay under the administration of a League of Nations commission or become part of France or Germany. In 1935, they voted to join Germany.

[11]**Prussian Moresnet:** Moresnet was annexed outright by Belgium. In Eupen and Malmédy, those who objected to transferring the areas to Belgium could sign their names in a public registry. Both areas became Belgian.

shall not take place before they have been put under Belgian sovereignty—comply in the least with such a solemn recognition of the right of self-determination.

The same is also true with regard to Alsace-Lorraine. If Germany has pledged herself "to right the wrong of 1871," this does not mean any renunciation of the right of self-determination of the inhabitants of Alsace-Lorraine. A cession of the country without consulting the population would be a new wrong, if for no other reason, because it would be inconsistent with a recognized principle of peace.

On the other hand, it is incompatible with the idea of national self-determination for two and one-half million Germans to be torn away from their native land against their own will. By the proposed demarcation of the boundary, unmistakably German territories are disposed of in favor of their Polish neighbors. Thus, from the Central Silesian districts of Guhrau and Militsch certain portions are to be wrenched away, in which, beside 44,900 Germans, reside at the utmost 3,700 Poles. . . .

This disrespect of the right of self-determination is shown most grossly in the fact that Danzig[12] is to be separated from the German Empire and made a free state. Neither historical rights nor the present ethnographical conditions of ownership of the Polish people can have any weight as compared with the German past and the German character of that city. . . . Likewise the cession of the commercial town of Memel, which is to be exacted from Germany, is in no way consistent with the right of self-determination. The same may be said with reference to the fact that millions of Germans in German-Austria are to be denied the union with Germany which they desire and that, further, millions of Germans dwelling along our frontiers are to be forced to remain part of the newly created Czecho-Slovakian State.

Even as regards that part of the national territory that is to be left to Germany, the promised right of self-determination is not observed. A Commission for the execution of the indemnity shall be the highest instance for the whole State. Our enemies claim to have fought for the great aim of the democratization of Germany. To be sure, the outcome of the war has delivered us from our former authorities, but instead of them we shall have in exchange a foreign, dictatorial power whose aim can and must be only to exploit the working power of the German people for the benefit of the creditor states.[13] . . .

The fact that this is an age in which economic relations are on a world scale, requires the political organization of the civilized world. The German Government agrees with the Governments of the Allied and Associated Powers in the conviction that the horrible devastation caused by this war requires the establishment of a new world order, an order which shall insure the "effective authority of the principles of international law," and "just and honorable relations between the nations." . . .

---

[12]**Danzig:** Danzig was administered by the League of Nations.

[13]**Commission for the execution . . . states:** After the Germans fell behind in their payments in 1923, the French-controlled reparations commission sent French, Belgian, and Italian technicians into Germany's Ruhr region to collect coal to make up for the delinquent payments.

There is no evidence of these principles in the peace document which has been laid before us. Expiring world theories, emanating from imperialistic and capitalistic tendencies, celebrate in it their last horrible triumph. As opposed to these views, which have brought unspeakable disaster upon the world, we appeal to the innate sense of right of men and nations, under whose token the English State developed, the Dutch People freed itself, the North American nation established its independence, France shook off absolutism. The bearers of such hallowed traditions cannot deny this right to the German people, that now for the first time has acquired in its internal polities the possibility of living in harmony with its free will based on law.

READING AND DISCUSSION QUESTIONS

1. What does the German delegation say is the real cause of the war?
2. What does the delegation mean when it invokes the "innate rights of nations"?
3. How does the peace proposed by the treaty differ from that which Germany expected and says it was promised, particularly by Wilson?
4. According to the Germans, in what ways does the treaty violate the right of self-determination?

VIEWPOINTS COMPARATIVE QUESTIONS

1. Do you think Konoe would have believed that the terms imposed on the Germans by the Versailles treaty were *justified* and *humane*, two terms he often uses in his essay?
2. On what might Konoe and the German delegates to the Paris Peace Conference have agreed? On what might they have disagreed?

28-5 | The Demilitarization of Germany Provisions in the Treaty of Versailles

Plane Scrapping (ca. 1919)

Signed exactly five years after the assassination of Archduke Franz Ferdinand, the Versailles treaty ended the state of war between the Allied Powers and Germany. One of the treaty provisions considered most humiliating and vindictive by the German people was the nearly complete disbanding of the German military forces and the destruction of its weapons. Germany was now limited to a standing army of less than 100,000 men, a navy of only 15,000, and no armored vehicles, submarines, capital ships, or aircraft of any kind. In this image, Germany's war planes are being dismantled and scrapped, and the same was done to tanks, fortresses, machine guns, ships, and even soldiers' helmets.

Germany was reduced from a global imperial power to a defenseless state in the heart of Europe. As you examine this image, consider what a former French or British soldier might think in seeing it. Did this justify their war sacrifices? What might a former German soldier feel?

Three Lions/Getty Images

READING AND DISCUSSION QUESTIONS

1. The three men in the image foreground, two of which have canes, are Germans, probably former (wounded) soldiers. Why did the photographer place them there? What audience might he be addressing? What reaction might he be seeking?

2. Air warfare made significant advances during the Great War, and Germans were proud of their air force and its pilots, such as Manfred Freiherr von Richthofen, the famous "Red Baron." How might images like this one create desires for revenge by Germans right after the war?

3. France and the United Kingdom worried that Germany might start another war without disarmament provisions written into the Versailles treaty. Could the victors have taken any other action besides the near total destruction of the Germany military, as portrayed in this image, to allay their fears?

■ COMPARATIVE QUESTIONS ■

1. The documents in this chapter range from intensely personal to geopolitical in nature. What connections can you draw between the emotions and experiences presented in the Albrights' letters and the political stances of the other authors?

2. How might Lenin have responded to the Paris peace talks? How would he have interpreted their course and outcome?

3. In your opinion, what were the most important problems with the treaties that formally ended World War I? What light do the documents and the image included in this chapter shed on this question?

29

Nationalism in Asia
1914–1939

Though the First World War is often cast as a European conflict, it reflected and exacerbated tensions throughout the world. The global network of empires and colonies that had formed by the turn of the century drew Asian peoples into the conflict, and the rhetoric of freedom and democracy mobilized during the war inspired nationalist sentiments in many contexts. For some in Asia, the war was an opportunity to fight for national sovereignty against imperial control. For others, the war created an opportunity to link their own popular nationalist causes with the stated goals of the victors. For Asians, the material and human cost of the war and the ensuing geopolitical reorganization were manifest in new ways of thinking about national identity. The documents in this chapter present a range of personal and political views on nations and national identity in Asia, exploring the complex mix of fear, hope, disappointment, and resolve of Asians who sought to build national identities out of the chaos of the early twentieth century.

29-1 | An Eyewitness to Genocide
MARY L. GRAFFAM, *An Account of Turkish Violence Against Armenians* (1915)

As young Turkish revolutionaries rose to power in Turkey after 1908, they sought to enforce a narrowly defined national identity that erased the country's multiculturalism and instead focused on Turkish language, culture, and race. Their efforts to consolidate what was left of the Ottoman Empire led to genocide against the Armenians. During World War I, while the international community was distracted by the war, the Turks massacred thousands of Armenians and deported others. Mary Graffam, a missionary from Massachusetts, was among the hundreds of U.S. and European workers and diplomats in Turkey who recorded

Mary L. Graffam, reprinted from the *Missionary Herald* (Boston), December 1915.

the killings, starvation, and brutal deportations. These eyewitness accounts were later printed in newspapers around the world.

When we were ready to leave Sivas,[1] the Government gave forty-five ox-carts for the Protestant townspeople and eighty horses, but none at all for our pupils and teachers; so we bought ten ox-carts, two horse arabas [wagons], and five or six donkeys, and started out. In the company were all our teachers in the college, about twenty boys from the college and about thirty of the girls'-school. It was as a special favor to the Sivas people, who had not done anything revolutionary, that the Vali [provincial governor] allowed the men who were not yet in prison to go with their families.

The first night we were so tired that we just ate a piece of bread and slept on the ground wherever we could find a place to spread a yorgan [blanket]. It was after dark when we stopped, anyway. We were so near Sivas that the gendarmes [armed Ottoman police] protected us, and no special harm was done; but the second night we began to see what was before us. The gendarmes would go ahead and have long conversations with the villagers, and then stand back and let them rob and trouble the people until we all began to scream, and then they would come and drive them away. Yorgans and rugs, and all such things, disappeared by the dozen, and donkeys were sure to be lost. Many had brought cows; but from the first day those were carried off, one by one, until not a single one remained.

We got accustomed to being robbed, but the third day a new fear took possession of us, and that was that the men were to be separated from us at Kangal. . . . Our teacher from Mandjaluk was there, with his mother and sisters. They had left the village with the rest of the women and children, and when they saw that the men were being taken off to be killed the teacher fled to another village, four hours away, where he was found by the police and brought safely with his family to Kangal, because the tchaoush [officer] who had taken them from Mandjaluk wanted his sister. I found them confined in one room. I went to the Kaimakam [district official] and got an order for them all to come with us.

At Kangal some Armenians had become Mohammedans, and had not left the village, but the others were all gone. . . . They said that a valley near there was full of corpses. At Kangal we also began to see exiles from Tokat. The sight was one to strike horror to any heart; they were a company of old women, who had been robbed of absolutely everything. At Tokat the Government had first imprisoned the men, and from the prison had taken them on the road. . . . After the men had gone, they arrested the old women and the older brides, perhaps about thirty or thirty-five years old. There were very few young women or children. All the younger women and children were left in Tokat. . . .

---

[1]**Sivas:** City in north-central Turkey, where Mary Graffam was the principal of a girls' school.

When we looked at them we could not imagine that even the sprinkling of men that were with us would be allowed to remain. We did not long remain in doubt; the next day we . . . had come to Hassan Tehelebi . . . and it was with terror in our hearts that we passed through that village about noon. But we encamped and ate our supper in peace, and even began to think that perhaps it was not so, when the Mudir [official in charge] came round with gendarmes and began to collect the men. . . .

The night passed, and only one man came back to tell the story of how every man was compelled to give up all his money, and all were taken to prison. The next morning they collected the men who had escaped the night before and extorted forty-five liras from our company, on the promise that they would give us gendarmes to protect us. One "company" is supposed to be from 1,000 to 3,000 persons. Ours was perhaps 2,000, and the greatest number of gendarmes would be five or six. In addition to these they sewed a red rag on the arm of a Kurdish villager and gave him a gun, and he had the right to rob and bully us all he pleased.[2]

Broken-hearted, the women continued their journey. . . .

As soon as the men left us, the Turkish drivers began to rob the women, saying: "You are all going to be thrown into the Tokma Su [river], so you might as well give your things to us, and then we will stay by you and try to protect you." Every Turkish woman that we met said the same thing. The worst were the gendarmes, who really did more or less bad things. One of our schoolgirls was carried off by the Kurds twice, but her companions made so much fuss that she was brought back. . . .

As we approached the bridge over the Tokma Su, it was certainly a fearful sight. As far as the eye could see over the plain was this slow-moving line of ox-carts. For hours there was not a drop of water on the road, and the sun poured down its very hottest. As we went on we began to see the dead from yesterday's company, and the weak began to fall by the way. The Kurds working in the fields made attacks continually, and we were half-distracted. I piled as many as I could on our wagons, and our pupils, both boys and girls, worked like heroes. One girl took a baby from its dead mother and carried it until evening. Another carried a dying woman until she died. We bought water from the Kurds, not minding the beating that the boys were sure to get with it. I counted forty-nine deaths, but there must have been many more. One naked body of a woman was covered with bruises. I saw the Kurds robbing the bodies of those not yet entirely dead. . . .

The hills on each side were white with Kurds, who were throwing stones on the Armenians, who were slowly wending their way to the bridge. I ran ahead and stood on the bridge in the midst of a crowd of Kurds, until I was used up

---

[2]**sewed a red rag . . . he pleased:** The "red rag" was an armband that gave the Kurds special status.

[exhausted]. I did not see anyone thrown into the water, but they said, and I believe it, that a certain Elmas, who has done handwork for me for years, was thrown over the bridge by a Kurd. Our Badvelli's wife was riding on a horse with a baby in her arms, and a Kurd took hold of her to throw her over, when another Kurd said: "She has a baby in her arms," and they let her go. . . .

The police for the first time began to interfere with me here, and it was evident that something was decided about me. The next morning after we arrived at this bridge, they wanted me to go to Malatia; but I insisted that I had permission to stay with the Armenians. During the day, however, they said that [I had been ordered] to come to Malatia, and that the others were going to Kiakhta. Soon after we heard that they were going to Ourfa, there to build villages and cities, &c.

In Malatia I went at once to the commandant, a captain who they say has made a fortune out of these exiles. I told him how I had gone to Erzeroum last winter, and how we pitied these women and children and wished to help them, and finally he sent me to the Mutessarif [district official]. The latter is a Kurd, apparently anxious to do the right thing; but he has been sick most of the time since he came, and the "beys" [Kurdish chiefs] here have had things more or less their own way, and certainly horrors have been committed. . . .

My friends here are very glad to have me with them, for they have a very difficult problem on their hands and are nearly crazy with the horrors they have been through here. The Mutessarif and other officials here and at Sivas have read me orders from Constantinople again and again to the effect that the lives of these exiles are to be protected, and from their actions I should judge that they must have received such orders; but they certainly have murdered a great many in every city. Here there were great trenches dug by the soldiers for drilling purposes. Now these trenches are all filled up, and our friends saw carts going back from the city by night. A man I know told me that when he was out to inspect some work he was having done, he saw a dead body which had evidently been pulled out of one of these trenches, probably by dogs. . . . The Beledia Reis [village chief] here says that every male over ten years old is being murdered, that not one is to live, and no woman over fifteen. The truth seems to be somewhere between these two extremes.

READING AND DISCUSSION QUESTIONS

1. What happened to the men after Graffam's group left Tokat? In what ways were they treated differently than the women and children?

2. Where were the Armenian exiles sent (and for what purpose) after Graffam was separated from them?

3. What does Graffam's account suggest about how the Armenian genocide was carried out? What role did government officials, military officers, and the police play? What about ordinary people?

29-2 | The British Government Supports a Jewish State in Palestine

ARTHUR JAMES BALFOUR, *Debating the Balfour Declaration* (1917)

The decision to support a Jewish homeland in Palestine posed a diplomatic dilemma for Great Britain. Though Lord Balfour, the British foreign secretary (1916–1919), would ultimately be authorized to endorse a Jewish homeland, the behind-the-scenes discussions excerpted below illustrate the War Department's concern about the consequences of such support. On the one hand, England hoped its actions might enlist American Zionists to push the U.S. Congress to back Britain in the war and would help Britain retain control of the Suez Canal. On the other hand, it risked its alliance with Arab leaders, who saw a separate Jewish state as contradictory to its government by majority rule.

The Balfour Declaration, 1917

Foreign Office
November 2nd, 1917
Dear Lord Rothschild,[3]
    I have much pleasure in conveying to you, on behalf of His Majesty's Government, the following declaration of sympathy with Jewish Zionist aspirations which has been submitted to, and approved by, the Cabinet.
    "His Majesty's Government view with favor the establishment in Palestine of a national home for the Jewish people, and will use their best endeavors to facilitate the achievement of this object, it being clearly understood that nothing shall be done which may prejudice the civil and religious rights of existing non-Jewish communities in Palestine, or the rights and political status enjoyed by Jews in any other country."
    I should be grateful if you would bring this declaration to the knowledge of the Zionist Federation.[4]
Yours sincerely,
Arthur James Balfour

Cambon Letter to Sokolow,[5] June 4, 1917

You were good enough to present the project to which you are devoting your efforts, which has for its object the development of Jewish colonization in Palestine. You consider that, circumstances permitting, and the independence of the

---

"The Balfour Declaration," *Times* (London), November 9, 1917, p. 1.

   [3]**Lord Rothschild:** Walter Lord Rothschild was a former member of Parliament (1899–1910) and an ardent English Zionist who was influential in shaping the Balfour Declaration.
   [4]**Zionist Federation:** The British Federation of Zionists, an organization that lobbied the British government to support a Jewish homeland in Palestine.
   [5]**Cambon . . . Sokolow:** Jules Cambon, secretary-general of the French Foreign Ministry; Nahum Sokolow, head of the Zionist Organization based in London (see note 6).

Holy Places being safeguarded on the other hand, it would be a deed of justice and of reparation to assist, by the protection of the Allied Powers, in the renaissance of the Jewish nationality in that Land from which the people of *Israel* were exiled so many centuries ago.

The French Government, which entered this present war to defend a people wrongfully attacked, and which continues the struggle to assure the victory of right over might, can but feel sympathy for your cause, the triumph of which is bound up with that of the Allies.

I am happy to give you herewith such assurance.

Official Zionist Formula, 18 July 1917

H. M. Government, after considering the aims of the Zionist Organization,[6] accepts the principle of recognizing Palestine as the National Home of the Jewish people and the right of the Jewish people to build up its National life in Palestine under a protection to be established at the conclusion of Peace, following upon the successful issue of the war.

H. M. Government regards as essential for the realization of this principle the grant of internal autonomy to the Jewish nationality in Palestine, freedom of immigration for Jews, and the establishment of a Jewish National Colonizing Corporation for the re-settlement and economic development of the country.

The conditions and forms of the internal autonomy and a charter for the Jewish National Colonizing Corporation should, in the view of H. M. Government, be elaborated in detail and determined with the representatives of the Zionist Organization.

Minutes of War Cabinet Meeting No. 227, Minute No. 2, 3 September 1917

The War Cabinet had under consideration correspondence which had passed between the Secretary of State for Foreign Affairs and Lord Rothschild on the question of the policy to be adopted towards the Zionist movement. In addition to the draft declaration of policy included in the above correspondence, they had before them an alternative draft prepared by Lord Milner. They had also before them a Memorandum by Mr. Montagu entitled "The Anti-Semitism of the present Government."

It was suggested that a question raising such important issues as to the future of Palestine ought, in the first instance, to be discussed with our Allies, and more particularly with the United States.

On the question of submitting Lord Milner's draft for the consideration of the United States Government, Mr. Montagu urged that the use of the phrase "the home of the Jewish people" would vitally prejudice the position of every

---

[6]**Zionist Organization:** An umbrella organization that merged Zionist groups in Europe and elsewhere to establish a Jewish state in Palestine.

Jew elsewhere and expand the argument contained in his Memorandum. Against this it was urged that the existence of a Jewish State or autonomous community in Palestine would strengthen rather than weaken the situation of Jews in countries where they were not yet in possession of equal rights, and that in countries like England, where they possessed such rights and were identified with the nation of which they were citizens, their position would be unaffected by the existence of a national Jewish community elsewhere. The view was expressed that, while a small influential section of English Jews were opposed to the idea, large numbers were sympathetic to it, but in the interests of Jews who wished to go from countries where they were less favorably situated, rather than from any idea of wishing to go to Palestine themselves.

With reference to a suggestion that the matter might be postponed, the Acting Secretary of State for Foreign Affairs pointed out that this was a question on which the Foreign Office had been very strongly pressed for a long time past. There was a very strong and enthusiastic organization, more particularly in the United States, who were zealous in this matter, and his belief was that it would be of most substantial assistance to the Allies to have the earnestness and enthusiasm of these people enlisted on our side. To do nothing was to risk a direct breach with them, and it was necessary to face this situation.

The War Cabinet decided that—

The views of [U.S.] President Wilson should be obtained before any declaration was made, and requested the Acting Secretary of State for Foreign Affairs to inform the Government of the United States that His Majesty's Government were being pressed to make a declaration in sympathy with the Zionist movement, and to ascertain their views as to the advisability of such a declaration being made.

Minutes of War Cabinet Meeting No. 245, Minute No. 18, 4 October 1917

With reference to War Cabinet 227, Minute 2, the Secretary of State for Foreign Affairs stated that the German Government were making great efforts to capture the sympathy of the Zionist Movement. This Movement, though opposed by a number of wealthy Jews in this country, had behind it the support of a majority of Jews, at all events in Russia and America, and possibly in other countries. He saw nothing inconsistent between the establishment of a Jewish national focus in Palestine and the complete assimilation and absorption of Jews into the nationality of other countries. Just as English emigrants to the United States became, either in the first or subsequent generations, American nationals, so, in future, should a Jewish citizenship be established in Palestine, would Jews become either Englishmen, Americans, Germans, or Palestinians. What was at the back of the Zionist Movement was the intense national consciousness held by certain members of the Jewish race. They regarded themselves as one of the great historic races of the world, whose original home was Palestine, and these Jews had a passionate longing to regain once more this ancient national home. Other Jews had become absorbed into the nations among whom they and their forefathers had dwelt for many generations. Mr. Balfour then read a very sympathetic declaration by the French Government which had been conveyed to the Zionists, and he stated that he knew that President Wilson was extremely favorable to the Movement.

Attention was drawn to the contradictory telegrams received from Colonel House and Justice Brandeis.

The Secretary was instructed to take the necessary action.

The War Cabinet further decided that the opinions received upon this draft declaration should be collated and submitted to them for decision.

Minutes of War Cabinet Meeting No. 259, Minute No. 12, 25 October 1917

With reference to War Cabinet 245, Minute 18, the Secretary mentioned that he was being pressed by the Foreign Office to bring forward the question of Zionism, an early settlement of which was regarded as of great importance.

Lord Curzon[7] stated that he had a Memorandum on the subject in course of preparation.

The question was adjourned until Monday, 29th October, or some other day early next week.

Minutes of War Cabinet Meeting No. 261, Minute No. 12, 31 October 1917

With reference to War Cabinet 245, Minute 18, the War Cabinet had before them a note by the Secretary, and also a memorandum by Lord Curzon on the subject of the Zionist movement.

The Secretary of State for Foreign Affairs stated that he gathered that everyone was now agreed that, from a purely diplomatic and political point of view, it was desirable that some declaration favorable to the aspirations of the Jewish nationalists should now be made. The vast majority of Jews in Russia and America, as, indeed, all over the world, now appeared to be favorable to Zionism. If we could make a declaration favorable to such an ideal, we should be able to carry on extremely useful propaganda both in Russia and America. He gathered that the main arguments still put forward against Zionism were twofold:—

(*a*.) That Palestine was inadequate to form a home for either the Jewish or any other people.
(*b*.) The difficulty felt with regard to the future position of Jews in Western countries.

With regard to the first, he understood that there were considerable differences of opinion among experts regarding the possibility of the settlement of any large

---

[7]**Lord Curzon:** George Nathaniel Curzon served in the British War Cabinet as Lord President of the Council (1916–1919).

population in Palestine, but he was informed that, if Palestine were scientifically developed, a very much larger population could be sustained than had existed during the period of Turkish misrule. As to the meaning of the words "national home," to which the Zionists attach so much importance, he understood it to mean some form of British, American, or other protectorate, under which full facilities would be given to the Jews to work out their own salvation and to build up, by means of education, agriculture, and industry, a real center of national culture and focus of national life. It did not necessarily involve the early establishment of an independent Jewish State, which was a matter for gradual development in accordance with the ordinary laws of political evolution.

With regard to the second point, he felt that, so far from Zionism hindering the process of assimilation in Western countries, the truer parallel was to be found in the position of an Englishman who leaves his country to establish a permanent home in the United States. In the latter case there was no difficulty in the Englishman or his children becoming full nationals of the United States, whereas, in the present position of Jewry, the assimilation was often felt to be incomplete, and any danger of a double allegiance or non-national outlook would be eliminated.

Lord Curzon stated that he admitted the force of the diplomatic arguments in favor of expressing sympathy, and agreed that the bulk of the Jews held Zionist rather than anti-Zionist opinions. He added that he did not agree with the attitude taken up by Mr. Montagu. On the other hand, he could not share the optimistic views held regarding the future of Palestine. These views were not merely the result of his own personal experiences of travel in that country, but of careful investigations from persons who had lived for many years in the country. He feared that by the suggested declaration we should be raising false expectations which could never be realized. He attached great importance to the necessity of retaining the Christian and Moslem Holy Places in Jerusalem and Bethlehem, and, if this were to be effectively done, he did not see how the Jewish people could have a political capital in Palestine. However, he recognized that some expression of sympathy with Jewish aspirations would be a valuable adjunct to our propaganda, though he thought that we should be guarded in the language used in giving expression to such sympathy.

READING AND DISCUSSION QUESTIONS

1. How do the various leaders think that creating a Jewish state will affect Jews living in other countries?

2. What reasons do the leaders give for the urgency to act on this matter and show support for Zionism?

3. What are their concerns about establishing a Jewish settlement within Palestine?

4. Why might some historians see the Balfour Declaration as the cause of later Palestinian-Jewish conflicts? Based on these excerpts, what might support that claim?

29-3 | An Indian Nationalist Condemns the British Government

SAROJINI NAIDU, *The Agony and Shame of the Punjab* (1920)

Despite British concerns, the First World War provoked strong support for Britain among the Indian population. Indians rallied around the British war effort, offering soldiers, food, and other essential resources. After the war, however, Indian nationalism grew rapidly, due in large part to disillusionment with Britain's continuing imperialist policies toward its colonies. In 1919, British troops were ordered to use live ammunition to disperse a peaceful crowd of men, women, and children celebrating a Sikh festival in the city of Amritsar. Hundreds were killed and more than a thousand wounded. Indian feminist and nationalist leader Sarojini Naidu (1879–1949) used this incident and other examples of British hypocrisy to justify Indian independence and self-rule.

I speak to you today as standing arraigned because of the blood-guiltiness of those who have committed murder in my country. I need not go into the details. But I am going to speak to you as a woman about the wrongs committed against my sisters. Englishmen, you who pride yourselves upon your chivalry, you who hold more precious than your imperial treasures the honor and chastity of your women, will you sit still and leave unavenged the dishonor, and the insult and agony inflicted upon the veiled women of the Punjab?

The minions of Lord Chelmsford, the Viceroy, and his martial authorities rent the veil from the faces of the women of the Punjab. Not only were men mown down as if they were grass that is born to wither; but they tore asunder the cherished Purdah,[8] that innermost privacy of the chaste womanhood of India. My sisters were stripped naked, they were flogged, they were outraged. These policies left your British democracy betrayed, dishonored, for no dishonor clings to the martyrs who suffered, but to the tyrants who inflicted the tyranny and pain. Should they hold their Empire by dishonoring the women of another nation or lose it out of chivalry for their honor and chastity? The Bible asked, "What shall it profit a man to gain the whole world and lose his own soul?" You deserve no Empire. You have lost your soul; you have the stain of blood guiltiness upon you; no nation that rules by tyranny is free; it is the slave of its own despotism.

Sarojini Naidu, "The Agony and Shame of the Punjab" [speech], in Padmini Sengupta, *Sarojini Naidu: A Biography* (London: Asia Publishing House, 1966), pp. 161–162.

[8]**Purdah:** Practice in which Indian women hide themselves from view behind veils or in special building enclosures.

READING AND DISCUSSION QUESTIONS

1. Why is Naidu angry?

2. According to Naidu, how does the treatment of Indian women by British officials differ from their treatment of English women?

3. Why does she say that the English "deserve no Empire"? What might this reveal about Indian values at the time?

VIEWPOINTS

Chinese Nationalism and Japanese Imperialism

Nationalist movements across Asia were united by a common set of commitments: resistance to foreign domination, the necessity of social and political reform, and the importance of creating a new sense of identity that transcended local, religious, and familial loyalties. Nonetheless, the interpretation of these objectives and the means by which Asian nationalists sought to achieve them varied widely, depending on the history, culture, and circumstances of the people in question. The document and image included in this feature illustrate this diversity. In China, nationalism was shaped by the failures of the imperial government in the face of Western incursions and by the political fragmentation that followed the collapse of imperial rule. In sharp contrast, Japanese nationalism included an element of colonialism, seeking to duplicate Western imperialism by creating colonies around Asia, which included seizing large areas of China. As you study the reading and image, compare and contrast the different nationalist goals of the Chinese and Japanese. Chinese nationalist Jiang Jieshi's recipe for progress is purely inward looking, while the Japanese nationalists are looking outward, seeking to spread the Japanese language and culture throughout Asia, just as the French and British had sought to do in their own colonies.

29-4 | A Chinese Nationalist Offers a Recipe for Progress
JIANG JIESHI, *The New Life Movement* (1934)

Following the death of Nationalist Party leader Sun Yatsen (see Document 26-5), his protégé Jiang Jieshi (known in the West as Chiang Kai-shek) (1887–1975) took control of the Nationalist movement. By 1927, Jiang had established control of a precariously unified China by

---

Sources of Chinese Tradition, ed. William Theodore de Bary and Richard Lufrano, 2 vols. (New York: Columbia University Press, 2001), 2:341–344. Copyright © 2001 Columbia University Press. Reprinted with permission of the publisher.

defeating or eliminating his opposition, including his former allies, the Communists. Jiang's rule focused on the unification and "education" of China, which he felt necessary before democracy could be practiced. To those ends, in 1934 Jiang gave a speech proclaiming his New Life Movement. Enforced with the help of Jiang's secret and quasi-fascist Blue Shirt Society, the New Life Movement set forth tradition, anti-individualism, and personal morality and hygiene as the foundation for a stronger, better China.

The Object of the New Life Movement

Why Is a New Life Needed?

The general psychology of our people today can be described as spiritless. What manifests itself in behavior is this: lack of discrimination between good and evil, between what is public and what is private, and between what is primary and what is secondary. Because there is no discrimination between good and evil, right and wrong are confused; because there is no discrimination between public and private, improper taking and giving [of public funds] occur; and because there is no distinction between primary and secondary, first and last are not placed in the proper order. As a result, officials tend to be dishonest and avaricious, the masses are undisciplined and calloused, youth become degraded and intemperate, adults are corrupt and ignorant, the rich become extravagant and luxurious, and the poor become mean and disorderly. Naturally it has resulted in disorganization of the social order and national life, and we are in no position either to prevent or to remedy natural calamities, disasters caused from within, or invasions from without. The individual, society, and the whole country are now suffering. . . . In order to develop the life of our nation, protect the existence of our society, and improve the livelihood of our people, it is absolutely necessary to wipe out these unwholesome conditions and to start to lead a new and rational life.

The Content of the New Life Movement

The Principles of the New Life Movement

The New Life Movement aims at the promotion of a regular life guided by the four virtues, namely, *li, yi, lian,* and *chi.* Those virtues must be applied to ordinary life in the matter of food, clothing, shelter, and action. The four virtues are the essential principles for the promotion of morality. They form the major rules for dealing with men and human affairs, for cultivating oneself, and for adjustment to one's surroundings. Whoever violates these rules is bound to fail, and a nation that neglects them will not survive.

There are two kinds of skeptics:

First, some hold that the four virtues are merely rules of good conduct. No matter how good they may be, they are not sufficient to save a nation whose knowledge and technique are inferior to others.

Those who hold this view do not seem to understand the distinction between matters of primary and secondary importance. People need knowledge and technique because they want to do good. Otherwise, knowledge and technique can only be instruments of dishonorable deeds. *Li, yi, lian,* and *chi* are the principal rules alike for the community, the group, or the entire nation. Those who do not observe these rules will probably utilize their knowledge and ability to the detriment of society and ultimately to their own disadvantage. Therefore, these virtues not only can save the nation but also can rebuild the nation.

Second, there is another group of people who argue that these virtues are merely formal refinements that are useless in dealing with hunger and cold. . . . [Yet] when these virtues prevail, even if food and clothing are insufficient, they can be produced by human labor; or, if the granary is empty, it can be filled through human effort. On the other hand, when these virtues are not observed, if food and clothing are insufficient, they will not be made sufficient by fighting and robbing; or, if the granary is empty, it will not be filled by stealing and begging. The four virtues, which rectify the misconduct of men, are the proper methods of achieving abundance. Without them, there will be fighting, robbing, stealing, and begging among men. . . .

The Meaning of *Li, Yi, Lian,* and *Chi*

Although *li, yi, lian,* and *chi* have always been regarded as the foundations of the nation, yet the changing times and circumstances may require that these principles be given a new interpretation. As applied to our life today, they may be interpreted as follows:

Li means "regulated attitude."
Yi means "right conduct."
Lian means "clear discrimination."
Chi means "real self-consciousness."

The word *li* (decorum) means *li* (principle). It becomes natural law when applied to nature; it becomes a rule when applied to social affairs; and it signifies discipline when used in reference to national affairs. A man's conduct is considered regular if it conforms with the above law, rule, and discipline. When one conducts oneself in accordance with the regular manner, one is said to have the regulated attitude.

The word *yi* means "proper." Any conduct that is in accordance with *li*—i.e., natural law, social rule, and national discipline—is considered proper. To act improperly, or to refrain from acting when one knows it is proper to act, cannot be called *yi.*

The word *lian* means "clear." It denotes distinction between right and wrong. What agrees with *li* and *yi* is right, and what does not agree is wrong. To take what we recognize as right and to forgo what we recognize as wrong constitute clear discrimination.

The word *chi* means "consciousness." When one is conscious of the fact that his own actions are not in accordance with *li, yi, lian,* and *chi,* one feels ashamed.

From the above explanations, it is clear that *chi* governs the motive of action, that *lian* gives the guidance for it, that *yi* relates to the carrying out of an action, and that *li* regulates its outward form. The four are interrelated. They are dependent upon each other in the perfecting of virtue.

Conclusion

In short, the main object of the New Life Movement is to substitute a rational life for the irrational, and to achieve this we must observe *li, yi, lian,* and *chi* in our daily life.

1. By the observance of these virtues, it is hoped that rudeness and vulgarity will be got rid of and that the life of our people will conform to the standard of art. By art we are not referring to the special enjoyment of the gentry. We mean the cultural standard of all the people, irrespective of sex, age, wealth, and class. It is the boundary line between civilized life and barbarism. It is the only way by which one can achieve the purpose of man, for only by artistically controlling oneself and dealing with others can one fulfill the duty of mutual assistance. . . . A lack of artistic training is the cause of suspicion, jealousy, hatred, and strife that are prevalent in our society today. . . . To investigate things so as to extend our knowledge, to distinguish between the fundamental and the secondary, to seek the invention of instruments, to excel in our techniques — these are the essentials of an artistic life, the practice of which will enable us to wipe out the defects of vulgarity, confusion, crudity, and baseness.

2. By the observance of these virtues, it is hoped that beggary and robbery will be eliminated and that the life of our people will be productive. The poverty of China is primarily caused by the fact that there are too many consumers and too few producers. Those who consume without producing usually live as parasites or as robbers. They behave thus because they are ignorant of the four virtues. To remedy this we must make them produce more and spend less. They must understand that luxury is improper and that living as a parasite is a shame.

3. By the observance of these virtues, it is hoped that social disorder and individual weakness will be remedied and that people will become more military-minded. If a country cannot defend itself, it has every chance of losing its existence. . . . Therefore our people must have military training. As a preliminary, we must acquire the habits of orderliness, cleanliness, simplicity, frugality, promptness, and exactness. We must preserve order, emphasize organization, responsibility, and discipline, and be ready to die for the country at any moment.

READING AND DISCUSSION QUESTIONS

1. What is the aim of the New Life Movement? What are its four components?

2. What criticisms does Jiang predict, and how does he answer them?

3. How does art figure into Jiang's vision of "New Life"? How is the promotion of art — or any other individual activity or attitude — supposed to have an impact on the nation?

4. Do you find Jiang's prescriptions for social improvement compelling? Why or why not?

29-5 | The Japanese Puppet Empire of Manchuria (Manchukuo)

Manchukuo Emperor Aisin-Gioro Puyi Visits Japan (1940)

In 1931, the Japanese invaded northeast China and established a puppet state in Manchuria (Manchukuo, in Japanese) and parts of Inner Mongolia. To legitimize their control over an ostensibly independent country, they made the dethroned last emperor of China, Puyi, first president, and then in 1934, emperor of Manchuria. Puyi had ascended the Chinese Dragon Throne in 1908 at the age of two years and ten months. Only three years later, in 1911, he was forced to abdicate following the Nationalist revolution of that year, thus becoming the last emperor of the Qing Dynasty. Puyi was forbidden to leave the imperial palace in Beijing from this time until 1924, when he was expelled and fled to the Japanese concession in the city of Tianjin. Here, he sought Japan's help in restoring him to the throne. Instead, in November 1931, the Japanese took him to Manchuria, where he was forced to become a puppet emperor entirely under Japanese control. Throughout his years as emperor, Puyi signed degrees, proclamations, and regulations — anything that the Japanese put in front of him. Puyi remained emperor until the Japanese surrender in August 1945 and was soon afterward taken prisoner by the Soviet Red Army. Declared a war criminal after the war, Puyi lived in Soviet, and then Chinese, prisons until being transferred to a government-sponsored hotel under the orders of Mao Zedong in 1959. He lived out the remainder of his life as a simple gardener until his death in Beijing in 1967. (An Oscar-winning biographical film of his life, *The Last*

The Asahi Shimbun/Getty Images

Emperor, appeared in 1987.) In the photo, the Japanese emperor Hirohito (left) greets Puyi at the Tokyo train station as he begins a state visit in June 1940. As you study the image, consider why the Japanese felt the need to go to such great lengths to legitimize their rule over Manchuria.

READING AND DISCUSSION QUESTIONS

1. Does this photo portray Emperor Puyi as an equal to Emperor Hirohito? Why or why not? Why might the Japanese want to make Puyi appear as an equal?

2. Both emperors are wearing military uniforms, not imperial court robes. Why? What is the significance of this?

3. Emperor Puyi would only be allowed to wear medals on his uniform that the Japanese approved. Why would they want him to appear highly decorated? What might all the medals on his uniform signify?

4. Puyi always believed that the Japanese would eventually restore him to the Chinese imperial throne. Did this justify his actions as a puppet ruler in Manchuria? How did signing documents consolidating Japanese control legitimize their rule? What do his actions say about his conception of Chinese nationalism?

VIEWPOINTS COMPARATIVE QUESTIONS

1. What steps did Jiang Jieshi believe the Chinese had to take to progress and come together as a nation? What did the Japanese believe was necessary for Japan to progress and become a great nation? What did each identify as the greatest threat to the nation?

2. The Chinese overthrew their emperor in 1911, while the Japanese still recognize their emperor today (although he has no official power). What does Japan's installation of a former Chinese emperor to legitimize their puppet empire of Manchuria say about the differences between Chinese and Japanese nationalism in the 1920s and 1930s?

■ COMPARATIVE QUESTIONS ■

1. In each of the documents in this chapter, the question of national identity is addressed either implicitly or explicitly. How does the author of each document take up the question of nationalism? What national identities are mentioned or described, and how?

2. How is nationalism presented as a positive or negative force in each document? Who is commenting on the value of nation and nationalism in each document, and what relationship can you identify between the author's identity and his or her views on nationalism?

3. How is nationalism connected to modernity in each document? How is nationalism linked to Western identity or Western ideas?

4. How does the use of foreign or Western ideas converge or differ in each text?

5. Lord Balfour and Sarojini Naidu represent the United Kingdom and its colony India, respectively. How do their writings reflect their position as imperial power or colony? Does any commonality of theme or purpose link them? On what do Balfour and Naidu agree, if anything?

30

The Great Depression and World War II

1929–1945

The Great Depression may have had its origins in the economy of the United States, but its effects were rapidly experienced throughout most of the world, and the hardships it generated added stress to the already fragile social and political situations that existed after the First World War. In the United States, the depression exacerbated social tensions; in Europe and elsewhere, it helped radicalize the political landscape, as men and women sought to create and make sense of new visions of state and citizen. New expressions of nationalism emerged, including the chilling racism of Hitler's Nazi Germany, Stalin's totalitarian order in the Communist Soviet Union, and Mussolini's Fascist control of Italy. While the Soviet Union's planned economy was largely spared the effects of the depression, citizens there also struggled to understand how their lives fit new forms of state and society. Universally, these social and political developments helped fuel the Second World War, which claimed millions of lives, ushered in the age of nuclear conflict, and reshaped the geopolitical landscape for decades.

30-1 | The Great Depression, London, 1930
One Man Demo (ca. 1930)

The Great Depression began in the United States, but it soon spread around the globe, reflecting how economically interconnected the world had become by 1929. In her 1993 novel *Consider the Lily*, author Elizabeth Buchan includes a letter from Kit, who lives in London, to his friend Matty. It is October 23, 1930. "I saw a man walking up

Elizabeth Buchan, *Consider the Lily* (New York: Penguin Books, 2005), p. 119.

and down the street by Marble Arch yesterday and I was very struck by the message on the placard." It is the man in the image here. After repeating the lines on the placard, Kit continues, "I watched him for a long time and his predicament made me boil with anger and pity. It can't be right that this is happening." Buchan must have seen this image and considered it so striking that she felt the need to refer to it in her book. As you study the image, what emotional response does it evoke? Anger and pity, like Kit, or other feelings?

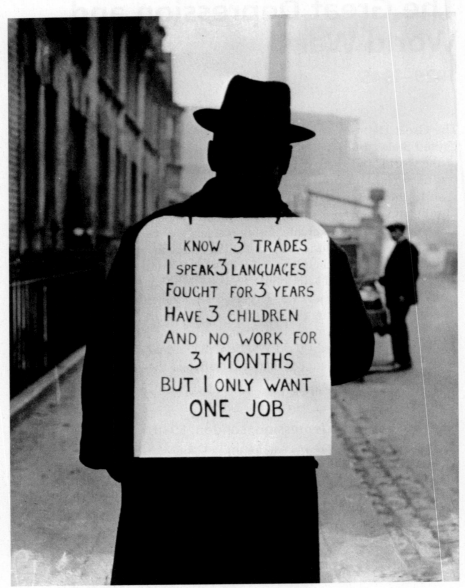

General Photographic Agency/Getty Images

READING AND DISCUSSION QUESTIONS

1. What skills does this man have that demonstrate how no one could escape the effects of the Great Depression?

2. This man fought for three years in the Great War. How might that experience make his current situation seem unfair or undeserved?

3. Millions of people around the world shared Kit's feeling of helplessness when he said, "It can't be right that this is happening." What are two or three actions you might have taken to combat helplessness and survive the depression?

30-2 | Legislating Racial Purity

The Nuremberg Laws: The Centerpiece of Nazi Racial Legislation (1935)

Adolf Hitler's beliefs about Germanic racial superiority, first articulated in his 1925 book *Mein Kampf*, became the foundation for the Nuremberg Laws, enacted after Hitler (1889–1945) seized power as German chancellor in 1933. Designed to preserve the purity of the German race, the laws—which were a manifestation of Hitler's fierce anti-Semitism—deemed Jews inferior, defined who was a Jew, and prohibited intermarriage between Germans and non-Germans (especially Jews). In the end, Jews lost not only citizenship rights and jobs but also their freedom and lives; ultimately, 6 million perished in the Holocaust.

Article 5

1. A Jew is anyone who descended from at least three grandparents who were racially full Jews. Article 2, par. 2, second sentence will apply.

2. A Jew is also one who descended from two full Jewish parents, if: (a) he belonged to the Jewish religious community at the time this law was issued, or who joined the community later; (b) he was married to a Jewish person, at the time the law was issued, or married one subsequently; (c) he is the offspring from a marriage with a Jew, in the sense of Section 1, which was contracted after the Law for the Protection of German Blood and German Honor became effective . . . ; (d) he is the offspring of an extramarital relationship, with a Jew, according to Section 1, and will be born out of wedlock after July 31, 1936. . . .

Law for the Protection of German Blood and German Honor of September 15, 1935

Thoroughly convinced by the knowledge that the purity of German blood is essential for the further existence of the German people and animated by

U.S. *Chief of Counsel for the Prosecution of Axis Criminality, Nazi Conspiracy and Aggression* (Washington, D.C.: U.S. Government Printing Office, 1946), vol. 4, doc. no. 1417-PS, 8–10; vol. 4, doc. no. 2000-PS, 636–638.

the inflexible will to safe-guard the German nation for the entire future, the Reichstag[1] has resolved upon the following law unanimously, which is promulgated herewith:

Section 1

1. Marriages between Jews and nationals of German or kindred blood are forbidden. Marriages concluded in defiance of this law are void, even if, for the purpose of evading this law, they are concluded abroad. . . .

Section 2

Relation[s] outside marriage between Jews and nationals of German or kindred blood are forbidden.

Section 3

Jews will not be permitted to employ female nationals of German or kindred blood in their household.

Section 4

1. Jews are forbidden to hoist the Reich and national flag and to present the colors of the Reich. . . .

Section 5

1. A person who acts contrary to the prohibition of Section 1 will be punished with hard labor.
2. A person who acts contrary to the prohibition of Section 2 will be punished with imprisonment or with hard labor.
3. A person who acts contrary to the provisions of Sections 3 or 4 will be punished with imprisonment up to a year and with a fine or with one of these penalties. . . .

READING AND DISCUSSION QUESTIONS

1. What makes someone a Jew, according to the Nuremberg Laws?
2. Why do you think so much attention is paid to "relations" between Germans and Jews in these laws?
3. Within the laws, what restrictions render Jews different from and inferior to other Germans?
4. What do the laws suggest about the place of race in Nazi ideology?

---

[1]**Reichstag:** The German legislative assembly.

30-3 | The Place of Women in Stalin's Soviet Union

Letters to Izvestiya: *On the Issue of Abortion* (1936)

As Joseph Stalin (1879–1953) rose to absolute power in the Soviet Union between 1922 and 1927, he launched an ambitious and strict campaign to solidify socialism by placing all economic development under government control and promoting new cultural values. Women, who had gained greater equality after the 1917 Bolshevik Revolution, became a key focus. As birthrates dropped by up to 50 percent from 1930 to 1935, Stalin's government released propaganda celebrating women's traditional roles as wives and mothers and enacted legislation outlawing abortion except to save the mother's life. The public's thoughts on this legal change ran in newspapers such as *Pravda* and *Izvestiya*.

Letter from a Student [K.B.]

I have read in the press the draft law on the prohibition of abortion, aid to expectant mothers, etc., and cannot remain silent on this matter.

There are thousands of women in the same position as myself. I am a student reading the first course of the second Moscow Medical Institute. My husband is also a student reading the same course at our Institute. Our scholarships amount jointly to 205 rubles. Neither he nor I have a room of our own. Next year we intend to apply for admission to a hostel, but I do not know whether our application will be granted. I love children and shall probably have some in four or five years' time. But can I have a child now? Having a child now would mean leaving the Institute, lagging behind my husband, forgetting everything I have learnt and probably leaving Moscow because there is nowhere to live.

There is another married couple in our Institute, Mitya and Galya, who live in a hostel. Yesterday Galya said to me: "If I become pregnant I shall have to leave the Institute; one cannot live in a hostel with children."

I consider that the projected law is premature because the housing problem in our towns is a painful one. Very often it is the lack of living quarters that is the reason behind an abortion. If the draft included an article assuring married couples, who are expecting a baby, of a room—that would be a different matter.

In five years' time when I am a doctor and have a job and a room I shall have children. But at present I do not want and cannot undertake such a responsibility. . . .

Answer to the Student K.B.

Your paper recently published a letter from a student, K.B., in which she raised objections to the prohibition of abortions. I think the author of the letter . . . has not grasped the full significance of the projected law. The difficulties about which K.B. writes and which, according to her, justify abortion are, she thinks, the difficulties of to-day which will have disappeared to-morrow. The writer of that letter completely ignored the fact that the government, by widening the network of child-welfare institutions, is easing the mother's task in looking after the child. The main mistake K.B. makes is, in my view, that she approaches the problem of childbearing as though it were a private matter. This would explain why she writes: "I shall have them (children) in four or five years' time." She hopes by that time to have completed her studies, obtained a medical diploma and found both a job and a room. But one must be logical! If during these years, K.B. intends to have recourse to abortions, who can vouch that by the time when she desires to have children she will still be able to do so? And for a normal woman to be deprived of the possibility of having children is as great a misfortune as the loss of a dear one.

I used to study in a factory and received a very small allowance while bringing up my small son whom I had to bring up on my own. (His father was dead.) It was a hard time. I had to go and unload trains or look for similar work that would bring in some money . . . that was in 1923. Now my son is a good, rough Komsomol[2] and a Red Army[3] soldier in the Far East. How great are my joy and pride that I did not shun the difficulties and that I managed to bring up such a son.

Letter from an Engineer [E.T.]

I am non-party [not Communist], married, with a 5-year-old son. I work as an engineer and have been and still am in a responsible position. I regard myself as a good citizen of the U.S.S.R.

I cannot agree with the prohibition of abortions. And I am very glad that this law has not entered into force but has been submitted to the workers for discussion.

The prohibition of abortion means the compulsory birth of a child to a woman who does not want children. The birth of a child ties married people to each other. Not everyone will readily abandon a child, for alimony is not all that children need. Where the parents produce a child of their own free will, all is well. But where a child comes into the family against the will of the parents, a grim personal drama will be enacted which will undoubtedly lower the social value of the parents and leave its mark on the child.

A categorical prohibition of abortion will confront young people with a dilemma: either complete sexual abstinence or the risk of jeopardizing their studies and disrupting their life. To my mind any prohibition of abortion is bound to mutilate many a young life. Apart from this, the result of such a prohibition might be an increase in the death-rate from abortions because they will then be performed illegally.

---

[2]**Komsomol:** Member of the Communist Youth Organization.
[3]**Red Army:** The reconstituted Soviet army founded by Commissar of Military and Naval Affairs Leon Trotsky (1879–1940) after the 1917 Bolshevik Revolution.

Letter from Professor K. Bogorekov, Leningrad

Abortions are harmful. One cannot disagree with that. But situations in life do exist when this harmful remedy will allow a woman to preserve normal conditions of life.

If a single child already ties a woman down, two, three, or four children leave her no possibility at all of participating in social life and having a job. A man suffers less. He gives the family his salary irrespective of the number of children—and the whole burden falls upon the mother.

Sometimes abortion is an extreme but decisive means of averting the disruption of a young woman's life. It may become imperative, through the accident of an unlucky liaison for a young girl-student without means for whom a child would be a heavy penalty, or through bad heredity of the parents or a number of other contingencies which play an important part in life and can often lead to its mutilation. All this must be taken into account.

It must not be thought that the majority of abortions are the result of irresponsible behavior. Experience shows that a woman resorts to abortion as a last resource when other methods of safeguard against pregnancy have failed and the birth of a child threatens to make her life more difficult.

Simple statistics show that in spite of this the birth-rate of our country is increasing rapidly.[4] And what is needed is not pressure, but a stimulation of the birth-rate by means of financial assistance, improved housing conditions, legal action against those who fail to pay alimony, etc. . . .

Abortions will become obsolete by themselves when knowledge of human anatomy spreads, methods of birth-control are more widely used and—last but not least—when housing conditions are improved. . . .

Letter from Professor M. Malinovsky

Performing an abortion is an operation undoubtedly involving great risks. There are few operations so dangerous as the cleaning out of the womb during pregnancy. Under the best of conditions and in the hands of the most experienced specialist this operation still has a "normal" percentage of fatal cases. It is true that the percentage is not very high. Our surgeons have brought the technique of performing abortions to perfection. The foreign doctors who have watched operations in our gynæcological hospitals have unanimously testified that their technique is irreproachable. And yet . . . here are still cases in which it is fatal. This is understandable. The operation is performed in the dark and with instruments which, so far as their effect on so tender an organ as the womb is concerned, remind one of a crowbar. And even the most gifted surgeons, virtuosi at their job, occasionally cause great and serious injuries for which the woman often pays with her life. . . .

---

[4]**birth-rate . . . increasing rapidly:** From what is known, this is a false statement.

The slave-like conditions of hired labor, together with unemployment and poverty, deprive women in capitalist countries of the impulse for childbearing. Their "will to motherhood" is paralyzed. In our country all the conditions for giving birth to and bringing up a healthy generation exist. The "fear of mother-hood," the fear of the morrow, the anxiety over the child's future are gone.

The lighthearted attitude towards the family, the feeling of irresponsibility which is still quite strong in men and women, the disgusting disrespect for women and children — all these must come before our guns. Every baseness towards women and every form of profligacy [extravagance] must be considered as serious antisocial acts. . . .

READING AND DISCUSSION QUESTIONS

1. Why does K.B. argue that abortion must remain legal? What solution for reducing the number of abortions does she propose? What generational differences do you notice between K.B.'s position and that of the woman who responds to her?

2. Why does E.T. oppose the ban on abortion?

3. Professor K. Bogorekov says that abortion will cease when what happens? Why does he think this is the case?

4. What comparison does Professor Malinovsky make between socialist and capitalist countries?

VIEWPOINTS

Hiroshima and Nagasaki

By the summer of 1945, Germany had surrendered and it was clear that the Allies would prevail against the Japanese in the Pacific. What was not clear was how long victory would take and how many lives it would cost. As they made plans for the invasion of the Japanese mainland, American commanders estimated that this final stage of the war would produce a million American casualties and result in the deaths of 10 to 20 million Japanese. It was in this context that President Harry Truman and his advisers decided to drop nuclear weapons on the Japanese cities of Hiroshima and Nagasaki. The decision was not reached without debate, and it remains controversial to this day. Some scholars believe that Japan was close to surrender even before the bombs were dropped. Others point out that American leaders could have taken a number of intermediate steps before resorting to the use of nuclear weapons. Still others argue that racial animus played a significant role in the decision to use nuclear weapons against Japan. As you read the documents included in this feature, formulate your opinion on this controversy. Were American leaders right to use nuclear weapons against Japan when they did? If so, why? If not, what should they have done instead?

30-4 | Truman Describes the Creation and Use of Nuclear Weapons

HARRY S. TRUMAN, *White House Press Release on Hiroshima* (August 6, 1945)

After the death of U.S. president Franklin Delano Roosevelt in April 1945, his vice president, Harry S. Truman (1884–1972), became president and inherited command of the Second World War. The U.S. government had engaged in nuclear weapons research since 1939, when notable scientists (including Albert Einstein) had signed a letter to the president warning of the possible military applications of atomic energy. The following press release, although formally issued after the August 6 nuclear attack on Hiroshima, was written by the War Department and submitted to President Truman on July 30, a full week earlier. In effect, Truman's approval of this press release was a final go-ahead for the first military nuclear strike in history. The release itself was the first official notice to the American people—and the world—of the age of atomic weapons.

Sixteen hours ago an American airplane dropped one bomb on [Hiroshima] and destroyed its usefulness to the enemy.[5] That bomb had more power than 20,000 tons of T.N.T. It had more than two thousand times the blast power of the British "Grand Slam" which is the largest bomb ever yet used in the history of warfare.

The Japanese began the war from the air at Pearl Harbor.[6] They have been repaid many fold. And the end is not yet. With this bomb we have now added a new and revolutionary increase in destruction to supplement the growing power of our armed forces. In their present form these bombs are now in production and even more powerful forms are in development.

It is an atomic bomb. It is a harnessing of the basic power of the universe. The force from which the sun draws its power has been loosed against those who brought war to the Far East.

Before 1939, it was the accepted belief of scientists that it was theoretically possible to release atomic energy. But no one knew any practical method of

---

"Statement by the President of the United States" [White House press release], August 6, 1945 (Harry S. Truman Library and Museum, Ayers Papers), www.trumanlibrary.org/whistlestop/study_collections/bomb/large/documents/index.php?documentdate=1945-08-06&documentid=59&studycollectionid=abomb&pagenumber=1.

[5][Hiroshima] . . . enemy: While Hiroshima was an important port and military center, it was also a thriving city. In the original release, the city's name is withheld.

[6]Pearl Harbor: The U.S. Navy base in Hawaii and the site of the 1941 Japanese attack on U.S. forces.

doing it. By 1942, however, we knew that the Germans were working feverishly to find a way to add atomic energy to the other engines of war with which they hoped to enslave the world. But they failed. We may be grateful to Providence that the Germans got the V-1's and V-2's[7] late and in limited quantities and even more grateful that they did not get the atomic bomb at all.

The battle of the laboratories held fateful risks for us as well as the battles of the air, land and sea, and we have now won the battle of the laboratories as we have won the other battles.

Beginning in 1940, before Pearl Harbor, scientific knowledge useful in war was pooled between the United States and Great Britain, and many priceless helps to our victories have come from that arrangement. Under that general policy the research on the atomic bomb was begun. With American and British scientists working together we entered the race of discovery against the Germans.

The United States had available the large number of scientists of distinction in the many needed areas of knowledge. It had the tremendous industrial and financial resources necessary for the project and they could be devoted to it without undue impairment of other vital war work. In the United States the laboratory work and the production plants, on which a substantial start had already been made, would be out of reach of enemy bombing, while at that time Britain was exposed to constant air attack and was still threatened with the possibility of invasion. For these reasons Prime Minister Churchill and President Roosevelt agreed that it was wise to carry on the project here. We now have two great plants and many lesser works devoted to the production of atomic power. Employment during peak construction numbered 125,000 and over 65,000 individuals are even now engaged in operating the plants. Many have worked there for two and a half years. Few know what they have been producing. They see great quantities of material going in and they see nothing coming out of these plants, for the physical size of the explosive charge is exceedingly small. We have spent two billion dollars on the greatest scientific gamble in history—and won.

But the greatest marvel is not the size of the enterprise, its secrecy, nor its cost, but the achievement of scientific brains in putting together infinitely complex pieces of knowledge held by many men in different fields of science into a workable plan. And hardly less marvellous has been the capacity of industry to design, and of labor to operate, the machines and methods to do things never done before so that the brain child of many minds came forth in physical shape and performed as it was supposed to do. Both science and industry worked under the direction of the United States Army, which achieved a unique success in managing so diverse a problem in the advancement of knowledge in an amazingly short time. It is doubtful if such another

---

[7]**V-1's and V-2's:** Guided missiles used by Germany against targets in Great Britain during the Second World War.

combination could be got together in the world. What has been done is the greatest achievement of organized science in history. It was done under high pressure and without failure.

We are now prepared to obliterate more rapidly and completely every productive enterprise the Japanese have above ground in any city. We shall destroy their docks, their factories, and their communications. Let there be no mistake; we shall completely destroy Japan's power to make war.

It was to spare the Japanese people from utter destruction that the ultimatum of July 26 was issued at Potsdam.[8] Their leaders promptly rejected that ultimatum. If they do not now accept our terms they may expect a rain of ruin from the air, the like of which has never been seen on this earth. Behind this air attack will follow sea and land forces in such numbers and power as they have not yet seen and with the fighting skill of which they are already well aware.

The Secretary of War, who has kept in personal touch with all phases of this project, will immediately make public a statement giving further details.

His statement will give facts concerning the sites of Oak Ridge near Knoxville, Tennessee, and at Richland near Pasco, Washington, and an installation near Santa Fe, New Mexico. Although the workers at the sites have been making materials to be used in producing the greatest destructive force in history they have not themselves been in danger beyond that of many other occupations, for the utmost care has been taken of their safety.

The fact that we can release atomic energy ushers in a new era in man's understanding of nature's forces. Atomic energy may in the future supplement the power that now comes from coal, oil, and falling water, but at present it cannot be produced on a basis to compete with them commercially. Before that comes there must be a long period of intensive research.

It has never been the habit of the scientists of this country or the policy of this Government to withhold from the world scientific knowledge. Normally, therefore, everything about the work with atomic energy would be made public.

But under present circumstances it is not intended to divulge the technical processes of production or all the military applications, pending further examination of possible methods of protecting us and the rest of the world from the danger of sudden destruction. I shall recommend that the Congress of the United States consider promptly the establishment of an appropriate commission to control the production and use of atomic power within the United States. I shall give further consideration and make further recommendations to the Congress as to how atomic power can become a powerful and forceful influence towards the maintenance of world peace.

---

[8]**the ultimatum of July 26 . . . at Potsdam:** The Potsdam Declaration of July 26, 1945, called for the "unconditional surrender" of Japanese military forces, warning of "prompt and utter destruction" unless Japan complied.

READING AND DISCUSSION QUESTIONS

1. Historians disagree about the U.S. motivation for using atomic weapons. How does Truman characterize Hiroshima and Japan in order to defend the use of the atomic bomb?

2. What points about the nuclear strike on Hiroshima does Truman emphasize? What details does he leave out?

3. What does Truman's press release suggest about the growth of Big Science? How did the Los Alamos project foreshadow postwar developments in the relationship between government and scientific research?

30-5 | The Impact of a Nuclear Weapon

TOSHIKO SAEKI, *Interview with a Survivor of Hiroshima* (1986)

On August 6, 1945, the U.S. military attacked the Japanese city of Hiroshima with a nuclear weapon. Casualty estimates range from slightly below to well over 100,000 deaths caused by the immediate attack, with many more deaths linked to radiation and other long-term injuries. Although the firebombing of Tokyo, Dresden, and other cities had produced similarly high death tolls, the shocking destructive power of the atomic weapon was unprecedented. The experiences of survivors—known by the Japanese term *hibakusha*—have been chronicled in many media and for a variety of reasons, including U.S. government studies on the effects of nuclear weapons on human populations. Here, a 1986 interview with a survivor by representatives of the Hiroshima Peace Cultural Center presents a firsthand account of the attack.

Ms. Toshiko Saeki, then 26. She was exposed to the atomic bomb when she entered the city to return to her parents' home in Yasufuruichi. She arrived in the city on the afternoon of August 6th and searched for members of her family every day after that. Thirteen people in her family, including her parents, perished as a result of the atomic bomb.

SAEKI: One of my older sisters lived about 12 kilometers from my house in Hiroshima and I had asked her to take care of my children. It was safer in the countryside. I was at my sister's house on August 5th, but when I moved to leave, my children started crying. My sister said it would be better if I spent the night, so I did.

INTERVIEWER: Where were you?

SAEKI: My sister's house was in present-day Numata-cho, about 12 kilometers from Hiroshima. After spending the night there, I was planning to return to Hiroshima the next morning on the 7:00 bus. But I ended up missing the bus

From the "Voice of Hibakusha" eyewitness accounts aired as part of *Hiroshima Witness*, produced by the Hiroshima Peace Cultural Center and NHK, the public broadcasting company of Japan. Translated into English and posted as "Testimony of Toshiko Saeki," AtomicArchive .com. Published in a limited edition by Andrew Mossberg.

so I would have to return to Hiroshima on foot. I went back to my sister's house and was chatting with her when an air-raid alert sounded. This warning was soon lifted, though. I then saw an airplane, a B-29, flying toward us from the mountains to the left of the house. It seemed strange that the anti-aircraft artillery on Hijiyama Hill wasn't firing at it. I watched the airplane fly off until it disappeared. But then another airplane flew in from the same direction. Suddenly, there was an eerie flash and I felt engulfed in heat—it was incredibly hot. I hit the floor, and as I heard a tremendous explosion, some sliding doors inside the house came flying in my direction. I looked up to see what had happened and discovered that the ceiling had collapsed and my sister and my children were buried beneath it. My sister called out for everyone to run to the safety of the storeroom, but I was frozen there on the floor. I was still in shock from seeing that flash in the sky—it's a sight I'll never forget. An enormous fireball then rose into the air, gradually becoming a great cloud of smoke. I burst into tears and cried out, "Hiroshima has been destroyed! Our mother is dead!" My sister came out of the storeroom and told me to stop crying. "Kure was attacked," she said, "not Hiroshima!" But I didn't think so, because smoldering debris was now falling from the sky, confirming a closer distance.

INTERVIEWER: Which part of Hiroshima did you live in?

SAEKI: I was living in Hirosemotomachi, only about a kilometer from the hypocenter. So I had a sense of the distance from my sister's house and that's why, when I saw the flash, I was afraid Hiroshima had been attacked. I asked my sister to pack some food for me so I could head back to Hiroshima to help our family. In the meantime, it started raining. At first, I welcomed the rain as I thought it would put out the fire. But the rain was black and it was pouring down. Some of the drops stuck to my hand and I tried to wipe them off, but they were really sticky. I didn't think it was rain, but I had no idea what it was. I smelled it, then licked it, but I still wasn't sure. Finally, I gulped some of it down to make sure it wasn't oil.

INTERVIEWER: You swallowed some of it?

SAEKI: Yes, because if it had been oil, I would have had to flee right away. I had a friend who lived in Kure and she had written me a letter at the end of July. In the letter, she told me that enemy aircraft had sprayed oil on the city and then dropped incendiary bombs. Actually, if the police had seen the text of this letter, we could have gotten into trouble—mention of Japan's losses during the war was forbidden. There were no air-raid shelters in the countryside, so I knew I would have to flee quickly if it was oil.

INTERVIEWER: Then what did you do?

SAEKI: I was convinced that it was rain after all, not oil. So I went to catch a bus back to Hiroshima to help my family. On the way, I ran into 50 or 60 people fleeing Hiroshima. They looked frightful, far worse than the figures in the Peace Memorial Museum.[9] I shouted at them to tell me what part

---

[9]**Peace Memorial Museum:** A museum in Hiroshima, Japan, established in 1955 to preserve artifacts and testimony from the U.S. nuclear attack, its aftermath, and related issues.

of Hiroshima had been bombed. But they would only reply that something terrible had happened there. As I ran on, I encountered a man who was naked. I hesitated for a moment, but then I called out to him to stop. When I asked him what part of Hiroshima had been bombed, he stared at me for a long moment. "You're Toshiko, aren't you?" he said. The man's face was so swollen that I couldn't recognize him right away. He continued, "It's me, Toshiko! Can't you recognize me?" And then I finally realized that he was one of my older brothers. He was in a terrible state—his whole body was badly burned. Just after my mother woke him up, the bomb exploded and he lost consciousness. When he came to, he heard an old woman shrieking for help as flames began to engulf her. My brother crawled frantically through the fire and managed to escape. If he had hesitated, he surely would have been burned to death. He told me that my mother went up to the third floor after waking him up and she was likely hit hard by the blast. He had to assume that she was killed. He also told me that my younger sister, 18 years old, had gone to the hospital in Hatchobori that morning. I asked him which part of the city had been bombed and he replied that the area west of Honkawa had been totally destroyed.

INTERVIEWER: How long did it take you to reach Hiroshima?

SAEKI: I'm not sure what time I left my sister's house, but it was probably about 10:00 that morning. I had to go on foot, and in addition to running into my brother, I spent some time helping the wounded along the way, so it took about two hours. I finally arrived in Hiroshima at about noon.

INTERVIEWER: And what did you experience then?

SAEKI: In Koi, everyone was being evacuated to the elementary school. When I got there, the school was full of victims, crying out for help. People who weren't injured were carrying out the bodies of the dead. I started to look for my parents, but it was hard to recognize people's misshapen faces, so I tried to identify them by their clothing. Out in the schoolyard were piles of bodies and I wondered if my parents were among them. But I was at a loss as to how I might find them within these piles. When I was crossing Fukushima Bridge, I saw a lot of cattle in the river—evidently, they had escaped from a slaughterhouse. This picture tries to capture that moment. After all, humans weren't the only victims of the bomb. The victims included birds, cats, and dogs—but there aren't really words to describe the awful sight of those cattle. Like the human victims, their bodies were burned and bloated. They were horribly disfigured.

INTERVIEWER: How long did you look for the missing members of your family?

SAEKI: I searched for them almost every day after the bombing.

INTERVIEWER: Did you find out what happened to your mother?

SAEKI: Despite my efforts, I could find no clues. But on September 6th, my older brother called us all together. He placed something on the table before us—it was wrapped up in a piece of cloth. He told me that I should be the one to open it since I had been looking for her so hard. I unwrapped the bundle, expecting to find some bones, but I found her skull instead, half of it charred black. Her skull had no eyes or nose, but a bit of skin and hair was still on the back. And some glasses were still stuck to it.

INTERVIEWER: How did you know it was your mother?

SAEKI: I could tell by the glasses—they had thick lenses, like my mother's pair of glasses.

INTERVIEWER: What happened to your older brother?

SAEKI: After my mother's skull was found, he had a mental breakdown. He told me to wrap his whole body up in white cloth, leaving only his eyes and mouth uncovered. He said he wanted to conduct an experiment designed to discharge the radiation that had accumulated in his body. He couldn't be dissuaded, so we wrapped him up in some cloth. Then he told me to place a bucket, half-full of water, between his legs, with a tube running to his mouth so he could drink from the bucket. We used a tube from a bicycle tire pump and we placed it in his mouth. He then started sucking sugar water from the bucket. He wasn't really drinking much, though—it was spilling out of his mouth and his nose. When I checked on him a little while later, I found that he had stripped off all the cloth and he was now lying naked on the floor. I thought he was dead and I started shouting at him. "You can't die!" I cried. "You have to go on!" At that point, he got up, claimed that his experiment was a failure, then began sobbing. I told him it didn't matter and he didn't need to cry. But he called me a fool. He said that he had hoped to treat all the people of Hiroshima—starting with me—if the experiment had been successful.

INTERVIEWER: What about your younger sister? Where was she when the bomb exploded?

SAEKI: She was at the hospital in Hatchobori. She wasn't seriously injured in the blast and one of the doctors then accompanied her to Kyobashi. But on August 9th or 10th, she began vomiting blood, her stools were bloody, and her hair was coming out in clumps. My brother started complaining about the foul smells and about becoming infected from her illness. Up to that point, I had always believed that love and compassion among family members couldn't be shaken, even in an emergency. The war not only wiped out human lives, it ravaged human hearts.

INTERVIEWER: How many family members did you lose?

SAEKI: Six members of my immediate family were killed. If relatives are included, I lost a total of 13 people. They all died a different death. When I reflect on what they might have been thinking when they died, or their last word, I feel guilty for having survived. In fact, I've wondered many times if it wouldn't have been better if I had died with them. But the fact that I survived would lose all meaning if I didn't go on living, if I didn't live for the members of my family who died. My hope is that, by telling my story, the tragedy of Hiroshima won't be forgotten and it might help prevent another war. The things we believed in at that time were turned upside-down by the bombing, but I didn't know where to direct my rage. As I staggered through the living hell that Hiroshima had become, I was aghast at the utter waste of war. This is why I continue to speak out and tell my story.

READING AND DISCUSSION QUESTIONS

1. Toshiko Saeki gives a disturbingly personal account of the nuclear attack on Hiroshima. What is the value of her testimony, if any, in evaluating the history of atomic warfare?

2. Conventional weapons killed millions of people in the Second World War. What aspect of Saeki's testimony, if any, makes the atomic attacks on Hiroshima and Nagasaki unique in the war's long history of carnage?

3. Saeki refers to the Peace Memorial Museum. What is the effect of bringing up the museum in her narrative? How does she compare or contrast the preservation of history with her own experiences? What does this suggest for your understanding of Saeki's experience and of the event?

VIEWPOINTS COMPARATIVE QUESTIONS

1. How might Saeki have responded to Truman's press release? How might he have responded to her account?

2. In your opinion, what lessons should be taken from the bombing of Hiroshima and Nagasaki?

■ COMPARATIVE QUESTIONS ■

1. The documents in this chapter present varying perspectives on individual lives and government policies during the Great Depression and the Second World War. What comparisons or contrasts can you draw among the documents based on the perspective of each author? Which documents present an "official" version, and which a more personal version? How does the author's perspective affect your reading of each document?

2. Both the Nuremberg Laws and Truman's press release reflect the efforts of very different governments to explain themselves or to further their own interests. Compare and contrast these two documents.

3. The press release on Hiroshima and the interview with Toshiko Saeki present two very different accounts of the nuclear strike on the city of Hiroshima. How is the atomic bomb described in each document? Compare and contrast the descriptions.

4. In what ways does each document in this chapter quantify human suffering? When they cite numbers, what effect do those numbers give? Are numbers more or less powerful than other forms of description? Cite examples.

31

Decolonization, Revolution, and the Cold War
1945–1968

Almost immediately following the end of the Second World War, the competing economic and social systems of the United States and its European allies, on the one hand, and the Soviet Union and its allies, on the other hand, spawned the Cold War. This period of heightened military tension and mutual suspicion lasted more than four decades, as each side struggled to expand its influence — and limit that of its rival — through economic, political, and occasionally military activity. The postwar decades were also times of revolutionary change outside the West. The war weakened the grip of European nations on their overseas colonies, and nationalist movements in Asia, the Middle East, and Africa won independence for former colonies. In many cases, decolonization proceeded relatively peacefully. In others, the struggle for independence produced violent clashes. In all cases, however, the process of decolonization and subsequent efforts at nation building were shaped by the battle between the United States and the Soviet Union for global influence.

VIEWPOINTS

The Cold War Begins

On March 5, 1946, former British prime minister Winston Churchill delivered his famous "Sinews of Peace" speech to more than forty thousand people at Westminster College in the small town of Fulton, Missouri. It was here that Churchill used the phrase the "iron curtain" for the first time, giving the speech its better-known name and coining the famous

417

phrase that soon became ubiquitous throughout the world to describe Russia's iron grip on eastern Europe.

A year later, on March 12, 1947, President Harry S. Truman addressed a joint session of the United States Congress to express his concern over the Soviet occupation of eastern Europe and the threat that communism posed to other countries in Europe, particularly Greece and Turkey. In his speech Truman set forth a new doctrine for American foreign policy, moving from a policy of "détente," or friendship with the Soviet Union, to a policy that aimed to directly confront and contain communism.

31-1 | An Iron Curtain Descends

WINSTON CHURCHILL, *"Sinews of Peace" Speech* (March 5, 1946)

After Winston Churchill's party lost the United Kingdom's 1945 elections, Churchill went from prime minister to leader of the opposition in Parliament. In this role he stressed what he saw as a growing threat from the Soviet Union as it imposed its allied governments upon the eastern European countries liberated and now occupied by its powerful Red Army. His speech in Missouri, often referred to as the "iron curtain" speech, sought to draw the United States into an alliance with Britain and other western European countries to respond to the perceived menace that Soviet control of eastern Europe presented.

A shadow has fallen upon the scenes so lately lighted by the Allied victory. Nobody knows what Soviet Russia and its Communist international organization intends to do in the immediate future, or what are the limits, if any, to their expansive and proselytizing tendencies. . . . We welcome Russia to her rightful place among the leading nations of the world. . . . It is my duty however, . . . to place before you certain facts about the present position in Europe.

From Stettin in the Baltic to Trieste in the Adriatic an iron curtain has descended across the Continent. Behind that line lie all the capitals of the ancient states of Central and Eastern Europe. Warsaw, Berlin, Prague, Vienna, Budapest, Belgrade, Bucharest and Sofia, all these famous cities and the populations around them lie in what I must call the Soviet sphere, and all are subject in one form or another, not only to Soviet influence but to a very high and, in some cases, increasing measure of control from Moscow. Athens alone — Greece with its immortal glories — is free to decide its future at an election under British, American and French observation. The Russian-dominated Polish Government has been encouraged to make enormous and wrongful inroads upon Germany, and mass expulsions of millions of Germans on a scale grievous and

Winston Churchill, "Sinews of Peace" (the Iron Curtain Speech), delivered at Westminster College in Fulton, Missouri, March 5, 1946, in Robert Rhodes James, ed., *Winston S. Churchill: His Complete Speeches, 1897–1963*, vol. 7: *1943–1949.*

undreamed-of are now taking place. The Communist parties, which were very small in all these Eastern States of Europe, have been raised to pre-eminence and power far beyond their numbers and are seeking everywhere to obtain totalitarian control. Police governments are prevailing in nearly every case, and so far, except in Czechoslovakia, there is no true democracy.

READING AND DISCUSSION QUESTIONS

1. What "shadow" is Churchill referring to in his speech?
2. Why does Churchill make use of the names of so many cities and locations in his speech? What do the geography and the long list of places convey?

31-2 | The Truman Doctrine

PRESIDENT HARRY S. TRUMAN, *Speech to Congress* (March 12, 1947)

In this speech to Congress, President Truman called for a means to contain the influence of the Soviet Union. This approach would come to be named the "Truman Doctrine," and it became one of the foundations of U.S. foreign policy during the Cold War. The speech came a year after Churchill warned of the "iron curtain," amid civil war in Greece, where Truman believed Soviet influence could impose another Soviet-aligned government. Note that when he proposes to support people "resisting attempted subjugation by armed minorities or by outside pressures," he is referring to those living in European countries, not to people under European colonial domination in Africa and Asia.

At the present moment in world history nearly every nation must choose between alternative ways of life. The choice is too often not a free one.

One way of life is based upon the will of the majority, and is distinguished by free institutions, representative government, free elections, guarantees of individual liberty, freedom of speech and religion, and freedom from political oppression.

The second way of life is based upon the will of a minority forcibly imposed upon the majority. It relies upon terror and oppression, a controlled press and radio; fixed elections, and the suppression of personal freedoms.

I believe that it must be the policy of the United States to support free peoples who are resisting attempted subjugation by armed minorities or by outside pressures.

I believe that we must assist free peoples to work out their own destinies in their own way.

I believe that our help should be primarily through economic and financial aid, which is essential to economic stability and orderly political processes.

Henry Steele Commager and Milton Cantor, *Documents of American History*, vol. 2: *Since 1898*, 10th ed. (Englewood Cliffs, N.J.: Prentice Hall, 1988), pp. 527–528.

The world is not static, and the status quo is not sacred. But we cannot allow changes in the status quo in violation of the Charter of the United Nations by such methods as coercion, or by such subterfuges as political infiltration. . . .

The seeds of totalitarian regimes are nurtured by misery and want. They spread and grow in the evil soil of poverty and strife. They reach their full growth when the hope of a people for a better life has died. We must keep that hope alive.

The free peoples of the world look to us for support in maintaining their freedoms.

If we falter in our leadership, we may endanger the peace of the world—and we shall surely endanger the welfare of our own nation.

READING AND DISCUSSION QUESTIONS

1. What does the word *free* mean in Truman's speech?

2. When Truman proposed to "support free peoples who are resisting attempted subjugation," whom was he claiming to support? Who was likely left out of or overlooked in this statement of support? What does this omission suggest about U.S. foreign policy?

3. What conditions make the world ripe for totalitarian regimes according to Truman?

VIEWPOINTS COMPARATIVE QUESTIONS

1. How do Churchill's speech and Truman's speech—considered by some scholars to be the opening acts in the Cold War—use language to persuade their audiences of the Soviet threat? What democratic ideals do they call upon?

2. How do the tones of Churchill's and Truman's speeches differ? What effects would each tone have? How are they attuned to their intended audiences?

31-3 | The United Nations Calls for an End to the Age of Empires

UNITED NATIONS GENERAL ASSEMBLY, *Declaration on the Granting of Independence to Colonial Countries and Peoples* (December 14, 1960)

After centuries of empire building and colonization, European countries began to move toward decolonization in the decades after World War II. Many former colonies obtained their freedom after 1945, driven in large part by the increasing quest for self-government

---

General Assembly of the United Nations, Resolution 1514 (XV), December 14, 1960.

in Africa and Asia. In 1960, the United Nations formalized the gradual process of granting independence to these once-colonized peoples, outlining basic assumptions about human rights and self-rule that would guide much of the decolonization process. Most UN member nations voted in favor of the declaration; the nine that abstained, however, were all imperialist nations, including the United States, Great Britain, France, Spain, and Portugal.

General Assembly Resolution 1514 (XV) of 14 December 1960

The General Assembly,

Mindful of the determination proclaimed by the peoples of the world in the Charter of the United Nations to reaffirm faith in fundamental human rights, in the dignity and worth of the human person, in the equal rights of men and women and of nations large and small and to promote social progress and better standards of life in larger freedom,

Conscious of the need for the creation of conditions of stability and well being and peaceful and friendly relations based on respect for the principles of equal rights and self-determination of all peoples, and of universal respect for, and observance of, human rights and fundamental freedoms for all without distinction as to race, sex, language, or religion,

Recognizing the passionate yearning for freedom in all dependent peoples and the decisive role of such peoples in the attainment of their independence,

Aware of the increasing conflicts resulting from the denial of or impediments in the way of the freedom of such peoples, which constitute a serious threat to world peace,

Considering the important role of the United Nations in assisting the movement for independence in Trust and Non-Self-Governing Territories,

Recognizing that the peoples of the world ardently desire the end of colonialism in all its manifestations,

Convinced that the continued existence of colonialism prevents the development of international economic co-operation, impedes the social, cultural, and economic development of dependent peoples and militates against the United Nations ideal of universal peace,

Affirming that peoples may, for their own ends, freely dispose of their natural wealth and resources without prejudice to any obligations arising out of international economic co-operation, based upon the principle of mutual benefit, and international law,

Believing that the process of liberation is irresistible and irreversible and that, in order to avoid serious crises, an end must be put to colonialism and all practices of segregation and discrimination associated therewith,

Welcoming the emergence in recent years of a large number of dependent territories into freedom and independence, and recognizing the increasingly powerful trends towards freedom in such territories which have not yet attained independence,

Convinced that all peoples have an inalienable right to complete freedom, the exercise of their sovereignty, and the integrity of their national territory,

Solemnly proclaims the necessity of bringing to a speedy and unconditional end colonialism in all its forms and manifestations;

And to this end

Declares that:

1. The subjection of peoples to alien subjugation, domination, and exploitation constitutes a denial of fundamental human rights, is contrary to the Charter of the United Nations, and is an impediment to the promotion of world peace and co-operation.
2. All peoples have the right to self-determination; by virtue of that right they freely determine their political status and freely pursue their economic, social, and cultural development.
3. Inadequacy of political, economic, social or educational preparedness should never serve as a pretext for delaying independence.
4. All armed action or repressive measures of all kinds directed against dependent peoples shall cease in order to enable them to exercise peacefully and freely their right to complete independence, and the integrity of their national territory shall be respected.
5. Immediate steps shall be taken, in Trust and Non-Self-Governing Territories or all other territories which have not yet attained independence, to transfer all powers to the peoples of those territories, without any conditions or reservations, in accordance with their freely expressed will and desire, without any distinction as to race, creed, or color, in order to enable them to enjoy complete independence and freedom.
6. Any attempt aimed at the partial or total disruption of the national unity and the territorial integrity of a country is incompatible with the purposes and principles of the Charter of the United Nations.
7. All States shall observe faithfully and strictly the provisions of the Charter of the United Nations, the Universal Declaration of Human Rights and the present Declaration on the basis of equality, non-interference in the internal affairs of all States, and respect for the sovereign rights of all peoples and their territorial integrity.

READING AND DISCUSSION QUESTIONS

1. According to this declaration, what goals do the peoples of the world share?
2. What problems would continued colonialism pose?
3. According to the declaration, what constitutes basic human rights?
4. How does the General Assembly describe its role in decolonization?

31-4 | The Challenges of Neocolonialism and Equitable Development

INDIRA GANDHI, *Address to the Fourth Congress of Non-Aligned Countries in Algiers* (1973)

India's prime minister Indira Gandhi (r. 1966–1977 and 1980–1984) was one of the leaders of the Non-Aligned Nations Movement, which was composed mainly of countries that had emerged from colonialism in the decades following the Second World War. The movement sought autonomy from the Cold War superpowers, as well as a path for development that broke the enduring bonds of colonialism in newly independent countries. Speaking to the assembly of the Non-Aligned Nations Movement in 1973, Prime Minister Gandhi described the ways in which powerful groups held on to colonial structures and inhibited the processes of transformation that many nonaligned political leaders had hoped would follow independence.

We have a part to play in the re-making of the world. Non-alignment was born as an assertion of our will to be sovereign and not be mere objects of imperial history. It came into being after the travails of the Second World War when the world appeared to be rent asunder irrevocably. We said then that these [Cold War] divisions were inconsistent with the real interests of the masses who have just emerged from the long night of imperial exploitation. It was a deliberate, though difficult, attempt to lower tensions and tempers at a time when these were considered the accoutrements of strength. It was a principled contribution to peace. Non-alignment has not lost any of its relevance even though the rigid attitudes of the Cold War have softened.

We often hear the phrase "third world." Is this not a product of the unconscious desire of the small affluent section of humanity to continue as oases of prosperity in the midst of vast waste lands of want? Surely our world is too small to be further fragmented. Mankind will survive together in hope and faith or give way to despair and destruction. . . .

When we became free, it was with high hopes of bringing about immediate changes in our society. We thought that the process of transformation, once initiated and pursued with fervor, would gather momentum. But political and economic interests, domestic as well as international, have proved to be formidable obstacles. As the economic struggle becomes more acute, the long suppressed voices of people sharpen. But with every step forward, the resistance of entrenched groups, often aligned with foreign interests, especially the faceless multinational corporations, becomes more vehement, unscrupulous and, at the same time, more subtle and even insidious, for it is no longer overt but indirectly subversive and provocative. In India we see these constraints in operation every day. Perhaps this is also the experience of other developing countries. Hence, the removal of poverty depends not merely on capital accumulation, important

Government of India Ministry of External Affairs, *Algiers Conference of Non-aligned Countries: Address of Prime Minister Indira Gandhi*, September 6, 1973, pp. 4–6.

as it is, but on the generation of conscious political forces to overcome these constraints.

Colonialism has left deep scars of inferiority which become all the more sensitive in the face of the staggering advance of science and technology in the affluent countries. It is right that we acquire knowledge and profit from the experience of others. But in doing so, we should not lose sight of the actual needs of the majority of our people. Technology must not be mere transplantation or widen disparities and impose heavier burdens than our society is capable of bearing. Step by step we are being pushed in a particular direction, imitating patterns and methods which do not necessarily fit into or benefit our society. The time has come for a re-assessment, not only to avoid the problems created by industrialization in other countries but more positively to clarify our own goals. For us the question of disparities and inequalities is not academic but one which affects our future even our survival. The aim of our socio-economic transformation is not merely to augment the Gross National Product or to build consumer societies but to balance growth, social justice and the inculcation of cultural values which are inspired by perception and compassion.

Economic and social development cannot just be a domestic effort for any of us. It has to be a major international concern. We the non-aligned do believe that the fight against poverty demand cooperation in which resources and technology are shared among nations. We are all familiar with the political fluctuations of 'aid' — with unfulfilled expectations and aid-weariness. . . . Perhaps one of the most interesting [interpretations of international aid] has been the Report of the Pearson Commission.[1] It might be worthwhile to remind ourselves of the conclusion reached by the Commission: "A good deal of bilateral aid has indeed been dispensed in order to achieve short-term political favours, gain strategic advantages, or promote exports from the donor. It is hardly surprising, therefore, that hopes of satisfactory development progress were disappointed." Subordinating aid policies to foreign policy aims has seldom been a successful exercise.

READING AND DISCUSSION QUESTIONS

1. What are the entrenched groups Gandhi mentions that make postcolonial transformations difficult?

2. What specifically does ending poverty depend upon?

3. In Gandhi's view, how does a Non-Aligned Nations Movement further national goals of transformation, economic justice, and development?

4. What are the problems with international aid identified by the Pearson Report?

---

[1]**Pearson Commission:** The Pearson Commission on International Development was formed by the World Bank in 1968 to investigate the effectiveness of international development aid.

31-5 | Revolutionary Brothers-in-Arms
Erich Honecker and Fidel Castro (1974)

The Cuban Revolution (1953–1959) provides a good example of the pervasive influence of the Cold War competition between the United States and the Soviet Union. Fidel Castro (1926–2016) and his fellow revolutionaries did not set out to create a Communist state. They wanted to level the economic playing field, but this desire was not driven by ideology or pursued in concert with the Soviet Union. Nonetheless, when the revolution finally succeeded in toppling the U.S.-backed dictator Fulgencio Batista (1901–1973), the United States, acting on Cold War imperatives, immediately launched a campaign to undermine the new government and depose Castro. These policies gave Castro little choice but to form an alliance with the Soviet Union, an alliance that only grew stronger over the course of the 1960s and 1970s. This photograph of Fidel Castro embracing East German leader Erich Honecker (1912–1994) illustrates the close ties that had developed by the mid-1970s between the Soviet Union and Cuba.

picture alliance/Getty Images

READING AND DISCUSSION QUESTIONS

1. How might this photograph have been interpreted by the majority of Americans in the mid-1970s? By the Cuban people? By the Soviet people?

2. Compare and contrast Cuba's relationship with the Soviet Union to the relationship between East Germany and the Soviet Union. What similarities and differences do you note? Did either Cuba or East Germany have much say in its own social and political development?

■ COMPARATIVE QUESTIONS ■

1. Was the Cold War an ideological struggle, as President Truman claimed, or were other forces at work as well? How do Castro and the Cuban Revolution support or refute this claim?

2. What factors were most important in shaping U.S. policy in Latin America in the 1950s and 1960s? What developments in Castro's Cuba shed light on this question?

3. How might Bolívar (Document 27-1) have responded to the UN *Declaration on the Granting of Independence to Colonial Countries and Peoples*? Would he have agreed, for example, that "inadequacy of political, economic, social or educational preparedness should never serve as a pretext for delaying independence"?

4. Compare and contrast the documents relating to decolonization and dependence in this chapter with those relating to nineteenth-century imperialism in Chapters 25 and 26. What similarities and differences do you note?

32

Liberalization and Liberation
1968–2000s

By the early 1970s, the postwar period of decolonization had come to an end. A host of new nations had been created, and the imperial order that had reached its apex in the late nineteenth and early twentieth centuries had been almost completely dismantled. This did not mean, however, that the unequal relationship between developing and developed nations had been fundamentally altered. Developing nations in Africa, Asia, the Middle East, and Latin America faced enormous political and economic challenges. These challenges were, in many cases, exacerbated by the actions and policies of the world's wealthiest and most powerful nations. Cold War competition prompted both the United States and the Soviet Union to intervene in the domestic politics of nations around the world, often in ways that ran counter to the interests of the nations involved. Moreover, starting in the 1970s, liberal political and economic ideology experienced a resurgence in the West. The United States in particular championed liberal economic policies and global free trade. Proponents of such policies argued that they would ultimately benefit all peoples because they would stimulate global economic growth. Opponents, including the leaders of a number of developing countries, saw liberalization as just the latest Western strategy to perpetuate global inequality.

32-1 | Remembering Argentina's Dirty War
Museo Sitio de Memoria ESMA (2019)

Between 1976 and 1983, Argentina's military junta waged a "Dirty War" against its political opponents, killing between 14,000 and 30,000 Argentines and imprisoning and torturing many thousands more. The most notorious of the detention and torture centers was the Navy Mechanics School (ESMA) in Buenos Aires. Thousands of political prisoners passed through the facility to be "disappeared" by the regime. The ESMA today is a museum committed to preserving the memory of both the state's acts of violence against its own citizens and of the people who disappeared after being taken there. The museum is administered by Argentina's Ministry of Justice and Human Rights. This image shows the museum entrance to the ESMA, with glass walls surrounding the entrance, upon which are printed photographs of people who were detained and disappeared there.

David Fernandez/EFE/Newscom

READING AND DISCUSSION QUESTIONS

1. What purpose do museums such as this one serve? Why is it important to pre-serve historical memory, particularly of tragic events?

2. Why would the ESMA be a protected site administered by the Ministry of Justice and Human Rights?

3. What impact do the photographs around the ESMA entrance have on viewers and visitors of the museum?

Race and Power in South Africa

The 1950s and 1960s saw the end of colonization and the establishment of new and independent nations across Africa. For the most part, this pro-cess was a peaceful one. In regions with large numbers of white settlers, however, decolonization was often accompanied by considerable violence. In French Algeria, for example, the large European population pressured the French government to resist calls for Algerian independence, sparking a long and bitter war between France and Algerian anticolonial forces (see Chapter 31). In South Africa, an even more entrenched European population made the preservation of the colonial racial hierarchy its highest priority, organizing the government, economy, and legal system of South Africa around that goal. As you read the documents included here, ask yourself if the racial policies of the South African government in the decades following World War II made political violence inevitable. How would Nelson Mandela have responded to this question? What about the leaders of the South African government under apartheid?

32-2 | The South African Government Justifies Apartheid

NATIONAL PARTY OF SOUTH AFRICA, *The National Party's Color Policy* (March 29, 1948)

When the Union of South Africa was established as a quasi-autonomous dominion of the British Empire in 1910, its legal and political system embraced the policies of segregation and disenfranchisement of nonwhites that had flourished in colonial times. Not until the 1948 South African parliamentary election, however, did the formal system of apartheid, or "separation," become official state policy. Inhabitants of South Africa were strictly defined according to government racial criteria that determined where they could live, whom they could marry or have sexual relationships with, what they could study, and whether they were in fact citizens. The resulting system of white supremacy emphasized the threat of decolonization and the need for unity among the white minority. Several points in the government's policy are laid out here in this 1948 government proclamation, as catalogued by the United Nations.

There are two sections of thought in South Africa in regard to the policy affecting the non-European community.[1] On the one hand there is the policy of equality, which advocates equal rights within the same political structure for all civilized and educated persons, irrespective of race or color, and the gradual granting of the franchise to non-Europeans as they become qualified to make use of democratic rights.

On the other hand there is the policy of separation (*apartheid*) which has grown from the experience of established European population of the country, and which is based on the Christian principles of Justice and reasonableness.

From U.N. General Assembly, Eighth Session. Supplement No. 16. *Report of the United Nations Commission on the Racial Situation in the Union of South Africa*, 1953. (A/2505 and A/2505/ADD.1). Official Record.

[1]**non-European community:** As used in this report, *European* loosely means "white," and *non-European* is approximately the same as "Colored" or "Native." South Asians in Africa are also nonwhite, but not native.

Its aim is the maintenance and protection of the European population of the country as a pure White race, the maintenance and protection of the indigenous racial groups as separate communities, with prospects of developing into self-supporting communities within their own areas, and the stimulation of national pride, self-respect, and mutual respect among the various races of the country.

We can act in only one of two directions. Either we must follow the course of equality, which must eventually mean national suicide for the White race, or we must take the course of separation (*apartheid*) through which the character and the future of every race will be protected and safeguarded with full opportunities for development and self-maintenance in their own ideas, without the interests of one clashing with the interests of the other, and without one regarding the development of the other as undermining or a threat to himself.

The party therefore undertakes to protect the White race properly and effectively against any policy, doctrine or attack which might undermine or threaten its continued existence. At the same time the party rejects any policy of oppression and exploitation of the non-Europeans by the Europeans as being in conflict with the Christian basis of our national life and irreconcilable with our policy.

The party believes that a definite policy of separation (*apartheid*) between the White races and the non-White racial groups, and the application of the policy of separation also in the case of the non-White racial groups, is the only basis on which the character and future of each race can be protected and safeguarded and on which each race can be guided so as to develop his own national character, aptitude and calling.

All marriages between Europeans and non-Europeans will be prohibited.

In their areas the non-European racial groups will have full opportunities for development in every sphere and will be able to develop their own institutions and social services whereby the forces of the progressive non-Europeans can be harnessed for their own national development (*volkeepbou*). The policy of the country must be so planned that it will eventually promote the ideal of complete separation (*algehele apartheid*) in a national way.

A permanent advisory body of experts on non-European affairs will be established.

The State will exercise complete supervision over the molding of the youth. The party will not tolerate interference from without or destructive propaganda from the outside world in regard to the racial problems of South Africa.

The party wishes all non-Europeans to be strongly encouraged to make the Christian religion the basis of their lives and will assist churches in this task in every possible way. Churches and societies which undermine the policy of *apartheid* and propagate doctrines foreign to the nation will be checked.

The Colored community takes a middle position between the European and the Natives. A policy of separation (*apartheid*) between the Europeans and Coloreds and between Natives and Coloreds will be applied in the social, residential, industrial and political spheres. No marriage between Europeans and Coloreds will be permitted. The Coloreds will be protected against unfair competition from the Natives in so far as where they are already established.

The Colored community will be represented in the Senate by a European representative to be appointed by the Government by reason of his knowledge of Colored affairs.

The present unhealthy system which allows Coloreds in the Cape to be registered on the same voters' roll as Europeans and to vote for the same candidate as Europeans will be abolished and the Coloreds will be represented in the House of Assembly by three European representatives.

These Colored representatives will be elected by a Colored representative council. They will not vote on:

(1) Votes on confidence in the Government.
(2) A declaration of war, and
(3) A change in the political rights of non-Europeans.

A State Department of Colored Affairs will be established.

The Colored community will be represented in the Cape Provincial Council by three Europeans elected by the Colored representative council.

A Colored representative council will be established in the Cape Province consisting of representatives elected by the Colored community, divided into constituencies with the present franchise qualifications, the head of the Department of Colored Affairs and representatives nominated by the Government. In their own areas the Colored community will have their own councils with their own public services which will be managed by themselves within the framework of the existing councils with higher authority.

Attention will be given to the provision of social, medical and welfare services in which the efforts of the Colored themselves can be harnessed, and in which they will be taught as far as possible to be self-supporting.

READING AND DISCUSSION QUESTIONS

1. Does this document represent the voice of Europeans or Africans? Who wrote this document?

2. What rationale does the national government present for the institution of apartheid?

3. How is religion used in this document, and to what end? What limitations, if any, are placed on religion?

4. What rights are given to "Colored" people, and what rights are denied to them? What can you imagine to be the probable outcomes of such restrictions?

32-3 | Mandela Explains the Need for Armed Struggle Against Apartheid

NELSON MANDELA, *The Rivonia Trial Speech to the Court* (April 20, 1964)

The white Afrikaner government that came to power in South Africa following World War II enacted extreme forms of legal segregation (apartheid) that relegated blacks to the lowest-paid jobs and the poorest regions of the country. In the 1950s and 1960s, the African National Congress (ANC), led by young attorney Nelson Mandela (1918–2013), protested these racist policies first peacefully and later violently. The organization was outlawed in 1961, but Mandela continued to run the ANC while in hiding for seventeen months before he was arrested, tried, and found guilty of treason. He was imprisoned until 1990. Mandela first presented this defense following the 1963 arrest of ANC leaders at Liliesleaf Farm, Rivonia, and later included it in reports he released after becoming the first democratically elected president of South Africa in 1994.

In my youth . . . I listened to the elders of my tribe telling stories of the old days. Amongst the tales they related to me were those of wars fought by our ancestors in defense of the father-land. . . . I hoped then that life might offer me the opportunity to serve my people and make my own humble contribution to their freedom struggle. This is what has motivated me in all that I have done in relation to the charges made against me in this case. . . .

I have already mentioned that I was one of the persons who helped to form Umkonto.[2] I, and the others who started the organization, did so for two reasons. Firstly, we believed that as a result of Government policy, violence by the African people had become inevitable, and that unless responsible leadership was given to canalize and control the feelings of our people, there would be outbreaks of terrorism which would produce an intensity of bitterness and hostility between the various races of this country which is not produced even by war. Secondly, we felt that without violence there would be no way open to the African people to succeed in their struggle against the principle of White supremacy. All lawful modes of expressing opposition to this principle had been closed by legislation, and we were placed in a position in which we had either to accept a permanent state of inferiority, or to defy the Government. . . .

But the violence which we chose to adopt was not terrorism. We who formed Umkonto were all members of the African National Congress, and had behind us the ANC tradition of non-violence and negotiation as a means of solving political disputes. We believed that South Africa belonged to all the people who lived in it, and not to one group, be it Black or White. We did not want an interracial war, and tried to avoid it to the last minute. . . .

Nelson Mandela, *No Easy Walk to Freedom*, ed. Ruth First (New York: Basic Books, 1965), pp. 163–168. Used by permission of The Nelson Mandela Foundation.

[2]**Umkonto:** Short for "Umkonto we Sizwe," or Spear of the Nation, a militant subgroup of the African National Congress that Mandela founded while in hiding in 1961.

The African National Congress was formed in 1912 to defend the rights of the African people. . . . For thirty-seven years — that is until 1949 — it adhered strictly to a constitutional struggle. It put forward demands and resolutions; it sent delegations to the Government in the belief that African grievances could be settled through peaceful discussion and that Africans could advance gradually to full political rights. But White Governments remained unmoved, and the rights of Africans became less instead of becoming greater. . . .

Even after 1949, the ANC remained determined to avoid violence. At this time, however, there was a change from the strictly constitutional means of protest which had been employed in the past. The change was embodied in a decision which was taken to protest against apartheid legislation by peaceful, but unlawful, demonstrations against certain laws. Pursuant to this policy the ANC launched the Defiance Campaign, in which I was placed in charge of volunteers. This campaign was based on the principles of passive resistance.[3] More than 8,500 people defied apartheid laws and went to jail. Yet there was not a single instance of violence in the course of this campaign on the part of any defier. . . .

In 1960 there was the shooting at Sharpeville,[4] which resulted in the proclamation of a state of emergency and the declaration of the ANC as an unlawful organization. My colleagues and I, after careful consideration, decided that we would not obey this decree. The African people were not part of the Government and did not make the laws by which they were governed. We believed in the words of the Universal Declaration of Human Rights,[5] that "the will of the people shall be the basis of authority of the Government," and for us to accept the banning was equivalent to accepting the silencing of the Africans for all time. The ANC refused to dissolve, but instead went underground. . . .

Each disturbance pointed clearly to the inevitable growth among Africans of the belief that violence was the only way out — it showed that a Government which uses force to maintain its rule teaches the oppressed to use force to oppose it. . . .

The avoidance of civil war had dominated our thinking for many years, but when we decided to adopt violence as part of our policy, we realized that we might one day have to face the prospect of such a war. . . . We did not want to be committed to civil war, but we wanted to be ready if it became inevitable.

Four forms of violence were possible. There is sabotage, there is guerrilla warfare, there is terrorism, and there is open revolution. We chose to adopt the first method and to exhaust it before taking any other decision.

In the light of our political background the choice was a logical one. Sabotage did not involve loss of life, and it offered the best hope for future race

---

[3]**passive resistance:** A form of nonviolent political protest used and popularized by Indian leader Mohandas Gandhi (1869–1948).

[4]**shooting at Sharpeville:** The Sharpeville Massacre of 1960, in which police killed 69 and wounded 178 anti-apartheid demonstrators.

[5]**Universal Declaration of Human Rights:** A declaration of the rights of every human being, adopted by the United Nations on December 10, 1948.

relations. Bitterness would be kept to a minimum and, if the policy bore fruit, democratic government could become a reality. . . .

Attacks on the economic lifelines of the country were to be linked with sabotage on Government buildings and other symbols of apartheid. These attacks would serve as a source of inspiration to our people. In addition, they would provide an outlet for those people who were urging the adoption of violent methods and would enable us to give concrete proof to our followers that we had adopted a stronger line and were fighting back against Government violence. . . .

Another of the allegations made by the State is that the aims and objects of the ANC and the Communist Party are the same. . . .

It is true that there has often been close cooperation between the ANC and the Communist Party. But cooperation is merely proof of a common goal—in this case the removal of White supremacy—and is not proof of a complete community of interests. . . .

It is perhaps difficult for White South Africans, with an ingrained prejudice against communism, to understand why experienced African politicians so readily accept communists as their friends. But to us the reason is obvious. Theoretical differences amongst those fighting against oppression is a luxury we cannot afford at this stage. What is more, for many decades communists were the only political group in South Africa who were prepared to treat Africans as human beings and their equals; who were prepared to eat with us, talk with us, live with us, and work with us. They were the only political group which was prepared to work with the Africans for the attainment of political rights and a stake in society. Because of this, there are many Africans who, today, tend to equate freedom with communism. . . .

Our fight is against real, and not imaginary, hardships or, to use the language of the State prosecutor, "so-called hardships." Basically, we fight against two features which are the hallmarks of African life in South Africa and which are entrenched by legislation which we seek to have repealed. These features are poverty and lack of human dignity. . . .

South Africa is the richest country in Africa, and could be one of the richest countries in the world. But it is a land of extremes and remarkable contrasts. The Whites enjoy what may well be the highest standard of living in the world, whilst Africans live in poverty and misery. Forty percent of the Africans live in hopelessly overcrowded and, in some cases, drought-stricken Reserves, where soil erosion and the overworking of the soil make it impossible for them to live properly off the land. Thirty percent are laborers, labor tenants, and squatters on White farms and work and live under conditions similar to those of the serfs of the Middle Ages. The other 30 percent live in towns where they have developed economic and social habits which bring them closer in many respects to White standards. Yet most Africans, even in this group, are impoverished by low incomes and [the] high cost of living. . . .

The lack of human dignity experienced by Africans is the direct result of the policy of White supremacy. White supremacy implies Black inferiority. Legislation designed to preserve White supremacy entrenches this notion. Menial tasks in South Africa are invariably performed by Africans. When anything has to be carried or cleaned the White man will look around for an African to do it for him, whether the African is employed by him or not. Because of this sort of attitude, Whites tend to regard Africans as a separate breed. They do not look upon them as people with families of their own; they do not realize that they have emotions—that they fall in love like White people do; that they want to be with their wives and children like White people want to be with theirs; that they want to earn enough money to support their families properly, to feed and clothe them and send them to school. And what "house-boy" or "garden-boy" or laborer can ever hope to do this? . . .

Poverty and the breakdown of family life have secondary effects. Children wander about the streets of the townships because they have no schools to go to, or no money to enable them to go to school, or no parents at home to see that they go to school, because both parents (if there be two) have to work to keep the family alive. This leads to a breakdown in moral standards, to an alarming rise in illegitimacy, and to growing violence which erupts, not only politically, but everywhere. Life in the townships is dangerous. There is not a day that goes by without somebody being stabbed or assaulted. And violence is carried out of the townships in the White living areas. People are afraid to walk alone in the streets after dark. Housebreakings and robberies are increasing, despite the fact that the death sentence can now be imposed for such offenses. Death sentences cannot cure the festering sore. . . .

During my lifetime I have dedicated myself to this struggle of the African people. I have fought against White domination, and I have fought against Black domination. I have cherished the ideal of a democratic and free society in which all persons live together in harmony and with equal opportunities. It is an ideal which I hope to live for and to achieve. But if needs be, it is an ideal for which I am prepared to die.

READING AND DISCUSSION QUESTIONS

1. What reason does Mandela give for the ANC's decision to defy the government decree that outlawed the group?

2. What form of violence did the formerly nonviolent ANC adopt, and how does Mandela justify this decision?

3. How does Mandela describe the experience of blacks under apartheid? Why did he believe that apartheid contributed to a host of social problems?

VIEWPOINTS COMPARATIVE QUESTIONS

1. According to the South African government, what were the intended consequences of apartheid? According to Mandela, what were the actual consequences of apartheid?

2. In your opinion, who bore the greater responsibility for the violence that rocked South Africa in the 1970s and 1980s: the South African government or the ANC? Why?

32-4 | Economic Change and Women's Roles in China
WANG XINGJUAN, *Interview for the Global Feminisms Project* (2004)

Wang Xingjuan is a pioneer in women's counseling and community education in China. She founded and directed the Maple Women's Counseling Center, which established China's first women's crisis hotline and provides counseling for women in situations of domestic violence. The center also provides training workshops for police, judges, doctors, and neighborhood committee officials to raise awareness of domestic violence and gender hierarchies. In this interview, part of the University of Michigan's Global Feminisms Project, Wang Xingjuan reflects on the impact of economic reforms (initiated by Premier Deng Xiaoping following the death of Mao Zedong) on women.

A lot of people have asked me why in 1988 I chose to devote attention to women's issues. Prior to this time period, I had always done work in the fields of culture and the media at a newspaper or a publishing house. But I had never worked in women's organizations. So why would I become involved with this and even become the leader to start this kind of non-governmental organization for women? I think at the very beginning I started to pay attention to women because of a kind of deep concern for the situation of women.

I think that you all know that in the 1980s China embarked on its policy of reform and opening. This policy of reform and opening really brought a new kind of life and new hope to the Chinese people. Regarding women, the policy has brought both advantages and disadvantages. As the economic system and the political system change, the status of some women will rise. They are transformed from ordinary workers and peasants to entrepreneurs, leaders and factory managers. People have said that women not only became white collar workers, but also even became higher status "gold collar" executives. However, only a very small portion of women have achieved this kind of success. The majority of women faced a situation where they had to start from scratch to find a position. Many women feel. . . . Women have lost their original economic status and their original social status and consequently are losing their status within their families. As the economic system gradually transforms from that of a planned economy to a market economy, a lot of factories are getting rid of their female workers.

I remember quite clearly that in 1988 — which was precisely the time when I was going to retire — *Chinese Women*, a magazine of the All-China Women's Federation, from the first issue in January to the year's end had a very active discussion called "1988, What Path for Women?" The articles in this discussion

University of Michigan Global Feminisms Project, "Global Feminisms: Comparative Case Studies of Women's Activism and Scholarship," interview with Wang Xingjuan, March 12, 2004. Translated by Kim Dorazio. Used with permission. https://globalfeminisms.umich.edu/sites/default/files//wangxingjuan_C_E_102806.pdf

raised such issues as: through the process of optimizing the composition of the labor force, women are being stripped of their positions; and after women are "downsized" what path should they take? I still remember very clearly that one of the articles talked about a female worker who was downsized and then returned home. In the beginning she was really happy. At first she thought, "Thank goodness, at last I do not have to work from very early in the morning until very late at night. I can stay home and be a good wife and mother. Yes, I can help out my husband and take good care of my child." To her surprise, after she returned home, her husband always seemed to scowl at her no matter how well she did at home, because he thought she was dependent on his income and should do a better job doing household chores. Her mother-in-law, who lived with them, also treated her poorly. She looked down upon her daughter-in-law and asked derisively, "Other people were not laid off. How come you were laid off? It must be because you did not work hard in your work unit." Her daughter also looked down upon her. She thought that because her mother was laid off, it brought dishonor to her and the family. This woman wrote down her own experience. She wrote that she had repeatedly paced back and forth at the edge of the river. She felt that her life had no meaningful future and several times she thought that she would jump in the river and end her own life. This was a very typical case for many women. It told about women's feelings. Many women since reform and opening felt that they did not have a meaningful path to follow. They did not understand why society was developing and moving forward, but their status had actually fallen. Women faced very many new questions and problems. At that time I was in the Marriage and Family Research Association of the All-China Women's Federation. They asked me to take the position of the editor of a magazine called *Marriage and Family*. At that time a lot of women came to interview me. They wanted to know why a whole generation of women needed to sacrifice themselves to pay the price for society's development. This issue really shook me up a lot.

Another issue that emerged during this time was women's participation in government. A moment ago I mentioned the discussions in the magazine, *Chinese Women*. Also in 1988, the *Chinese Women's Newspaper* also launched a very big discussion about women's participation in government. At that time China was in the process of reforming its electoral system. In the past there were the same number of seats as there were number of candidates. They were working to change elections so that there would be more candidates than seats. For example, originally if there were nine seats available, then you would be given a ballot with nine names. Everybody would draw a circle around the nine choices. Now if there were nine seats available, you would be given a ballot with eleven names. Two people would not be elected. However, the people that would not be elected were always women. Thus at that time in some provinces and cities there were no women cadres in the four groups of administrative leaders.

READING AND DISCUSSION QUESTIONS

1. According to Wang Xingjuan, how did the 1980s economic reforms affect Chinese women?

2. What kinds of workplace and family pressures did women face? How were these related?

3. What impact did reforms of the political system have on women, and why?

32-5 | Building a Meaningful Life in Contemporary Japan

MALE JAPANESE CITIZENS, *"Ikigai"* (2003)

Following Japan's cataclysmic defeat in the Second World War, the American-led occupation forces worked closely with Japanese political and industrial leaders to rebuild the war-torn country and, during the Cold War, to make Japan a bulwark against communism in East Asia. Close relationships between industry and government, a hallmark of the prewar economy, continued to drive Japan's postwar economic recovery, though in slightly different forms. Within the corporate world, a highly gendered Japanese workforce also depended on long-term relationships, and lifetime employment at a single company became the norm for Japanese men. After the collapse of the economic "bubble" in the early 1990s, however, Japanese men began to question their relationship with Japan's economy and society. The selections here present a range of contemporary Japanese male voices on the changing definition of *ikigai*—that which makes life worth living.

Corporate Executive

For the past thirty years, my *ikigai* has been the companies I've worked for; they've been more important to me than my family. I don't expect much from my family; they don't expect me to be at home on weekends anymore. Yes, I can't say that I'm a family man. I have more human communication with the young girls . . . in my office than I do with my own daughters. . . .

There are fewer and fewer company men like me these days; there are many more "my home" types—these kind of people aren't at all happy if I tell them to come to the office on Sunday! I've never said no to any of my job assignments—I was always there when they needed me. I like men who do that: manly men . . . , like Western cowboys! Men living for their companies are better than those who live for their families; that's why Japan's developed! I get upset when I see a young man with dyed hair driving around in a fancy car with a pretty girl. Fifty years ago, people his age all died in the war; they didn't have the chance to enjoy their youth! I want to drag that young man out of his car and put a judo hold on him, teach him a lesson!

Gordon Mathews, "Can a Real Man Live for His Family? *Ikigai* and Masculinity in Today's Japan," in James Roberson and Nobue Suzuki, eds., *Men and Masculinities in Contemporary Japan* (New York: RoutledgeCurzon, 2003), pp. 109–225. Reprinted by permission of Gordon Mathews.

High School Teacher

Maybe Americans can separate business and private life, but I can't, and most Japanese can't. If you don't have business, you can't have any private life. . . . In my house, my wife was like a widow; I was busy, even on Sundays, with my school clubs. So now, if I'm not home, everyone feels more relaxed! . . .

Young people today overwhelmingly value being with their families. They calmly say, "My child's sick. I'll take the day off." Nobody ever did that when I was young! Today's young people don't have any fighting spirit! They relax with their families before they think about work!

Sarariman (White-Collar Worker) 1

The problem was that we worked too hard, generated too much money, that had to be plowed back into the system, into stocks and land, creating "the bubble economy." . . . If only Japanese hadn't worked so hard, maybe the economic downturn would never have happened.

Sarariman 2

If you ask my coworkers whether they find *ikigai* in work for this company, they might say they do. But they'd be lying. . . . But, then, maybe they really do find *ikigai* here. If you don't have time to do anything but work, then isn't that your *ikigai*?

Retired Railroad Worker

You know how work is. The husband has to be subservient to his boss, and so when he comes home, he wants to boss around his wife and children: "Turn off the TV! Put the kids to bed!" And communication between husband and wife, father and children, goes bad.

Self-Employed Repairman

I believe that the husband's the boss of the family. A wife should know what her husband is thinking by looking at his face. She should properly send him off to work in the morning; and when he comes home at night, there should be a drink and some good food waiting for him. A husband should educate his wife to do that. . . . When I got married, my wife fell in love with me; I didn't care whether I married her or not. She works part-time at the supermarket as a cashier—she's a little overbearing now, since she's got her own money.

Sarariman 3

Early in our marriage, my wife was always angry because I came home late from work, and because I wasn't *yasashii* (affectionate); I didn't take her anywhere on weekends, I didn't convey to her that I loved her. We came very close to divorce several times. Once my wife left with the kids and didn't come home for three days; I still don't know where they went. I wasn't thinking much about my family then; that's why my wife got so upset. I realized that I'd have to change. My wife made me promise that, unless I was out of town on business, I'd have breakfast with the family no matter how late I came home the previous night. I also spend every Sunday—at least half the day—with my family. Saturdays I use for myself: I go fishing. . . . I feel exhausted because of the stress on my job—that's why I need Saturdays for myself. When I'm with my family, I just can't get rid of stress.

Bank Worker

I don't like my work—I really hate it—but I wouldn't want to stay at home either, taking care of my children. Maybe that's my pride—maybe I don't want to deviate from the ideal image of a man. A man is supposed to work outside the home. In Japan, if a man says his child rather than his work is his *ikigai*, he'll be considered a sissy. . . . I could never say that. . . . In Japan women are discriminated against in the workplace, but at the same time they have less obligation; they have more time to follow their own pursuits. Do I wish I could be a woman instead of a man? Well . . . I could never say that; but it's possible that it's true.

Junior High School Teacher

I want to be with my wife when she gives birth; I'll need to take three days off from school for that. When I told that to the mothers in the PTA, they said, "That's great—go ahead!" I thought they were going to say, "What? Why so long a vacation!" But they didn't. They really appreciate me! . . . I usually get home by 7:30 or 8:00; sometimes not until 9:00 or 10:00. All I can do after I come home so late is bathe, eat and sleep; that's tough on my wife. I'm really tired. Sometimes it's just too much trouble to listen to her, to be honest. I'd really like more free time. . . . My family—my wife and child to be—is more important than my work. I'd quit my work, if I had to, for my family. My family is my *ikigai*. I just wish I had more time to be with my family.

Construction Worker and Former Rock Musician

I like myself now because I'm working hard for my family, but I hate myself because I gave up music. I'm not a bad father—I'm supporting my family—but maybe it'd be better for my two kids if I showed them a father who's pursuing his dream. Life isn't only a matter of making money; that's why I half regret my life now. I want to quit my job and play music again. But it'd be hard. The older you get, the less courage you've got. Compared to five years ago, I'm much more of a coward than I used to be. Maybe I've become a better husband and father to the extent that I've grown chicken-hearted! . . . I live for my dream of music, but

I also live for my wife: she too is my *ikigai*. But yeah, I guess that my real *ikigai* is music. I don't play the guitar much these days, but I have that desire—I'll have that for the rest of my life.

READING AND DISCUSSION QUESTIONS

1. How do these accounts of *ikigai* present Japan's economic success in the postwar era?

2. Some of these accounts deal explicitly with Japanese history, including the Second World War. How does history inform each of these accounts? Why might history play a larger role in some accounts than in others?

3. How does each of these accounts talk about gender? What women's roles are described here? Based on these accounts, what can you say about gender roles in contemporary Japan?

▪ COMPARATIVE QUESTIONS ▪

1. What connections can you make between the military governments that took power in South America in the 1970s (see Document 32-1) and the caudillos who rose to power in the nineteenth century (see Chapter 27)?

2. Compare the roles of women and men in China and Japan as described in Documents 32-4 and 32-5. How did economic changes affect gender roles and gender identity in these countries?

3. How might Gandhi (see Chapter 26) have responded to Mandela's defense of violent struggle in South Africa (see Documents 32-2 and 32-3)? What differences might Mandela have identified between India and South Africa to justify his position?

4. What similarities and differences do you see between the civil rights movement in the United States in the 1950s and 1960s and the fight against apartheid in South Africa (see Documents 32-2 and 32-3)? How did the civil rights movement shape American public opinion about apartheid in the 1970s and 1980s?

5. Compare and contrast the National Party's Color Policy with the Nazis' Nuremberg Laws (Document 30-2). In what ways are the two policies similar?

33

The Contemporary World in Historical Perspective

The 1990s marked the beginning of a new era in world history. The Cold War was over, new human rights initiatives were springing up in long repressed countries, and the so-called age of globalization was under way. By the early twenty-first century, the political and economic systems of all countries were more intricately linked and interdependent than ever before. Booms and busts, environmental issues, terrorism, war, and the spread of multinational corporations had become concerns for all nation-states. Throughout the world, new economic and political frameworks produced rising discontent, particularly as income inequalities, poverty, and job insecurity became increasingly prominent outcomes of neoliberalism. In many cases this resentment led to the election of right-wing nationalists who scapegoated foreigners and migrants. The contemporary world has also been shaped by the intensifying effects of climate change. State inaction despite increasing public concern about climate change has given rise to vocal social movements advocating for change.

33-1 | Defining and Defending Torture

JOHN YOO, *Memoranda Regarding U.S. Military Interrogations* (2002, 2003)

Following the attacks of September 11, 2001, the United States' most visible responses were military action against and invasion of Afghanistan (2001) and Iraq (2003). Domestically, President George W. Bush's administration moved to clarify the legal and political grounds for what was termed the war on terrorism, an effort that involved the detention and interrogation

---

John Yoo, Deputy Assistant Attorney General of the United States, to Alberto R. Gonzales, Counsel to the President, August 1, 2002, Office of Legal Counsel, U.S. Department of Justice, Washington, D.C. John Yoo, Deputy Assistant Attorney General of the United States, to William J. Haynes II, General Counsel of the Department of Defense, March 14, 2003, Office of Legal Counsel, U.S. Department of Justice, Washington, D.C.

of both U.S. citizens and aliens. Deputy Assistant Attorney General of the United States John Yoo was asked by then-Counsel to the President Alberto R. Gonzalez, and later by General Counsel of the Department of Defense William J. Haynes II, to provide a legal opinion on the power of the president to interrogate prisoners and whether such interrogation was prosecutable as torture. His responses, excerpted here from fifty- and eighty-page letters, respectively, were widely understood to condone interrogation techniques such as waterboarding, adding to the controversy surrounding the U.S. response to the attacks of September 11.

Memorandum for Alberto R. Gonzales, Counsel to the President

August 1, 2002

Re: Standards of Conduct for Interrogation
Under 18 U.S.C. 2340–2340A

You have asked for our Office's views regarding the standards of conduct under the Convention Against Torture and Other Cruel, Inhuman and Degrading Treatment or Punishment as implemented by Sections 2340–2340A of title 18 of the United States Code.[1] As we understand it, this question has arisen in the context of the conduct of interrogations outside of the United States. We conclude . . . that Section 2340A proscribes acts inflicting, and that are specifically intended to inflict, severe pain or suffering, whether mental or physical. Those acts must be of an extreme nature to rise to the level of torture within the meaning of Section 2340A and the Convention. We further conclude that certain acts may be cruel, inhuman, or degrading, but still not produce pain and suffering of the requisite intensity to fall within Section 2340A's proscription against torture. . . .

We conclude that for an act to constitute torture as defined in Section 2340, it must inflict pain that is difficult to endure. Physical pain amounting to torture must be equivalent in intensity to the pain accompanying serious physical injury, such as organ failure, impairment of bodily function, or even death. For purely mental pain or suffering to amount to torture under Section 2340, it must result in significant psychological harm of significant duration, e.g., lasting for months or even years. We conclude that the mental harm also must result from one of the predicate acts listed in the statute, namely: threats of imminent death; threats of infliction of the kind of pain that would amount to physical torture; infliction of such physical pain as a means of psychological torture; use of drugs or other procedures designed to deeply disrupt the senses, or fundamentally alter an individual's personality; or threatening to do any of these things to a third party. The legislative history simply reveals that Congress intended for the statute's definition to track the Convention's definition of torture and the reservations, understandings, and declarations that the United States submitted with its ratification. We conclude that the statute, taken as a whole, makes plain that it prohibits only extreme acts. . . .

---

[1]**Sections 2340–2340A . . . United States Code:** United States Code Title 18, Part I, Chapter 113C, Sections 2340 and 2340A, define torture and make it illegal both within and beyond the United States.

We conclude that the treaty's text prohibits only the most extreme acts by reserving criminal penalties solely for torture and declining to require such penalties for "cruel, inhuman, or degrading treatment or punishment." This confirms our view that the criminal statute penalizes only the most egregious conduct. . . .

We examine international decisions regarding the use of sensory deprivation techniques. These cases make clear that while many of these techniques may amount to cruel, inhuman or degrading treatment, they do not produce pain or suffering of the necessary intensity to meet the definition of torture. From these decisions, we conclude that there is a wide range of such techniques that will not rise to the level of torture.

. . . We discuss whether Section 2340A may be unconstitutional if applied to interrogations undertaken of enemy combatants pursuant to the President's Commander-in-Chief powers. We find that in the circumstances of the current war against al Qaeda and its allies, prosecution under Section 2340A may be barred because enforcement of the statute would represent an unconstitutional infringement of the President's authority to conduct war.

Memorandum for William J. Haynes II, General Counsel of the Department of Defense

March 14, 2003

Re: Military Interrogation of Alien Unlawful Combatants
Held Outside the United States

You have asked our Office to examine the legal standards governing military interrogations of alien unlawful combatants held outside the United States. . . .

We conclude that the Fifth and Eighth Amendments,[2] as interpreted by the Supreme Court, do not extend to alien enemy combatants held abroad. . . . Federal criminal laws of general applicability do not apply to properly authorized interrogations of enemy combatants, undertaken by military personnel in the course of an armed conflict. Such criminal statutes, if they were misconstrued to apply to the interrogation of enemy combatants, would conflict with the Constitution's grant of the Commander in Chief power solely to the President. . . .

Given the ongoing threat of al Qaeda attacks, the capture and interrogation of al Qaeda operatives is imperative to our national security and defense. Because of the asymmetric nature of terrorist operations, information is perhaps the most critical weapon for defeating al Qaeda. Al Qaeda is not a nation-state, and has no single country or geographic area as its base of operations. It has no fixed, large-scale military or civilian infrastructure. It deploys personnel,

---

[2]**Fifth and Eighth Amendments:** U.S. constitutional amendments guaranteeing citizens protection against government abuse in legal procedures and prohibiting the federal government from imposing cruel and unusual punishments, respectively.

material, and finances covertly and attacks without warning using unconventional weapons and methods. As the September 11, 2001 attacks and subsequent events demonstrate, it seeks to launch terror attacks against purely civilian targets within the United States, and seeks to acquire weapons of mass destruction for such attacks. Because of the secret nature of al Qaeda's operations, obtaining advance information about the identity of al Qaeda operatives and their plans may prove to be the only way to prevent direct attacks on the United States. Interrogation of captured al Qaeda operatives could provide that information; indeed, in many cases interrogation may be the only method to obtain it. Given the massive destruction and loss of life caused by the September 11 attacks, it is reasonable to believe that information gained from al Qaeda personnel could prevent attacks of a similar (if not greater) magnitude from occurring in the United States. . . .

One of the core functions of the Commander in Chief is that of capturing, detaining, and interrogating members of the enemy. . . . It is well settled that the President may seize and detain enemy combatants, at least for the duration of the conflict, and the laws of war make clear that prisoners may be interrogated for information concerning the enemy, its strength, and its plans. Numerous Presidents have ordered the capture, detention, and questioning of enemy combatants during virtually every major conflict in the Nation's history, including recent conflicts such as the Gulf, Vietnam, and Korean wars. Recognizing this authority, Congress has never attempted to restrict or interfere with the President's authority on this score. . . .

We conclude below that the Fifth Amendment Due Process Clause is inapplicable to the conduct of interrogations of alien enemy combatants held outside the United States for two independent reasons. First, the Fifth Amendment Due Process Clause does not apply to the President's conduct of a war. Second, even if the Fifth Amendment applied to the conduct of war, the Fifth Amendment does not apply extraterritorially to aliens who have no connection to the United States. We address each of these reasons in turn. . . .

Under traditional practice as expressed in the customary laws of war, the treatment of unlawful belligerents is left to the sovereign's discretion. . . . Under our Constitution, the sovereign right of the United States on the treatment of enemy combatants is reserved to the President as Commander-in-Chief. In light of the long history of discretion given to each nation to determine its treatment of unlawful combatants, to construe these statutes to regulate the conduct of the United States toward such combatants would interfere with a well-established prerogative of the sovereign. While the Geneva Convention (III) Relative to the Treatment of Prisoners of War, Aug. 12, 1949, . . . imposes restrictions on the interrogations of prisoners of war, it does not provide prisoner of war status to those who are unlawful combatants. . . . Those restrictions therefore would not apply to the interrogations of unlawful belligerents such as al Qaeda or Taliban members.

The second exception recognized by the Supreme Court arises where the application of general laws to a government official would create absurd results, such as effectively preventing the official from carrying out his duties. In Nardone, the Supreme Court pointed to "the application of a speed law to a policeman pursuing a criminal or the driver of a fire engine responding to an alarm" as examples of such absurd results. . . . For the reasons we explain above, the application of these general laws to the conduct of the military during the course of a war would create untenable results. . . .

In the context of interrogations, we believe that interrogation methods that do not involve physical contact will not support a charge of assault resulting in substantial injury or assault resulting in serious bodily injury or substantial bodily injury. Moreover, even minimal physical contact, such as poking, slapping, or shoving the detainee, is unlikely to produce the injury necessary to establish either one of these types of assault. . . .

[On Maiming]

Another criminal statute applicable in the special maritime and territorial jurisdiction is 18 U.S.C. § 114. Section 114 makes it a crime for an individual (1) "with the intent to torture (as defined in section 2340), maim, or disfigure" to (2) "cut, bite, or slit the nose, ear, or lip, or cut out or disable the tongue, or put out or destroy an eye, or cut off or disable a limb or any member of another person." . . . It further prohibits individuals from "throw[ing] or pour[ing] upon another person any scalding water, corrosive acid, or caustic substance" with like intent. . . .

The offense requires the specific intent to torture, maim or disfigure. . . . Moreover, the defendant's method of maiming must be one of the types the statute specifies—i.e., cutting, biting, slitting, cutting out, disabling, or putting out—and the injury must be to a body part the statute specifies—i.e., the nose, ear, lip, tongue, eye, or limb. . . . Similarly, the second set of acts applies to a very narrow band of conduct. It applies only to the throwing or pouring of some sort of scalding, corrosive, or caustic substance. . . .

Here, so long as the interrogation methods under contemplation do not involve the acts enumerated in section 114, the conduct of those interrogations will not fall within the purview of this statute. Because the statute requires specific intent, i.e., the intent to maim, disfigure or torture, the absence of such intent is a complete defense to a charge of maiming. . . .

[On Criminal Prohibitions Applicable to Conduct Occurring Outside the Jurisdiction of the United States]

There are two criminal prohibitions that apply to the conduct of U.S. persons outside the United States: the War Crimes Act, 18 U.S.C. § 2441, and the prohibition against torture, 18 U.S.C. §§ 2340–2340A. We conclude that the War Crimes Act does not apply to the interrogation of al Qaeda and

Taliban detainees because, as illegal belligerents, they do not qualify for the legal protections under the Geneva or Hague Conventions that section 2441 enforces. In regard to section 2340, we conclude that the statute, by its terms, does not apply to interrogations conducted within the territorial United States or on permanent military bases outside the territory of the United States. Nonetheless, we identify the relevant substantive standards regarding the prohibition on torture should interrogations occur outside that jurisdictional limit. . . .

Section 2340A of Title 18 makes it a criminal offense for any person "outside the United States [to] commit or attempt to commit torture." The statute defines "the United States" as "all areas under the jurisdiction of the United States including any of the places described in" 18 U.S.C. § 5, and 18 U.S.C.A. § 7. 18 U.S.C. § 2340(3). Therefore, to the extent that interrogations take place within the special maritime and territorial jurisdiction, such as at a U.S. military base in a foreign state, the interrogations are not subject to sections 2340–2340A. If, however, the interrogations take place outside the special maritime and territorial jurisdiction and are otherwise outside the United States, the torture statute applies. Thus, for example, interrogations conducted at GTMO[3] would not be subject to this prohibition, but interrogations conducted at a non-U.S. base in Afghanistan would be subject to section 2340A. . . .

Thus, to establish the offense of torture, the prosecution must show that: (1) the torture occurred outside the United States; (2) the defendant acted under the color of law; (3) the victim was within the defendant's custody or physical control; (4) the defendant specifically intended to cause severe physical or mental pain or suffering; and (5) that the act inflicted severe physical or mental pain or suffering. . . .

To violate section 2340A, the statute requires that severe pain and suffering be inflicted with specific intent. . . . For a defendant to act with specific intent, he must expressly intend to achieve the forbidden act. . . .

Here, because section 2340 requires that a defendant act with the specific intent to inflict severe pain, the infliction of such pain must be the defendant's precise objective. . . .

[In Summary]

Section 2340's definition of torture must be read as a sum of these component parts. . . . Each component of the definition emphasizes that torture is not the mere infliction of pain or suffering on another, but is instead a step well removed. The victim must experience intense pain or suffering of the kind that is equivalent to the pain that would be associated with serious physical injury so severe that death, organ failure, or permanent damage resulting in a loss of significant body function will likely result. If that pain

---

[3]**GTMO:** The military abbreviation for the prison maintained by the U.S. government at Guantánamo Bay, Cuba.

or suffering is psychological, that suffering must result from one of the acts set forth in the statute. In addition, these acts must cause long-term mental harm. Indeed, this view of the criminal act of torture is consistent with the term's common meaning. Torture is generally understood to involve "intense pain" or "excruciating pain," or put another way, "extreme anguish of body or mind." . . . In short, reading the definition of torture as a whole, it is plain that the term encompasses only extreme acts. . . .

As we have made clear in other opinions involving the war against al Qaeda, the Nation's right to self-defense has been triggered by the events of September 11. If a government defendant were to harm an enemy combatant during an interrogation in a manner that might arguably violate a criminal prohibition, he would be doing so in order to prevent further attacks on the United States by the al Qaeda terrorist network. In that case, we believe that he could argue that the executive branch's constitutional authority to protect the nation from attack justified his actions. This national and international version of the right to self-defense could supplement and bolster the government defendant's individual right.

Conclusion

For the foregoing reasons, we conclude that the Fifth and Eighth Amendments do not extend to alien enemy combatants held abroad. Moreover, we conclude that different canons of construction indicate that generally applicable criminal laws do not apply to the military interrogation of alien unlawful combatants held abroad. Were it otherwise, the application of these statutes to the interrogation of enemy combatants undertaken by military personnel would conflict with the President's Commander-in-Chief power.

We further conclude that CAT[4] defines U.S. international law obligations with respect to torture and other cruel, inhuman, or degrading treatment or punishment. The standard of conduct regarding torture is the same as that which is found in the torture statute, 18 U.S.C. §§ 2340–2340A. Moreover, the scope of U.S. obligations under CAT regarding cruel, inhuman, or degrading treatment or punishment is limited to conduct prohibited by the Eighth, Fifth and Fourteenth Amendments. Customary international law does not supply any additional standards.

Finally, even if the criminal prohibitions outlined above applied, and an interrogation method might violate those prohibitions, necessity or self-defense could provide justifications for any criminal liability.

Please let us know if we can be of further assistance.

John C. Yoo
Deputy Assistant Attorney General

---

[4]**CAT:** The UN Convention Against Torture and Other Cruel, Inhumane, or Degrading Punishment, to which the United States is a signatory.

READING AND DISCUSSION QUESTIONS

1. How do these memos define torture?

2. What arguments does Yoo put forward concerning the power of the presidency?

3. These memos provide a legal framework for interrogations conducted by representatives of the U.S. government according to U.S. law. How does Yoo address international law? Judging by these memos, how does the United States balance international and domestic concerns?

VIEWPOINTS

Immigration and Assimilation in Postwar Germany

The migration of foreign workers to Germany in the decades following World War II began at the invitation of the German government. During the 1950s and 1960s, as Germany recovered from the devastation of the war, the key limiting factor in German economic growth was a shortage of labor. By the early 1960s, there were more unfilled jobs in Germany than there were Germans on the official unemployment lists. The government responded by signing agreements with a number of countries to allow the temporary migration of "guest workers." When those guest workers defied government expectations and sought to settle in Germany, it raised a host of unexpected questions. How would these "foreigners" fit into German society? What adjustments would Germans have to make as their country grew more diverse? How did the permanent presence of guest workers challenge prevailing notions of what it meant to be German?

33-2 | A Management Expert Explains How to Make Guest Workers Feel Welcome

GIACOMO MATURI, *The Integration of the Southern Labor Force and Its Specific Adaptation Problems* (1961)

As more and more guest workers made their way into the German labor force, German employers struggled to come to terms with their "differentness." When problems arose in

---

Deniz Gokturk, David Gramling, and Anton Kaes, eds., *Germany in Transit: Nation and Migration, 1955–2005* (Berkeley: University of California Press, 2007), pp. 32–33. © 2007 by the Regents of the University of California. Reprinted with permission.

the integration of the new workers into existing production regimes, employers tended to explain those problems in cultural terms. From employers' point of view, German industrial norms reflected German culture and the German character. If Spanish, Portuguese, or Italian workers failed to fit in, it was, in essence, because they were not German. In this excerpt from a paper delivered at a 1961 convention of German employers, Giacomo Maturi, an industrial psychologist employed by the Ford Motor Company, presented his views on the cultural differences between southern European and German workers, as well as his suggestions for overcoming those differences.

Many of the difficulties in the integration of foreign labor power in the German economy originate in the *differentness* of these southern people. These are psychological difficulties, which cannot always be resolved by adapting these people to the German mentality and German forms. These difficulties can only be mastered by getting to know the eccentricities of these foreigners. They arise primarily when one tries to handle these people like Germans. It is only when one knows foreignness that a right-minded negotiation with them is possible, in which case the difficulties cease to exist, or are not that bad after all. They are only new manifestations that one must take into account; they can even be useful for the business milieu. . . .

The roots of these differences lie in the climate, in the landscape, in the historical development, in the culture and education, and in the societal structure of these peoples. The depth and momentousness of these factors show that it is impossible and irrational to demand a quick and total adaptation.

The Influence of the Climate on Life Rhythms

The southern climate demands and enables a different life rhythm than here in the north. Life is livelier; it is less strict and regulated. Without affecting actual productive potential, the climate has an effect on people and demands a different daily schedule, conditioning the distinct habits of these people, in private as well as in business life. Labor takes place in a different way than in the northern countries; it does not have the haste and the tempo that is common here. These people are no less willing to work or capable of work. This fact needs no further proof, because everyone praises the industriousness and the joy in working evident among the Italians. The legend of lazy Italians is, after all, a thing of the past. The overtly negative aspects can also be attributed to the climatic influences; it is also true, nonetheless, that southerners have another understanding of work.

The Southerner's Idea of Labor

Southerners are more conscious than others that they do not live to work but work to live. They are, after all, the heirs to the ancient Roman and Greek societies that regarded handiwork as slave labor and saw life's ideal as an *otium*—meaning liberation from material handiwork—in order to devote oneself to the greater values of life. They carry themselves with a distinct sense for the truly human aspects of life, because they do not really need to give themselves over to a hasty industriousness in order to drive away boredom. They value many things much more than financial affluence and the comfort of technology. Moreover, their deeply religious, sometimes fatalistic sense for life leads them to undervalue many external things.

The beauty of the landscape, the mild climate, the clear blue sky and sea on the heavenly coasts are not inconsequential for them, in that they encourage a more contemplative and nature-bound way of living.

The pressure of work and income has, however, become great among these people of late. This fact is evident in their desire for overtime and their thrifty intentions to send as much money back home as possible. But one may not forget the conventional attitude of these people toward material labor if one wants to understand this or that particular manifestation. Their lack of hardiness and reliability, which is cause for complaint here and there, can certainly be understood from this point of view. . . .

The Psychological Differences Between Germans and Southerners

The southerner wants to be dealt with in a very personal manner; he does not want to be a number. He needs warmth, sympathy, open and affectionate friendship, as well as recognition for work performed. Equality of rights and compensation is not sufficient for him; he is receptive and looks for a smile from his boss or employer.

The German, in contrast, is cold and objective; he is usually honest, just, and shies away from playing favorites, but he smiles too infrequently. For the southerner, he is not human enough. The tone one finds in the businesses here, particularly in construction work, is too tough and raw for southerners and sometimes appears almost brutal to them. These people are not exactly sensitive but they do tend to react more quickly. Even their voices sound different, particularly when they are fighting. They are impulsive and sometimes violent, but this behavior is only their passions coming to the surface. . . .

Most German employers are happy with the performance of these newly recruited foreigners, but the latter are too often conceived of only as labor power, as an economic factor, not as people. This perception does not mean that too little is being done for them; many firms even provide housing and supplies for them. But the human contact is missing. Coworkers also do not do much to foster intimacy with these people, to understand them. Foreign labor power is certainly not merely "foreign workers" anymore, but these people are still not perceived as full humans; they are isolated. Families living in the area also tend to avoid contact with these people as much as possible. There are no free rooms to rent for them; they are not wanted.

One should greet them, invite them in, receive them warmly, in order to introduce them into the new society. The economic problems of immigration should not overshadow the purely human problems. Inclusion in the economy demands inclusion in society.

READING AND DISCUSSION QUESTIONS

1. According to Maturi, what are the key differences between Germans and southern Europeans? How does he explain these differences?

2. What suggestions does Maturi offer employers seeking to facilitate the adaptation of foreign workers to German conditions? What does his advice suggest about German attitudes toward foreign workers in the early 1960s?

33-3 | German Academics Take a Stand Against Immigration

Heidelberg Manifesto (1982)

By the early 1970s, the unbridled economic growth that had accompanied the rebuilding of Germany had come to a halt. Recession, inflation, and rising unemployment became the economic watchwords in Germany and, indeed, throughout the West. The guest workers who had arrived in the previous decades did not leave when economic conditions changed. Despite official policy to the contrary, many guest workers put down roots in Germany, starting families and building communities. This combination of economic hard times and the increasingly apparent reality that former guest workers and their families intended to become permanent residents fueled widespread anti-immigrant sentiment in Germany. This 1982 manifesto, authored by a group of leading German academics, captures prevailing German attitudes toward immigration in the 1970s and early 1980s.

We are observing a development with great concern, a development initiated by a euphorically optimistic economic policy that has resulted in a state of affairs in which approximately 5 million guest workers and their families are now living and working in our country. Obviously, it has not been possible to halt the influx, despite a moratorium on recruitment. In 1989 alone, the number of registered foreigners rose by 309,000; 194,000 of those were Turks.

The situation has been exacerbated by the fact that little more than half of the necessary amount of children are being born in order to maintain zero growth of the German population in West Germany. A renewal of the procreative function of the German family is urgently needed.

Many Germans already feel foreign in their own neighborhoods, workplaces, and homeland in general—just as foreign as the guest workers are in their new surroundings.

The government's decision to promote the influx of foreigners in an era of unbridled economic growth is now widely recognized as questionable. Up to this point, the German population has not been informed of the significance and consequences of this process. We believe that the establishment of a politically independent consortium is necessary, one that will work in dialogue with politicians toward a (preferably) universal solution. This problem must be resolved if it is not to become a fateful impasse for guest workers as well as the host country.

One complication in the search for a solution to this problem is the fact that one can no longer pose the necessary questions in public debate without incurring accusations of Nazism. For this reason, we must stress that we stand firmly on the foundation of the Basic Law in all our efforts toward a solution. We emphatically oppose ideological nationalism, racism, right- and left-wing extremism.

The integration of large masses of non-German foreigners is not possible without threatening the German people, language, culture, and religion. Every people, including the Germans, has a natural right to preserve its identity and character in its residential areas. Respect for other peoples necessitates their preservation as well, not their assimilation ("Germanization"). We perceive Europe as an industrious community of peoples and nations that gives rise to a coherent higher order through culture and history. As Solzhenitsyn suggests, "Every nation is a one-time facet of a divine plan." On April 5, 1981, the voters of a multiracial nation, Switzerland, approved a model.

Although we know about the abuse of the word *Volk*, we must remind the reader that the Basic Law emanates from the term *Volk*, indeed from the German *Volk*, and that the federal president and the members of the government take this oath: "I swear that I will dedicate my energies to the good of the German *Volk*, further its interests, and prevent injury to it." Whoever understands this oath cannot deny that it is the German people whose "preservation" is at stake. And those who decide that there are no peoples worth preserving disregard the rules of scientific hermeneutics and grossly misinterpret our concerns.

We do not hesitate to remind you that the goal of reunification—an obligation established in the preamble of the Basic Law—could be most grievously endangered through the current foreigner policy.

How is reunification to remain a possibility when many regions of Germany are becoming ethnically foreign? What hope for the future do the hundreds of thousands of guest-worker children have if they are illiterate in both their native language and German? What hope do our own children have when they are being educated predominantly in classes with foreigners? Only active and viable German families can preserve our people for the future.

Technological advancement continues to offer various possibilities to make the employment of guest workers superfluous. The highest priority of economic management must be to bring machines to people, not people to machines. Solving this problem means improving the living conditions of the guest workers in their own countries through targeted development assistance—not here with us. Reuniting guest workers with their families in the ancestral homeland—on a voluntary basis, of course—will relieve the burden on our overindustrialized country, a country suffering from environmental destruction.

Almost none of the responsible persons or the functionaries from prominent social institutions have dared to face facts, let alone to propose a realistic concept for a long-term policy. To this end, we believe the formation of a politically independent consortium is necessary, one that will encourage organizations, associations, and individuals to collaboratively dedicate themselves to the preservation of our people—its language, culture, religion, and way of life.

We as university instructors, a profession with lofty tasks and responsibilities that compel us to ensure an appropriate and reasonable education for foreigners in our country (especially those from the so-called third world), must, on the grounds of our professional legitimacy, point out the seriousness of the current situation and the menacing consequences of a trend already under way.

READING AND DISCUSSION QUESTIONS

1. How do the authors define what it means to be a German? Why do they believe that immigrants threaten the survival of a distinct German identity?

2. How might the German experience under the Third Reich have shaped the debate about German cultural diversity in the early 1980s? Why do the authors of the Heidelberg Manifesto feel compelled to defend themselves against "accusations of Nazism"?

VIEWPOINTS COMPARATIVE QUESTIONS

1. What differences do Maturi and the authors of the Heidelberg Manifesto identify between native Germans and immigrants working and living in Germany? What importance do they attach to these differences?

2. How would you account for the very different attitudes toward immigrant workers revealed in these two documents? What had changed in Germany between 1961 and 1982?

3. On what, if anything, might Maturi and the authors of the Heidelberg Manifesto have agreed? What solutions might Maturi have suggested to the problems identified by the manifesto's authors?

33-4 | Glaciers as Evidence of Climate Change

Greenland: A Laboratory for the Symptoms of Global Warming (July 17, 2013)

The study of glaciers has yielded fundamental insights into the nature of climate and climate change. It was not until the mid-nineteenth century that scientists began to understand the historical role of glaciers in shaping the earth's landscapes over millions of years. The flatness of the U.S. Midwest and the formation of the Great Lakes, for instance, are now understood to have been the work of glaciers. The development of that early research formed the basis for the scientific understanding of climate change: that long periods of warming and cooling of the earth's atmosphere and oceans cause glaciers to expand and recede. Building upon this nineteenth-century foundation, glaciologists, geologists, and atmospheric scientists began to study glaciers to better understand historical temperatures, precipitation levels, and particles of matter in the atmosphere that are deposited over time in glaciers' thick layers. This line of research grew during the industrial age as the planet began to warm from greenhouse gas emissions and the earth's glaciers began to shrink. Scientists could extract cylinders of ice (known as cores) from glaciers, and read them the way that the rings of a tree can be read to show age, rate of growth, and periods of stress. Glaciers became a tool to study not only long-term changes in climate but also the sudden changes brought on by the industrial age. The rapidly accelerating melting of glaciers is a visible marker that sheds light on the vast, complex, and often imperceptible phenomenon of climate change. It also gives scientists, like the ones in the photo below, a concrete way to document the suddenness and severity of contemporary global warming in the context of historical patterns.

Joe Raedle/Getty Images

READING AND DISCUSSION QUESTIONS

1. Why do scientists study glaciers?

2. How do receding glaciers help us to better understand global warming?

3. Can you think of other ways to visualize or interpret climate change?

33-5 | A Generational Rift on Climate Change

GRETA THUNBERG, *Address to the United Nations Climate Action Summit* (2019)

In October 2019, students around the world walked out of classes to protest political inaction on the global crisis of climate change. The striking students opened a new front in the struggle to enact and implement public policy measures that would sharply reduce the carbon and methane emissions that cause global warming. They argued that the generation currently holding political power was failing the generation of students that would have to live with the consequences of today's inaction or inadequate action. The most prominent advocate in this social movement is Swedish teenager Greta Thunberg, who sailed to the United States to speak at the United Nations Climate Action Summit and the U.S. Congress about the cost that government inaction to regulate and reduce greenhouse gas emissions will have on future generations.

My message is that we'll be watching you.

This is all wrong. I shouldn't be up here. I should be back in school on the other side of the ocean. Yet you all come to us young people for hope. How dare you!

You have stolen my dreams and my childhood with your empty words. And yet I'm one of the lucky ones. People are suffering. People are dying. Entire ecosystems are collapsing. We are in the beginning of a mass extinction, and all you can talk about is money and fairy tales of eternal economic growth. How dare you!

For more than 30 years, the science has been crystal clear. How dare you continue to look away and come here saying that you're doing enough, when the politics and solutions needed are still nowhere in sight.

You say you hear us and that you understand the urgency. But no matter how sad and angry I am, I do not want to believe that. Because if you really understood the situation and still kept on failing to act, then you would be evil. And that I refuse to believe.

The popular idea of cutting our emissions in half in 10 years only gives us a 50% chance of staying below 1.5 degrees [Celsius], and the risk of setting off irreversible chain reactions beyond human control.

Fifty percent may be acceptable to you. But those numbers do not include tipping points, most feedback loops, additional warming hidden by toxic air pollution or the aspects of equity and climate justice. They also rely on my generation sucking hundreds of billions of tons of your CO_2 out of the air with technologies that barely exist.

So a 50% risk is simply not acceptable to us—we who have to live with the consequences.

National Public Radio, "Transcript: Gretha Thunberg's Speech at the U.N. Climate Action Summit," September 23, 2019. https://www.npr.org/2019/09/23/763452863/transcript-greta-thunbergs-speech-at-the-u-n-climate-action-summit

To have a 67% chance of staying below a 1.5 degrees global temperature rise — the best odds given by the [Intergovernmental Panel on Climate Change] — the world had 420 gigatons of CO_2 left to emit back on Jan. 1st, 2018. Today that figure is already down to less than 350 gigatons.

How dare you pretend that this can be solved with just "business as usual" and some technical solutions? With today's emissions levels, that remaining CO_2 budget will be entirely gone within less than 8½ years.

There will not be any solutions or plans presented in line with these figures here today, because these numbers are too uncomfortable. And you are still not mature enough to tell it like it is.

You are failing us. But the young people are starting to understand your betrayal. The eyes of all future generations are upon you. And if you choose to fail us, I say: We will never forgive you.

We will not let you get away with this. Right here, right now is where we draw the line. The world is waking up. And change is coming, whether you like it or not.

Thank you.

READING AND DISCUSSION QUESTIONS

1. What specific action is Greta Thunberg asking for?

2. What does she say stands in the way of significant action on climate change?

3. How does Thunberg make use of age to advocate for policy change?

▪ COMPARATIVE QUESTIONS ▪

1. What does John Yoo's memorandum suggest about the way the author saw the relationship between the United States and the rest of the world? In your opinion, does the memorandum reflect a significant departure from earlier U.S. viewpoints and policies? Why or why not?

2. Compare and contrast the postwar surge in immigration with the similar surge that occurred in the late nineteenth and early twentieth centuries (see Chapter 27). What similarities and differences do you note?

3. Compare the memoranda by John Yoo with the speech by Greta Thunberg. How do they build moral arguments for their positions?

4. How do you think the themes in these documents — war, terrorism, human rights, migration, and climate change — are perceived by peoples in different parts of the world? What would contribute to differing perceptions of these issues?